WHAT IS THE HUMAN?

Australian Voices from the Humanities

edited by
L. E. Semler, Bob Hodge and Philippa Kelly

AUSTRALIAN SCHOLARLY

© L. E. Semler, Bob Hodge and Philippa Kelly 2012

First published 2011, by Australian Scholarly Publishing Pty Ltd
7 Lt Lothian St Nth, North Melbourne, Vic 3051 TEL: 03 9329 6963 FAX: 03 9329 5452
EMAIL: aspic@ozemail.com.au WEB: scholarly.info

ISBN 978-1-921875-60-1

Copyediting Nick Walker   *Design and typesetting* Art Rowlands   *Printing and binding* BPA Print Group

The main chapters of this book are typeset in Adobe Garamond Pro 11/19pt

Contents

Part Three: **What was the Human? Then and Now**

The editors would like to acknowledge with thanks the financial and intellectual support for this book from the Australasian Universities Language and Literature Association, the School of Letters, Art and Media (University of Sydney) and the English Department (University of Sydney).

Introduction

What is the Human?
The Reach of the Imagination

Philippa Kelly and L. E. Semler

What does it mean, and what does it take, to be human? This ancient issue will continue to puzzle people as long as there are humans on earth (or elsewhere) and it is a question in which everyone, presumably equally, has a stake. At one level it is profoundly simple to be human – if one *is* human, that is, but not so easy if one is not as some chapters in this book will demonstrate. But things are more complicated than this. As anyone on the wrong side of state law, cultural norm, adequate health or personal aggression might testify (but of course, frequently they are not given the chance) the pain of being refused, diffused or abused, of enduring bare life or a state of exception, of being swept backwards out of the definition of the human, is excruciating beyond description.[1]

Beyond description? Not entirely. Description is what humans are good at—definitively so. In his influential account of human nature, Thomas Hobbes theorised that human curiosity and the ability to apply names to things, to reason and remember, and thence to develop conceptual lines of argument and communicate these to one's fellows, all these amount to a defining capacity of the human (Hobbes 94–118). Unlike forgetful beasts, who lack *scientia* and are ever subject to their appetites, the human possesses a rational soul evidenced, as Descartes also argued in his *Discourse on Method* (1637), by agile mental and discursive ability (Descartes 40–42). The perceived world can be put into trains of thought, into variously meaningful stories that can be shared and built upon. Stories that in turn shape further realities and on it goes in ever increasing complexity. Postmodernism would seem to affirm, rightly or wrongly, the Romantic truth that the imagination in part, perhaps in large part, creates the world.

Hobbesian and Cartesian accounts of the human clearly had implications not merely for the animal, but also for the divine. While these issues were explored at length in antiquity (Sorabji), early modernity in the West (roughly from 1550–1750) was a watershed moment of renegotiation of the rights and oligations of the human, a tipping point in the secularisation of the western mind that was bound up with the rise of global economies of cultural and economic exchange. The incipient atheism of Hobbesian theory and the self-empowered, system-building drive of new philosophers like Descartes, joined an upsurge in empirical inquiry in science and medicine to create a launch pad for the human as many now live it.

The ever present murmur of scepticism and relativism – from Sextus Empiricus through to Montaigne and Shakespeare's Hamlet, and then on to Nietzsche and postmodern theorists such as Baudrillard and Lyotard – has thrived in modern times where total war, economic rationalism and terroist ambush have fuelled and been fuelled by technological advances. This astonishing, modern melange, powerfully inflected by the now historical theories of Freud and Darwin and the still unfolding electronic and bioscientific revolutions, necessarily strains the relationships human beings might have with animals, nature and God. Definitions of the transhuman and posthuman are becoming ever more credible in the developed world,[2] while at the same time religious conservatism and fundamentalism are vivid realities. In a world that is increasingly wealthy and populated, what does it mean that between one to two billion people remain living in poverty?

How are we to make our way in such a world? And when we do manage to chart a personally acceptable path, what degree of freedom to think our own thoughts and be our own selves are we really experiencing? A world where irresistible cultural tides preform or co-opt our thoughts and plans, and our deepest beliefs feel vulnerable to casual deconstruction or local politics; a world where the structures that our species has developed – biotechnology, capitalism, disciplinarity, for example – overshadow quintessential human values, urges and capacities that refuse to die; a world ultimately of fraught freedoms and contradictions that puzzle the will (as Hamlet might say), all this seems a mixed blessing indeed.

It is remarkable that we can think at all, or, once we start that we can stop. And yet the contradiction is that while the Danish prince is crippled by simply entertaining notions of being, the English play *Hamlet* succeeds beyond measure as creative expression. Albeit as 'tragedy', but also as a stretching of the imagination, something positive because artful, affective and insightful, and the same could be said of Beckett's *Waiting for Godot* or Cimino's *The Deer Hunter*. Vexed we may be, but the long record of human aesthetic and cultural production is unequivocally affirming – from dystopias to deathworlds and memorials, from doll culture to manga and CG humans, and from primeval demonology to secular leadership and soaring religious verse. It is this reach of imagination that is the lens through which our contributors explore the problematics of being human. Literature, philosophy, cultural studies and history – key disciplines represented in this collection – are the frames around these cultural mirrors.

While the fundamental tenets of our humanity are of crucial importance to how we live and think about our world, they are often left in the hands of 'experts' while the rest of us get on with the exigencies of day-to-day life. But Socrates spoke a deep human truth when he said that the unexamined life is not worth living.[3] The purpose of this collection is to stimulate thought and debate, and to have voices from the past converse with those of our present day. These are global concerns that can only be addressed via analyses of local exemplars that are dazzling in their diversity.

Part 1 of this collection, 'What is the Human? Expressions and Suppressions', considers aspects of 'humanity' through the prism of evolution and simulation, a prism that blends theory, technics and texts and throws uncanny light on formerly familiar subjects, transforming them and us in the process. The first chapter, Elizabeth Grosz's 'The Inhuman in the Humanities: Darwin and the Ends of Man,' explores Darwin's theory of evolution as a reinstatement of the animal in understandings of the human, and suggests that Darwin's categories of being are mutually supportive and life-enhancing. All forms of life enter the realm of art when they exceed the basic requirements of existence. Darwin, according to Grosz, defines two processes that regulate all of life; one is natural selection and the other is sexual selection. Natural selection is about survival, and sexual selection, for Darwin, is largely about reproduction or a kind of sexual *seduction*. Grosz sees the origin of art as pertaining to the realm of seduction: so that all forms of art are an expression of the body, and all forms of life express this artistic intention.

In the following essay, 'Narratives of Identity and Authenticity: The Humanities meets Leadership Studies,' Jan Shaw prompts us to ask: how possible is it to articulate stories of one's identity that are both professionally functional and authentic? When a leader tells an inspirational story of his or her rise to the top, how 'true' does this life story need to be in order to connect actuality to ideal leadership? If real change and philosophical clarity are to occur in the theory and practice of human leadership, the starting point must be a properly nuanced understanding of the problematics of authenticity, storytelling and truthfulness.

'[I]t is only by being "recognized" by another, by many others, or – in the extreme – by all others, that a human being is really human, for himself as well as for others,' writes Alexandre Kojève as cited in Hannah Stark's chapter, 'A Critical Politics of the Human: Judith Butler and Gilles Deleuze'. The question here, Stark argues, is not just 'who is endowed with recognition?' but 'what are the frameworks we use to create and announce those forms of recognition?' Stark explores this conundrum via two philosophers, Judith Butler and Gilles Deleuze, whose work overlays Hegel's thinking on what 'humanity' constitutes and how it can be expressed and analysed, and engages with the insights of Elizabeth Grosz, the author of our book's first chapter. In what ways can we use palimpsestic layers of philosophical thinking from past and present to stretch and re-formulate what it means to be human?

In Chapter 4, 'Not Quite Human: Traversing the Uncanny Valley,' Kathy Cleland examines the uncanny space between robotic human simulations and the human physiognomies and functions they replicate. The more technically 'human' these robots seem to be, the more we expect from them, while failures in technical function can lead to notions that they are 'unconvincing'. Powerful gaming computers such as IBM's upgraded Deep Blue seemingly can beat even the best human chess players – and yet no one has created a robot or a digital animation that can pass as human. The real problem is not just that these near-human creations don't pass as human, but that they can generate decidedly uncanny responses in audiences. This fundamental unease about the nearly human and the havoc it might wreak on our deepest assumptions, ethics and species identity no longer exists solely in the fictive realms of *Blade Runner* and *Frankenstein*, but is finding more general release via the provocations of real science, entertainment and art.

Mio Bryce's chapter, 'Diffused Reflection of Body Imageries: Dolls as Humans and Humans as Dolls,' probes the importance of dolls in contemporary Japanese culture. Toy and religious dolls, along with dolls in manga and anime, serve an extraordinary range of purposes that cut to the heart of human needs for play, transcendent meaning and power. Bryce explores how doll culture bridges the human and its material and spiritual environments as well as raising complex questions about the internal mind-body relation and human emotions and interactivity. Living doll stories and the fictional possibility of humans morphing into dolls have disturbing power and brings us back to the uncanny that Cleland approached by another route.

The concluding chapter in Part 1, Rebecca Suter's 'Human and Superhuman in Contemporary Japanese Girls' Manga,' examines the role and importance of science fiction animations that focus on the machine's 'encroachment' on the human and the place of sexuality in these stories. A central theme in Japanese comics and animation has for a long time been the question 'what is human?' Suter adds to the conversation about manga in the previous chapter by demonstrating how *shôjo* (girl's manga) and *shônen ai* (the 'boy's love' subgenre) present complex visions of race, gender and sexuality.

Part 2 of the collection, 'Spaces for the Human: Personal and Political Frontiers,' concentrates attention on literary and cultural analysis as a way of opening out notions of humanness. In Chapter 7, 'Frontiers of Life and Death: The Human, New Wars and World Literary Sensibilities,' Debjani Ganguly argues for a new configuration of the 'human' via exploration of contemporary world literatures in English. This global literary space, she suggests, has emerged at the intersection of post-1989 geographies of violence, hyperconnective information technology, and a new humanitarian sensibility in a context where suffering has a presence in everyday life through the shocking immediacy of digital images. But even in this context, people can simply 'turn it off'. They can control and mediate exactly how much 'reality' they allow in, and what this reality means. This has profound implications for any overarching understanding of, or ethics of, or sympathy for, the human and its actors and patients.

In Chapter 8, 'Neurology is Destiny: Character and Consciousness in Ian McEwan's *Saturday*', Nicole Heber teases out the kind of direct emotional expression that McEwan puts in dialogue with the tendency of Henry Perowne, *Saturday's* protagonist, to abstract and categorize. Expert at keeping life at one remove, Perowne is confronted by the challenging figure of a character called Baxter who suffers Huntington's disease. There is Baxter's shocking interjection of himself into Perowne's household; and then there is the diminished responsibility that is the effect of his disablement. Perowne is helpless against the force of this unreason, although his own clinical faculties compulsively chart it all the while, in the process illuminating for us core vulnerabilities of the human.

Peter Goodall follows with his chapter, 'Human Values in a Mass Society: A Reading of George Orwell's Novels,' which demonstrates the fruitfulness of literary analysis to understandings and expressions of 'the human' in Orwell's *Nineteen Eighty-Four*. This novel is usually read as political satire, but is at heart a sustained meditation on what it means to be human and on the future of human-ness as it has been traditionally understood and valued in society. Goodall follows Orwell's journey to the proles of *Nineteen Eighty-Four* from his early work and sets it in the context of an evolving presentation of the poor in modern society that developed from the late nineteenth to the early twentieth century.

In Chapter 10, 'Telling Stories at the Permeable Borders of the Human in David Malouf's *Ransom*,' Yvonne Smith explores Malouf's ongoing desire to grasp through the working of the imagination what the past can bring to the present. In the process Smith shows how how old myths and tales might become untold tales we need to hear as we make meaning in today's societies.

The final chapter in Part 2, Matthew Graves's 'Displacing Geographies of Memory: The Australian and New Zealand Memorials, London,' also deals with the past's significance in the present. He examines the Australian and New Zealand Memorials in London and the repatriation of Unknown Soldiers to the southern hemisphere as recent developments in the ANZAC landscape that highlight paradoxes in the geographies of remembrance. Graves probes the way memorials produce landscapes of human memory that are political, cultural and artistic.

Part 3 of the collection, 'What was the Human? Then and Now', explores the 'translation' of old stories into contemporary identity practices. In Chapter 12, 'Must Humanity perforce Prey upon Itself? *King Lear*, War and the Humanities', R. S. White uses Shakespeare's bleakest war-play to consider the place and value of human pacifism. The play has always been seen to have a parable-like quality, and yet any parable drawn differs from age to age. White shows how *King Lear* speaks to the present via its representation of political and personal ruptures. The characters illustrate fundamental human flaws and needs as the plot carries them to the heights of human art, evil and suffering.

In Chapter 13, 'Defining the Demonic in Ancient China,' Jeffrey Riegel considers the human in tension with the demonic and its other world. He draws on the history of Chinese tales of ghosts and spirits from their earliest written forms to text messages of today. It is salutary to consider ancient traditions of demonic stories that frighten us, especially stories woven into quite specific cultures and times, for they reveal as much about their moment of origin or popularity as they do about the limits and commonalities of other human cultures and times.

Bob Hodge and Marina Gerzic offer essays on that most famous of identity puzzles, Shakespeare's *Hamlet*. In Chapter 14, 'Hamlet and the Crisis in the Humanities,' Hodge delivers a dynamic and wry portrait of what the 'businessman' Hamlet can teach us today. Hamlet has often been thought of as a soft scholar, 'fat and scant of breath', full of scrupulous cogitation but not the model of efficacy. He declares that he has 'that within', but what does he have to reveal to modern business? Hodge illuminates the gap and overlap between the humanities and the world of business via a novel approach to Hamlet's most famous question. Marina Gerzic follows with, 'Reel Life: Representing the Human in Michael Almereyda's *Hamlet*', an analysis of the mediatized, postmodern Hamlet constantly replacing human interactions with virtual ones. He obsessively replays, reconfigures and manipulates images in an unsuccessful attempt to make the virtual 'real'. What happens to humans in this *Hamlet* is conveyed most strongly by the character of Fortinbras, who is completely disembodied, and also by the pandemic of surveillance that infects us all.

Chapters 16 and 17 offer two views of John Milton's enduring impact on modern readers: silent readers of his complex printed words and vocal readers of his verse as sound performance. Ronald Bedford's 'Milton and the Fit Reader' explores a continuing paradox of the human activities of writing and reading: that is, the way in which readers cannot be counted on to read in ways desired by authors, nor can readers always agree among themselves about the 'meaning' of what they read. The example of Milton's attempt to create a 'fit audience', or readership, for his epic poem, *Paradise Lost*, raises fascinating questions of readerly – and writerly – competence, which might turn, for instance, on the perception of irony, or of its absence, or on the differences between legitimate figuration and mere lies. And radical differences may issue forth between equally competent readers as they mobilise the author for one cause or another.

Beverley Sherry's chapter, '*Paradise Lost* Aloud: Then and Now,' takes account of the high priority Milton placed on the sound of poetry and the fact that the blind poet dictated the poem to amanuenses. Since it first appeared in 1667, *Paradise Lost* has stayed alive through readings. Sherry asks: how was *Paradise Lost* heard in the past and how is it heard today? Beginning with scant reports from Milton's own time, Sherry moves to more substantial evidence from the eighteenth and nineteenth centuries and finally to the late 20th and early 21st centuries, where she documents ear-witness accounts of public readings, including the popular 'Milton marathons.' If speech is a defining trait of the human – as Cicero (13), Hobbes, and Descartes affirm – surely sounds carry potent meanings when poetic art is read aloud.

******

This book, *What is the Human? Australian Voices from the Humanities*, as its title suggests, presents a range of Australian scholarly voices speaking about the human. They do so via reflection on its cultural products and from various disciplinary locations within the humanities. The essays indicate something crucial about the notion of humanity – its parameters are forever shifting, so that it is, in a sense, always a retrospective consideration as we race toward the next phase of what humanity entails. Perennial issues such as evil and suffering, meaning and art, the animal and the divine, persist. Yet, massive cultural revolutions continue to unfold through the realms of medicine, philosophy, gender, politics and science and technology. Continuity and change in the zone of the human together produce astonishing and relentless art. This artistic response testifies to the reach of human imagination, a reach so profound that it troubles us, yet so enabling that it reshapes the world before it. The human may not be the final or sole arbiter of reality, but is undoubtedly a player on that stage and a shaper of its stories. The human reimagining of humanity in all its forms deserves the scrutiny we apply here because it is through both creativity and analysis that we bequeath new worlds to new generations.

Works Cited

Agamben, Giorgio. *Homo Sacer: Sovereign Power and Bare Life*. 1995. Trans. Daniel Heller-Roazen. Stanford: Stanford University Press, 1998

———. *State of Exception*. trans. Kevin Attell. Chicago: University of Chicago Press, 2005

Baudrillard, Jean. *Simulations*. Trans. Paul Foss, Paul Patton and Philip Beitchman. New York: Semiotext(e), 1983

Beckett, Samuel. *The Complete Dramatic Works of Samuel Beckett*. London: Faber and Faber, 2006.

Cicero, Marcus Tullius. *De inventione, De optimo genere oratorum, Topica*. Trans. H. M. Hubbell. 1949; rpt. London: Heinemann, 1976

Cimino, Michael (dir.). *The Deer Hunter*. Universal Pictures, 1978

Darwin, Charles. *The Origin of Species*. Ed. by Gillian Beer. Oxford: Oxford University Press, 1996

Descartes, Rene. *Discourse on Method and Related Writings*. Trans. Desmond M. Clarke. 1999. Rev. London: Penguin, 2003

Empiricus, Sextus. *Outlines of Scepticism*. Ed. by Julia Annas and Jonathan Barnes. 2000. Rpt. Cambridge: Cambridge University Press, 2002

Extropy Institute, The. <URL: http://www.exropy.org/resources.htm> Accessed 25 June 2010

Freud, Sigmund. *The Complete Psychological Works*. 24 vols. Trans. James Strachey. Norton, 1976

Hobbes, Thomas. *Leviathan*. 1651. Ed. by C. B. MacPherson. Harmondsworth: Penguin, 1985

Humanity+. <URL: http://humanityplus.org/> Accessed 25 June 2010

Lyotard, Jean-François. *The Postmodern Condition: A Report on Knowledge*. Trans. Geoff Bennington and Brian Massumi. 1984. Rpt. Manchester: Manchester University Press, 2004

Montaigne, Michel de. *The Complete Essays*. Trans. M. A. Screech. London: Penguin 1991

Nietzsche, Friedrich. *Basic Writings of Nietzsche*. Trans. Walter Kaufmann. Modern Library, 2000

Plato. *The Last Days of Socrates: Euthyphro, Apology, Crito, Phaedo*. Trans. Hugh Tredennick and Harold Tarrant. 1954. Rev. Harmondsworth: Penguin, 1993

Scott, Ridley (dir.). *Blade Runner (The Director's Cut)*. Warner Home Video, 1982

Shakespeare, William. *Hamlet*. Arden3. Ed. Ann Thompson and Neil Taylor. 2 vols. London: Thomson, 2006

Shelley, Mary. *Frankenstein or The Modern Prometheus: The 1818 Text*. Ed. Marylin Butler. Oxford: Oxford University Press, 1998

Sorabji, Richard. *Animal Minds and Human Morals: The Origins of the Western Debate*. London: Duckworth, 1993

Transhumanist Arts and Culture. <URL: http://www.transhumanist.biz/> Accessed 25 June 2010

Notes

1   On bare life and the state of exception, see Agamben 1998, 2005.
2   See the websites of: The Extropy Institue, Humanity+, and Transhumanist Arts and Culture.
3   Plato, *The Apology* 38a, in Plato 63.

Part One
What is the Human? Expressions and Suppressions

Chapter 1

The Inhuman in the Humanities. Darwin and the Ends of Man

Elizabeth Grosz
Rutgers University

> *In truth, there are only inhumanities, humans are made exclusively of inhumanities, but very different ones, of very different natures and speeds.*
>
> Deleuze and Guattari (190)

> *Writing is a question of becoming, always incomplete, always in the midst of being formed, and goes beyond the matter of any livable or lived experience. It is a process that is, a passage of Life that traverses both the livable and the lived.*
>
> Deleuze (1)

I am honoured to have this opportunity to reflect on the place of the animal and the inhuman in our conceptions of the human, and their place in the humanities, those disciplines and interdisciplines devoted to the study of humans and their cultural and expressive relations, especially in any humanities to come. The place of the animal – what is before, beyond and after the human, the uncontainable condition of the human, the origin of and trajectory immanent within the human – will be the object of my reflections: in doing so, I am merely continuing a tradition that resurfaced in the final Nietzschean decade of the twentieth century: not only do Deleuze and Guattari address the question of becoming-animal through the writings of Spinoza, Nietzsche and Bergson, Derrida makes the animal the object of interrogation of his final book, and Agamben places the animal at the center of his reflections on man as political being. The animal is that from which the human precariously emerges; and the animal is that inhuman destination to which the human always tends. The animal surrounds the human at both ends: it is the origin and the end of humanity, the destiny to which the human always tends.

We have dealt with the intangible and evasive line that divides the animal from the human since Ancient Greece, by creating an oppositional structure that denies to the animal what it grants to the human as a power or ability: whether it is reason, language, thought, consciousness, or the ability to dress, to bury, to mourn, to invent, to control fire, this division – constitutive of the humanities as they developed from the nineteenth century onward – has cast man on the other side of the animals.[1] Philosophy has attributed to man a power that animals (and often women, children, slaves, foreigners and others) lack. What makes man human is the power of reason, speech, shame and so on, that animals lack. Man must be understood as fundamentally different from the animal, an animal perhaps, but one with at least one added category – a rational animal, an upright animal, an embarrassed animal – that lifts it out of the categories it shares with all other living beings and marks man's separateness, his distance, his movement beyond the animal. If philosophy from the time of Plato to Descartes affirmed man's place as a rational animal, a speaking animal, a conscious animal, an animal perhaps in body but a being distinguished through mind, and if the Cartesian and Greek roots have largely structured the ways in which contemporary philosophy functions (Derrida affirms the continuity that links the Greeks and Descartes to the work of phenomenological and psychoanalytic theory running through the texts of Kant, Hegel, Heidegger, Levinas, and Lacan) through the relegation of the animal to man's utter other, an other bereft of humanity, this tradition is sorely challenged and deeply compromised by the eruption of Darwinism in the second half of the nineteenth century. Philosophy has yet to recover from this eruption, has yet to recompose its concepts of man, reason and consciousness to accommodate the Darwinian explosion that, according to Freud, produced one of the three major assaults by science on man's narcissism: along with the (first) Copernican revolution that demonstrated that the earth circulated the sun; and the (third) Freudian revolution that demonstrated that consciousness is not master of itself was a perhaps far more profound insult to mankind's sense of self, the (second) Darwinian revolution that demonstrated that man descended from animals and remains animal still.[2]

1. Darwin in the Humanities

I want to explore Darwin's place in the humanities. His conception of animals, the world of the living, which addresses the animal, the vegetal and the human alongside of the protozoa, bacteria and viruses, has yet to fully impact the humanities though it has often problematically dominated the biological sciences. It is now perhaps appropriate to reevaluate Darwin's conception of the descent of man and to explore what it means for philosophies of the human that might develop in Darwin's wake. What would a humanities, a knowledge of and for the human, look like that placed the animal in its rightful place, not only before the human but within and after the human? What is the trajectory of a newly considered humanities that seeks to know itself not in opposition to its inhuman 'others' but in continuity with them?

What would the study of, say, literature and language look like which did not privilege the human as its paradigm? Is it possible for us to understand language differently, beyond and outside the limits of the human? Could there be an ethology of language? Or of expression? (Derrida asks of post-Cartesian philosophy: What would a theory of language, signification or the trace look like that did not, through logocentric techniques, privilege not only the human but a particular kind of (white, European, masculine, upright and erect carnivorous – a carnophallologocentric) subject and discourse? What would a theory of language be like that understood language in its full resonance as trace, as the material and incorporeal incision that marks and hides its own movement? Isn't such an ethology precisely what Derrida has searched for as a language beyond logocentrism? And isn't language that erupts from the animal already a language beyond the model of signification, such as Deleuze seeks, a language linked not only to the signification of what is absent, but a language that acts and transforms, a language more amenable to a pragmatism than a linguistics?[3]

How open-endedly must we understand language, representation, and art – those qualities that we have up to now relegated to the human only to the extent that they are denied to the animal – if we are to problematize the opposition between animal and human and place the human in the midst of the world(s) of the animal? What is distinctively human in the humanities if man is again, in the light of Darwin's rearrangement of the universe, placed in the context of animals and animal-becomings? What would the humanities, a knowledge of the post-human, be like far in the future, after mankind has evolved beyond man? What are the limits of knowing, the limits of relevance of the humanities?

Perhaps this is another way of asking: at what point do the humanities find themselves inevitably connected to the natural sciences? And at what point is it that the sciences nevertheless find that they need another framework or perspective from which to understand their various objects, not from outside, as the natural sciences do, but from within, as the humanities attempt? In other words, if man is understood, following Darwin, as one among many animals, an animal who has perhaps different degrees of development of what may also be viewed in undeveloped form in other animals, then perhaps we may understand that the natural sciences, even as they may be augmented by the social sciences, nevertheless remain unable to grasp the qualitative nuances that only the humanities – each in their different ways – address.

Darwin understood the extent to which man has regulated and ordered the natural world according to his own various interests. 'If man had not been his own classifier, he would never have thought of founding a separate order for his own reception' (*Descent* 1. 191). This seems remarkably close to Derrida's claim: '*Animal* is a word that men have given themselves the right to give. These humans are found giving it to themselves, this word, but as if they had received it as an inheritance' (32). The sciences as much as the humanities require other perspectives than those which have dictated what counts as human, which entails an evaluation also of which humans are classified as borderline, less than human or already on the animal-side of the human/ animal divide. This question of what constitutes the human is one of the most intense and fraught questions of the modern era: it constitutes the center of feminist, anti-racist and class-based struggles. These struggles have been elaborated around precisely the question of who to include or exclude when characterizing the human. Ironically, what Darwin may make explicit, in ways that his own, humanities-based writings attest, is that there can be no scientific accounts of the world which are not also embedded in, surrounded by and associatively connected with other kinds of ('humanist') knowledge, knowledge framing the world in terms of its lived possibilities, in terms of its possibilities of becoming other, that the sciences cannot address. Derrida claims that this very act of naming 'the animal' is already a containment of the animal as mute inarticulateness, the granting of the power of political and cultural representation to the human alone.[4] We need a humanities in which the human is no longer the norm, rule or object, but where life itself, in its open multiplicity, comes to provide the object of analysis and poses its questions about man's (and woman's) specificity as species, as a social collective, as political order or economic structure.

2. Darwin and the Distinctively Human

Darwin published *The Descent of Man* (1871) in part as an attempt to demonstrate that the principles he outlined for explaining the origin and evolution of species in *On the Origin of Species* (1859) were as relevant for an analysis of man, mankind in all its sexual and racial variations, as they are for the analysis of the descent of animal species from pre-existing species. While he famously delayed the publication of his book on man after the also long-delayed publication of *On the Origin of Species*, fearing a wide-scale backlash, this was a book that he wisely understood needed to address why, in 'man' there are two sexes, and why among all the forms of man, there are different races with different qualities even if there is no measure that could hierarchically order these races. He needed to show both that the principles broadly regulating the genealogy of species applied also to man, and that these principles are able to address very wide variations in behavior and appearance that distinguish the different types of man from each other.

Darwin's argument, in brief, is that the differences between man and other animal species are differences of degree not differences in kind; and that the differences between the races and cultures of mankind are one of degree and not a difference in kind:

> We must ... admit that there is a much wider interval in mental power
> between one of the lowest fishes, as a lamprey or lancelet, and one of the
> higher apes, than between an ape and man; yet this immense interval is
> filled up by numberless gradations ... Differences ... between the highest
> men of the highest races and the lowest savages, are connected by the
> finest gradations. Therefore it is possible that they might pass and develop
> into each other. (*Descent* 1. 35)

The idea of 'numberless gradations,' of the 'finest gradations,' of 'no
fundamental difference' (35) anticipates one of the most profound and
motivating of concepts in twentieth century thought and beyond, the idea of
difference, of differences without the central organizing principle of identity,
not a difference between given things, a comparison, but a difference which
differentiates itself without having clear-cut or separable terms. Darwin
affirms that the differences between the lowliest fish and mankind is not
a difference in kind but a difference of degree, a difference that can be
obtained by insensible gradations, the slowest movements of transformation
that link the existence of one species to the emergence of another. To affirm
as he does that 'there is no fundamental difference between man and the
higher mammals in their mental faculties' (35) is to affirm both that man
and all other living things are linked through 'numberless gradations' but
also that there may not be two different kinds of knowledge about these
two kinds of living beings (one human the other animal) but also a new
kind of hybrid knowledge, somewhere perhaps between the natural sciences
(which encompasses man's knowledge of other animals, man's knowledge
from outside) and the humanities (which include man's knowledge of man
and his various social institutions and products) that can more adequately
address the implications of this fundamental continuity, indeed genealogy,
between man and all other living species.

This is precisely the affront to the privilege of consciousness, language
and reason that Freud understood as one of science's insults to human
narcissism: what we consider most special about our status as a species –
that we speak, that we reason and comprehend, we hide ourselves or cover
our tracks, that we know ourselves, that we deceive – while uncontested by

Darwin are not accorded any special privilege by him either. The conditions for the emergence of all these, and every other 'distinctively human' capacity or quality are already there in animal existence. It is Darwin who most adequately addresses Derrida's concern: why must we assume that all language, all reason, all knowledge must accord with the model of its European history? Why is language (or any distinctively human capacity) conceived as a uniquely human attribute when it must have come from somewhere, elaborated itself in its prehistorical forms, connected itself to some animal origin?[5] In Darwin's understanding, all the qualities that have been variously used to characterize man's specific uniqueness from animals are already developed in some less elaborated form in animal species.[6] This is his broad argument regarding not only reason, moral feelings, even an aesthetic sense (this occupies chapter two of *The Descent of Man*) but perhaps most unusual in the light of the structuralist and post-structural privileging of language, it is also his argument regarding language and instrumental thought.

Language, which for him functions primarily as a mode of sexual attraction or appeal, is what man shares with many species, each of which may have the capacity to elaborate and develop simpler sign systems into languages fully blown. Language originates neither in communication nor in defense: its function is *not* to enhance natural selection, to provide techniques for survival. Rather, it begins as a form of sexual allure, a mode of enhancement and intensification, as a musical form that only gradually develops itself into a language which in turn may help facilitate the qualities of reasoning, communication and information transmission that aid the survival of social groups. While it may serve to facilitate survival, Darwin insists on the primarily erotic and attractive nature of vocalization, its rhythmic and melodic force in explaining the origins of language. It begins, as Deleuze recognizes, as a mode of sexual intensification. Languages, like species, while they may not have a clear-cut or singular origin, nevertheless proliferate, compete with each other and submit to the exigencies of their own forms of 'natural selection' in the competition between individuals words within a single language as well as between different languages and language speakers.[7] Once they exist – and their origin and existence is contingent upon their (random) erotic appeal – they are submitted to precisely the same criteria of natural and cultural selection that evaluate all other biological and cultural forms. This for me is the most provocative and unusual element in Darwin's understanding of language, that supposedly uniquely human characteristic, language, along with all of the arts, along with all moral and intellectual accomplishments, is animal in its origins, sources and forces to the extent that it resides within and operates according to the logic of sexual selection, the attraction, enhancement and appeal of sexually attracted members of the same species.[8]

Language is not the uniquely human accomplishment that post-Enlightenment thought has assumed, but is already a tendency, residing within the voice and in other organs capable of resonating sound, to articulate itself, to express itself, to vibrate and thus in some way to affect bodies. Articulation, vocalization, resonance are possibilities inherent in a wide variety of organs, ranging from body parts to organs specifically devoted to or capable of emitting sounds.[9] Language is not a unique and singular accomplishment, but, like Darwin's account of convergent development of the eye or other organs in different species that are not directly linked through descent, relies on the notion that there are tendencies that many forms of life share, whether these tendencies are actualized or not. Such tendencies may be the heritable results of variations, random acquisitions. Yet life, as will-to-power, as impulse to maximize action, enables these acquisitions to come into a new form or place in those beings who do maximize actions. Such tendencies regulate the evolutionary development of various organs, such as eyes, but also such complex behaviors as articulation and vocalization: life in general must be understood as the ongoing tendency to actualize the virtual, to explore organs and activities so as to facilitate and maximize the actions they make possible. Living bodies are the ongoing provocation for inventive practice, for inventing widely varying practices, for using organs and activities in unexpected and potentially expansive ways, for making art out of the body's capacities.

If language begins as song, as cadence or musical resonance, a force which in some sense excites, intensifies, and marks both the bodies that articulate song and those that hear it, then there are clearly strong affiliations between human language and the sometimes remarkably complex songs of birds (remarked upon and fully elaborated musically in the work of Messiaen[10]), whales, dolphins and other song-forming species. Human vocalization is one form of articulation, one form of language-becoming and by no means the only path to language. The human represents one branch of an anthropoid line of language; birds a different line, and bees and other insects another line altogether. Each develops languages, forms of articulated becoming, sign-systems, according to its own morphological capacities, its own sexual interests and its own species-specific effects. Each 'speaks' as it can, elaborating a line of movement that brings sound, movement, resonance into being, that composes songs, sound-lines, statements, expressions as complex and rich as each species can bear.

Are there not a hundred thousand potential languages, romantic themes, urges, impulses to be transmitted and acted on? Is not language (and music), connected to stirring, enhancing and elaborating emotions, affections, passions? Is not the language of bees as open to elaboration, to musicality, to poetry, that is, to dissemination or the trace, as any human language? Karl von Frisch's observations of the remarkable dancing language of bees, used by Lacan as a form of proof that human language is of a fundamentally different order, regulated by its own signifying chain rather than through a fixed code which correlates only with real objects in the world (Lacan distinguishes the internal structure of signification from the external structure of reference), demonstrate so much more: they attest not just to the indexical or demonstrative nature of signs, but to the contaminating effects of musicality. As Frisch describes it, bees do not transmit a message that precisely locates a source of food in the so-called round dance: they transmit something less specific but equally motivating. They impart information that there is nutrition, but not unambiguously, and not without the bees themselves fanning out and seeking nutrition in a wide area without a precise location for the source of the food. Above all they generate a wave of excitement, a wave of activity to the bees in the vicinity of the dance. Bees, pleased with their discovery of rich sources of food, dance joyously – the happier they are, the more vigorous is their dance. Other bees do not observe the round dance (or its companion in communication, the waggle dance) which is commonly performed in a darkened hive; they feel it, with their bodies, their antennae, in the contagious movements they themselves come to enact.[11] If there are a hundred thousand potential languages, expressive impulses, and modes of bodily communication, ranging from the pheromonal language of ants, to the dancing vibratory movements of bees and the song performances of birds, to the chemical language of cells themselves, then new notions of collectivity, new notions of social production, new modes of linguistic analysis are waiting to be born, commensurate with and adequate to the multiplicity of life-forms to which they apply. A new humanities becomes possible once the human is placed in its properly inhuman context.

3. Animal Ethics, Aesthetics and Rationality

Darwin has suggested in a most surprising and provocative fashion that if we place man in his rightful place as one among many animal species, it is no longer clear whether the qualities that man defines as uniquely his own – the forms of reason that enable abstraction, logic, arguments, deductions, inferences and so on, or the forms of moral, religious, ethic or aesthetic discernment and commitments and practices that others have specified as uniquely human – do in fact serve to distinguish man from other animals. If man is not the only species that produces and judges reason, morality, art or religion, this not only problematizes all of the humanities that have made the human the mark and measure of social creativity, it also obscures the animal conditions for the emergence of so-called human qualities. It obscures the fundamental relativity of knowledges, aims, goals and practices (a relativity not according to given values, but a perspectivalism that is always relative to the perceiving, moving, acting body and its particular morphology), the ways in which each species, from the humblest to the most complex, orients its world according to its interests, capacity, knowledge and use.

Darwin makes it clear that he does not believe that it is possible to understand a single (God-given) morality, reason or logic to regulate all of life on earth. Rather, each species, each bodily form, orients the world, and their actions in it, according to its ability to maximize action in the world, the kinds of action that its particular bodily form enables. He speculates that we cannot assume that the kinds of morality that we as humans find 'natural' or conducive to our well-being (as widely conflicting as these are among different categories of the human) are of the same kind that would regulate other species. He argues that if other social animals – and he refers here primarily to bees, a favorite among philosophers! – can be rightfully attributed a sense of beauty, morality or well-being, a very different type of ethics, aesthetics and technics would come into existence, just as language of a very different kind than the human has now been elaborated as the masterful and complex language of bees:

> I do not wish to maintain that any strictly social animal, if its intellectual faculties were to become as active and as highly developed as in man, would acquire exactly the same moral sense as ours….If, for instance, to take an extreme case, men were reared under precisely the conditions of hive-bees, there can hardly be a doubt that our unmarried females would, like the worker-bees, think it a sacred duty to kill their brothers, and mothers would strive to kill their fertile daughters; and no one would think of interfering. Nevertheless the bee, or any other social animal, would in our supposed case gain, as it appears to me, some feeling of right and wrong, or a conscience. (*Descent* 1. 73)

We have here an insect ethics, a morality that accords with the morphologies and life-cycle of bees, in which the self-interest of various categories of bees drives a way of living, a mode of morality which maximizes what bees privilege. Were men to be brought up as bees, Darwin suggests, they too would elaborate a bee-morality as if this were given only to man. Our sense of right and wrong, of fellow-feeling and antagonism to enemies and outsiders, is not derived from a uniquely human sensibility or from a social organization that is purely man-made. Ethics, he suggests, is an effect of how we live, what we need to enhance and transform that mode of living and is thus as open to the forces of natural selection as every other evolving phenomenon. An insect ethics is as elaborate and developed as are forms of insect taste and insect discernment; to accompany any insect ethics, there is also one, or indeed many, insect aesthetics, insect pleasures, insect desires, insect forms of life, insect modes of intensification.

Darwin implies that the different morphological and social structures that regulate species life, that privilege certain organs and activities, imply an ethics, aesthetics and technics, or at least their most rudimentary forms. The different needs and tastes of different species imply a wide variety of forms of intelligence, sociality and creativity which are themselves submitted to the forces of natural selection. These various forms of ethics, aesthetics and technics are the elementary resources for group and individual survival.

There are, in short, a multiplicity of forms of reason, love, curiosity, conscience, tool-making, art-making, invention if we focus not only on the vast range of human cultures but also at the open tendencies of various animal species, each on its own path of evolutionary elaboration. There are as many forms of beauty and artfulness as there are forms of sexual attraction, and as many forms of sexual attraction as there are different body ideals and pleasing forms. There are as many forms of reason, and thus modes of knowing, forms of apprehension, as there are organs of perception and modes of reliably informed action. There are as many modes of ethics or morality as there are bonds that bind together individuals and groups through relations of affection, convenience, safety or comfort and separate them from their enemies or competitors. There are as many forms of political and social organization as there are collections of large numbers, populations.

If these inventions are all forms of becoming, forms of self-transformation and part of the evolutionary becoming in which all of life partakes, then reason, language, culture, tools, and other distinctively human accomplishments must now take their place, not as the overcoming or surpassing of an animal ancestry but as its most recent elaboration, as one of the many possible lines of elaboration that life has made possible. The human is no longer in the position of speaking for and authorizing the analysis of the animal as other, no longer takes on the right to name, to categorize, the rest of the world but is now forced, or at least enticed, to listen, to respond, to observe, to become attuned to a nature it was always part of but had only aimed to master and control.

Darwin has effected a new kind of humanity, a new kind of 'enlightenment,' neither modeled on man's resemblance to the sovereignty of God nor on man's presumed right to the mastery of nature, but a fleeting humanity whose destiny is self-overcoming, a humanity that no longer knows or masters itself, that does not regulate or order materiality but that becomes other in spite of itself, that returns in spite of itself, to those animal forces which enables all of life to ceaselessly become.

Darwin has helped multiply, pluralize, proliferate all kinds of becomings, becomings in directions that cannot be known in advance, becomings which sweep up man in their forces along with all kinds of other living things. In the process, he has engendered a concept of man as a being as much at the prey of the random forces of becoming and self-overcoming, of natural selection, as any other forms of life. Man is not the center of animal life just as the earth is not the center of the universe. The human is but a momentary blip in a history and cosmology that remains fundamentally indifferent to this temporary eruption. What kind of new understanding of the humanities would it take to adequately map this decentering that places man back within the animal, within nature, and within a space and time that man neither regulates, understands or can control? What new kinds of science does this entail? And what new kinds of art?

Works cited

Darwin, Charles. *The Descent of Man, and Selection in Relation to Sex*. 1871. Princeton: Princeton University Press, 1981
————. *The Origin of Species*. 1859. Oxford: Oxford University Press, 1996
Deleuze, Gilles. *Essays Critical and Clinical*. Tr. Daniel W Smith and Michael A Greco. Minneapolis: University of Minnesota Press, 1997
————, and F. Guattari. *A Thousand Plateaus. Capitalism and Schizophrenia*. Tr. Brian Massumi. Minneapolis: University of Minnesota Press, 1987
Derrida. Jacques. *The Animal That Therefore I Am*. Tr. David Wills. New York: Fordham University Press, 2008
Freud, Sigmund. 'Fixation to Traumas – The Unconscious.' 1916. *The Standard Edition of the Complete Psychological Works of Sigmund Freud*. 24 vols. Ed. & tr. James Strachey. London, 1953–74. Vol. 16.
————. 'A Difficulty in the Path of Psychoanalysis.' 1917. *The Standard Edition of the Complete Psychological Works of Sigmund Freud*. 24 vols. Ed. & tr. James Strachey. London, 1953–74. Vol. 17
Frisch, Karl von. *Bees. Their Vision, Chemical Senses and Language*. Ithaca: Cornell University Press, 1950.
————. *The Dancing Bees. An Account of the Life and Sense of the Honey Bee*. Tr Dora Ilse. New York: Harvest, 1953

Grosz, Elizabeth. *The Nick of Time. Politics, Evolution and the Untimely.* Durham, NC: Duke University Press, 2004

Lacan, Jacques. 'The Function and Field of Speech and Language in Psychoanalysis.' *Écrits.* Tr. Bruce Fink. New York: Norton, 2006

Notes

1   Derrida's 2008 text *The Animal that Therefore I Am* provides a moving testament to the intimate connectedness of man, this man at any rate, and the various and multiple worlds of animals. Derrida makes it apparent how much has been conceptually invested in ensuring that we, the all-too-human, are not cast into this animal world as one among many, but only as the one who rules, the one who need not know, and does what he can not to know, what the animal shares with all that is living, what it feels, acts, suffers (27).

2   Freud well understood the affront to the primacy of consciousness that science offered, seeing his own revelation of the unconscious as the third and most decisive blow to human self-conception (Freud, 1916, 284-5) The first blow is cosmological, it displaced man, and the earth from the centre of the universe; the second is a biological wound to human narcissism; and the third is a psychological injury that human narcissism sustains in the advances that science makes in spite of the wishes of consciousness itself. (See also Freud, 1917, 140–141). It is significant that for Derrida it is no longer the first or third traumas with which philosophy must now deal but only the second, in whose wake we live today (Derrida 136)

3   Linguistics relies on a pragmatics, for language is itself diagrammatic, it enacts rather than represents:
'If the external pragmatics of nonlinguistic factors must be taken into consideration, it is because linguistics itself is inseparable from an internal pragmatics involving its own factors' (Deleuze and Guattari 91).

4   '[Humans] have given themselves the word in order to corral a large number of living beings within a single concept: "The Animal," they say. And they have given it to themselves, this word at the same time according to themselves, reserving for them, for humans, the right to the word, the naming noun, the verb, the attribute, to a language of words, in short to the very thing that the others in question would be deprived of, those that are corralled within the grand territory of the beasts: The Animal' (Derrida 32).

5   Derrida is highly critical of Lacan's attempts in 'The Function and Field of Speech and Language in Psychoanalysis' to distinguish between human language, based as it is on the signifying chain and the internal and potentially infinite relation of signifiers, and animal coding, which Lacan considers to be a fixed relation between a sign and reality, a feature he attributes to the dancing language of bees that Karl von Frisch discerned. For Lacan, we can say that [a code such as that of the dancing bee] is distinguished from language precisely by the fixed correlation between its signs and the reality they signify. For in a language, signs take on their value from their relations to each other in the lexical distribution of semantemes as much as in the positional, or even flectional use of morphemes – in sharp contrast to the fixity of coding used by bees. The diversity of human language takes on its full value viewed in this light. (Lacan 245-46)
Derrida problematizes this distinction between a language and a code by affirming that all codes, like languages, 'take on their value from their relations to each other' (124), implying that there is no logical gulf between the self-sustaining signifying

chain Lacan affirms as truly language and those systems of code that animals use to communicate.

6 Darwin remains skeptical of any unbridgeable gap between man and other animal species. First he claims that all the qualities that are to be uniquely attributed to man are also there in a less developed form in other species; and second, he claims that there is so little agreement among men themselves about what uniquely characterizes the human, that it seems the gap is not as impermeable as it first appears: …
many authors have insisted that man is separated through his mental faculties by an impassable barrier from all of the lower animals. I formerly made a collection of above a score of such aphorisms, but they are not worth giving, as their wide difference and number prove the difficulty, if not impossibility, of the attempt. It has been asserted that man alone is capable of progressive improvement; that he alone makes use of tools or fire, domesticates other animals, possesses property, or employs language; that no other animal is self-conscious, comprehends itself, has the power of abstraction, or possesses general ideas; that man alone has a sense of beauty, is liable to caprice, has the feeling of gratitude, mystery, etc.; believes in God, or is endowed with a conscience. (*Descent* 1. 49)

7 Darwin has convincingly argued that the origins of species and of languages are remarkably similar and the criteria by which competing languages are assessed accords with the criteria of natural selection that regulate natural selection: 'Languages, like organic beings, can be classed either naturally according to descent, or artificially by other characters. Dominant languages and dialects spread widely and lead to the gradual extinction of other tongues. A language, like a species, when once extinct, never… reappears. The same language never has two birthplaces. Distinct languages may be crossed or blended together…' (*Descent* 1. 59-69).

8 Darwin writes:
With respect to the origin of articulate language….I cannot doubt that language owes its origin to the imitation and modification, aided by signs and gestures, of various natural sounds, the voices of other animals, and man's own instinctive cries. When we treat of sexual selection we shall see that primeval man, or rather some early progenitor of man, probably used his voice largely as does one of the gibbon-apes at the present day, in producing true musical cadences, that is in singing; we may conclude from a wide-spread analogy that during the courtship of the sexes, serving to express various emotions, as love, jealousy, triumph, and serving as a challenge to their rivals. The imitation by articulate sounds of musical cries might have given rise to words expressive of various complex emotions. (*Descent* 1. 56)

9 See *Descent* 2. 330–31:
'Although the sounds emitted by animals of all kinds serve many purposes, a strong argument can be made out, that the vocal organs were primarily used and perfected in relation to the propagation of the species. Insects and some few spiders are the lowest animals which voluntarily produce any sound; and this is generally effected by the aid of beautifully constructed stridulating organs, which are often confined to the males alone. The sounds thus produced consist, I believe in all cases, of the same note, repeated rhythmically; and this is sometimes pleasing even to the ears of man. Their chief, and in some cases exclusive use appears to be either to call or to charm the opposite sex.'

10 Messiaen makes birds themselves appear in musical form in the string quartet, *Quartet for the End of Time*, but also his only opera *Saint-Francois d'Assise* as well as his solo piano of birdsong melodies, *Catalogue d'oiseaux*. His *L'Oiseau-lyre et la Ville-Fiancee* aims to capture the movement, both vocal and behavioral of the lyre bird.

11 Frisch describes in considerable detail in a number of central texts, how the language of bees consists primarily in forms of communication transmitted through forms of dancing (Lacan talks of a 'dancité,' the kind of density or force of the dance) that are more forms of rhythmic contamination than unambiguous messages. See *The Dancing Bees* 101–103; see also *Bees* 56–58.

Chapter 2

Narratives of Identity and Authenticity: The Humanities meets Leadership Studies

Jan Shaw
University of Sydney

The human sciences have been engaged in reassessing the relationship between 'the human' and 'the scientific' and, in so doing, have left the empirical or positivistic straight and narrow to wander off into somewhat more meandering intellectual territory. A map of this now more circuitous route would have to start with the *linguistic turn* ... and then move on to the *rhetorical turn*, the *interpretative turn*, and even the *historical turn*, before approaching our destination, the *narrative* or ... *narrativist turn*. (Kreiswirth 297)

In the last 25 years or so narrative has burgeoned as an alternative epistemological process. It has spread outwards from its more traditional base in literary studies, through the other interpretative sciences (history and philosophy), and can now be found across a range of disciplines which could loosely be described as 'the arts and human sciences' (Kreiswirth 297). Narrative has been adopted as a methodological approach within the human sciences because it presents possibilities for creating new kinds of knowledge.

While there is ample opportunity for cross-fertilization within disciplines that recognise both narrative and empirical forms of knowledge, there are also incommensurabilities between the two that need to be acknowledged and articulated. Most fundamentally, empiricism is an archaeological project based upon the recovery of pre-existing facts, for example, on broad-ranging statistical data or the results of repeatable, observable experiments. In other words, empirical knowledge is based upon the tenets of retrievability through the traditional mechanism of the scientific method. Narrative, on the other hand, operates within the realm of discourse. It is simultaneously an effect and a cause of discursive formations, existing at any moment as one of a range of possibilities. In other words, it is an approach to knowledge based upon the production of meaning rather than the excavation of facts. Therefore, the acceptance of narrative as an approach to knowledge necessarily undercuts the assumption that there is one truth out there waiting to be discovered.

Being explicit about narrative denies claims to transcendence and enables the localities of practice to be examined in terms of their complexity, contradictions and multivocity. (Rhodes and Brown 179)

While narrative has been embraced by disciplines that traditionally privilege empirical methods, questions remain as to whether the translation of narrative into these disciplines has sustained its potential multivocality, or whether one possibility is privileged over others and thus becomes the 'truth' discovered. Martin Kreiswirth has questioned the validity of the distinctive and individualistic appropriation of narrative methods into different disciplines, particularly the 'human sciences' (294). He argues particularly that inappropriate slippages in argument occur because of the difficulty in sustaining distinctions between process and artefact, and between different kinds of truth claims. This paper takes Kreiswirth's critique and applies it to the life stories approach to authentic leadership as delineated by Shamir and associates (Shamir et al.; Shamir & Eilam), and thereby demonstrates that the construction of knowledge through narrative can indeed slip into inappropriate claims to truth.

Narrative & Identity

Narrative approaches to identity have been enthusiastically adopted in business and organisational studies. Many of these approaches have centred around narrative's potential to organise one's life into some kind of meaningful trajectory. Narrativisation has become a mechanism to overcome the anxiety of a fragmented and apparently random life, giving it continuity and meaning, and perhaps even unity (Giddens). This has developed, in some cases, into an active appropriation of narrative to consciously script a teleology into one's life (Shamir & Eilam; Shamir et al.). These approaches highlight the 'unique ability' of narrative to show 'causality, temporal interrelation, and teleology' (Kreiswirth 309). The effect is a structuring of inevitability into the outcome of one's chosen actions. Privileging agency imputes personal responsibility to success, but also to failure, thus connecting morality with success. Success becomes a matter of choice, and choice a matter of 'character' (Collinson 530). In this way these approaches focus on the development of 'moral agents, with pasts, presents, and futures' (Kreiswirth 309).

While such narratives might be successfully traced, identity is not simply a matter of adopting a favoured script. Aspiration is not necessarily enough to secure full coherency of the desired identity (Alvesson & Sveningsson). Indeed, a misplaced reliance on the agency of the self to intervene in the life-story narrative can lead to a number of difficulties. Sveningsson and Larsson have shown that, while a preferred identity can be invoked through the operation of identity work, this can in fact lead to the creation of a 'fantasy' of identity rather than connecting identity with 'actual practice' (Sveningsson and Larsson). Others have shown that the self actually contains a number of structural ambiguities. For example, Knights and Willmott have noted that one experiences oneself simultaneously as agent in one's life and also as an external viewer of oneself in one's life, as both narratee and narrator (Knights and Willmott). Further, Collinson has argued that the self is not one, but a number of coexisting identities drawn from the many different aspects of life: 'body, ethnicity, religion, possessions, family status, gender, age, class' and so on (Collinson 534). In this view, attempts to consciously secure a unified identity are necessarily doomed to failure, and can thus reinforce insecurity (Collinson 534). Indeed, conscious identity work (rather than unconscious) has been associated with self-doubt, with worry about or threat to self-identity (Alvesson and Willmott). Deliberating engaging with conscious identity work, with drafting one's own narrative identity, might therefore be productive of its own anxieties.

One particular ambiguity produced by opening identity up in this way is an exaggerated sense of agency. Knights and Willmott (1989) argue that a narrow or limited freedom, coupled with self-discipline and a sense that the 'right' choice will remedy anxiety and isolation, is in fact a form of subjugation. Indeed, the discursive privileging of particular dominant narratives can have extraordinary and counter-intuitive effects. Discourse can rework coercion into apparent voluntarism (Grey, 1994), the local effect of which might be the production of an apparently self-produced narrative identity which is in fact the result of targeted organisational control mechanisms (Alvesson and Willmott). Indeed, Collinson argues that intensifying material and symbolic insecurity is a conscious motivational mechanism for contemporary management (541). Granting agency to the self in the production of narrative identity could therefore be seen as, at best, risking an increase in anxiety, at worst, a deliberate ploy to increase anxiety and insecurity, and thereby motivation, consequently also increasing complicity and dependency.

While it could be argued that these divergent views are the result of the multivocality of narrative, it is not within the individual narratives of identity themselves where the divergence is found. Rather, it is within the narrative of narrative; it is the overarching frame of disciplinary narrative which differs. It is this narrative that Kreiswirth critiques. Kreiswirth urges a re-examination of the ways in which the stories which come from narrative methods are 'formulated, used and considered' (Kreiswirth 294). His enquiry goes much further than simply considering the meaning that is ascribed to stories. It is not only a question of content and form, but also of the content and form of content and form, and of context and process in their broadest and most multivalent terms.

Kreiswirth proposes that the production of flawed narrative truths is the result of confusions, or slippages, which easily occur when narratives are mined for meaning in the human sciences. First, he cites misunderstandings and confusion around the fundamental 'bivalency' of narrative: 'the 'what' of the story told and the 'how' of its telling' (302). The 'what' is the representation, the sequence of depicted events, that which is told, the 'conceptualized or reified content'; in other words, the tale (302–3). The 'how' is the crafting of the narrative, the sequences of signs produced and their ongoing method of organisation, the 'discursive performance'; in other words, the telling (302–3). Kreiswirth argues that failing to distinguish between the tale and the telling results in a slippage of truth and knowledge claims from one spatiotemporality to another, most significantly, from the process of telling, or the authority of the teller, to the referential accuracy of the tale itself.

Kreiswirth extends his concern to another distinction which is often elided in narrative methods, that between truth claim and truth value. Traditionally, narrative has been associated with literary studies where claims to referential truth or representational accuracy have little significance. In the broader human sciences, however, narrative has moved into a different discursive space, a space that interacts directly with the real world, a space in which narrators want to make claims to referential truth. These claims to truth, however, mean very little if they are not perceived as such. Kreiswirth thus emphasises not only the claims made by narrators, but also the 'web of responses to these claims' (314). In other words, Kreiswirth argues that just as much attention should be paid to the reception of narratives, to the contexts of dissemination and the meaning attributed to them by audiences, as to the asserted or attributed claims of narrators and the texts themselves. For Kreiswirth, while truth claims can be made by narrators or texts, it is only the audience within the context of reception of the narrative which can determine the truth value.

The next two sections of this paper consider Kreiswirth's problematics and apply them to a the life-stories approach to authentic leadership. Shamir and associates propose a 'life-stories' approach to explore issues of identity and authenticity as they arise in the recent formulations of authentic leadership. Authentic leadership developed as a response to the corporate collapses of the late 1990s and early 2000s, and the unethical leadership practices which came to light in the analyses that followed. Authentic leadership revolves around the idea of 'being true to one's core beliefs and values and exhibiting authentic behaviour' (Gardner et al 345). Authenticity 'involves "owning" who one truly is' (Sparrowe 421). The life-stories approach is an examination of leaders' life stories, or in some cases published autobiographies, in order to shed light upon the 'true' self (Shamir & Eilam 397, 402). These life stories, however, are not 'truth' in terms of referential truth or representational accuracy. They are explicitly subjective, and aligned with narrative constructions of identity (Shamir et al. 17; Shamir & Eilam 402). It is an approach based on positive psychology which promotes personal agency in identity creation through narrative processes. As such, the life-stories approach is itself a narrative, and it is this narrative which provides an ideal example from the field to explore Kreiswirth's largely theoretical position.

From the telling to the told

Narrative by its very signification and cultural use is both presentation and presented; the narratological problematic, the basic formal relationship between the what and the how, is thus contained within the term itself and infects, to some degree, any attempt to define, legitimize, or criticize it. (Kreiswirth 303)

The narrative approach to leaders' life stories, as delineated by Shamir and associates, examines the text of life stories as enabling self-constructs rather than as a representation of actual lives or histories. In this view, life stories are based upon life events, but are active and conscious constructions which work as self-justification mechanisms, both to the self and to others. The focus is on the agency of the narrator in making the life story into an appropriately enabling leadership narrative, rather than the story itself. This section will show, however, that once the story is constructed, the truth claim carefully argued in relation to the process of the telling slides onto the tale itself. This happens almost imperceptibly as explicit and implicit truth claims play themselves out in the complex interrelationship, the narratological problematic, between the tale and its telling.

In the life-story approach there is explicitly no assumption that the coherence, linearity or causality in the leader's story objectively reflect a real life situation.

> [T]he life story ... is not a testimony to the objective events that happened, but the manifestation and expression of the events as perceived and interpreted by the individual that experienced them ... (Shamir et al. 17)

In this view, life stories are based upon perception, interpretation and individual experience. Thus the first-person subjective experience is foregrounded. This is an interesting rhetorical move which presents complicated shifts in partial truth claims.

The truth claims in first person narratives are complex, operating at a number of levels. The truth claim in relation to referentiality is always necessarily partial, but the truth claim in relation to experiential knowledge cannot be so easily pinned down. Explicitly, it cannot be proven but also cannot be effectively refuted. Implicitly, the first person narration invokes personal identification and an empathic response which aligns the audience with the narrator's position. The audience is literally invited into the narrator's world, to see what they see, and experience what they experience. If the perspectival position of the audience is successfully conflated with that of the narrator, then the experiential knowledge of the narrator, however personal it might be, becomes, at least vicariously, the audience's own. Therefore, while the explicit truth claims of the first person narrative are always partial, the implicit truth claim is entirely personal, both yours and mine, and it is complete.

Having established the legitimacy of the first-person account, Shamir and associates' argument takes another step, introducing an active authorial agency.

> Personal narratives are much more than remembered. They are *constructed* and involve *thinking* more than memory ... This *storied construction* of reality has less to do with facts and more to do with *meanings* ... narrators *select* the elements of the story *to confer* meaning on prior events ... *highlighting* certain participants and parts and *ignoring* or *hiding* others. (my emphasis, Shamir et al. 17)

This authorial agency is presented as involving quite conscious and strategic choices. The first-person subjective perspective of 'memory' is here leveraged up to 'thinking', and consciousness is further foregrounded in process such as 'select', 'to confer', 'highlighting', 'ignoring', 'hiding'. Further, the life stories are 'constructed', they are 'storied construction', associated with 'meaning' and disassociated from 'fact'. Life stories are constructed retrospectively. This allows not only for the more innocent result of rendering a coherence to life as it has been lived, but can also be used to justify actions and explain outcomes: 'the outcome serves as the organizing principle around which the story is told' (17). By foregrounding agency in this way, the truth claim is slipping further away from the narrative itself and onto the processes of narrativisation.

The narrativisation process itself serves an agentive function. Retrospectively creating a narrative of one's life necessarily suggests that other choices could potentially have been made; different events could have been determined to be significant, different people influential, different causal connections made. Shamir and associates make a causal link between the determination of these choices and the identity of the narrator. However, rather than making identity the determiner of choice, it is choice that is the determiner of identity:

> the story-teller's identity ... is a product of the relationship between life experiences and the organized stories of these experiences. Some writers claim that life stories are a way of fashioning identity ... Others advocate that personal narratives *are* people's identities. They view identity as a story created, told, revised and retold throughout life. (Shamir et al. 17)

By this account, identity is a product of the life story. Life comes first, then the life story is retrospectively and actively constructed, and finally identity is drawn from that life story. Identity is therefore not innate, it does not pre-exist the life story. Rather, one is an active agent in the construction not only of the life story, but also of identity. Indeed the distinction between the two is somewhat unclear at this point. What is clear, however, is that the truth claim revolves around agency in the process of narrativisation, the truth is in the telling rather than the story told.

Unfortunately, the lack of clarity between identity and the life-story does become an issue. The introduction of the term 'identity' seems to trigger assumptions about truth, and consequently what truth claims can be made. First, there is confusion about the cause and effect relation of the life story and identity. To quote the first sentence of the above-cited paragraph in full:

> Life stories express the story-teller's identity, which is a product of the relationship between life experiences and the organized stories of these experiences. (Shamir et al. 17)

These few additional words demonstrate the confusion. If life stories 'express' the story teller's identity, then identity precedes the story. But then, as noted above, even in the same sentence, identity is presented as a 'product' of the stories, meaning that the story precede identity. This chicken-and-egg confusion is not itself undermining of the argument as a whole, as long as the notion is sustained that identity and the life-story remain in a close and mutually constructive relationship. However, the problem is seriously compounded by an immediately following, and somewhat startling, truth claim:

> [W]e *know* or *discover* ourselves, and *reveal* ourselves to others, by the stories we tell about ourselves. Life stories provide an explanation of *what the person is* at present. (Shamir et al. 17)

All of a sudden, life stories have become a source of truth. The terms 'know', 'discover', 'reveal' suggest that life stories have the power to uncover some kind of pre-existing or underlying truth, and that truth is no less than 'what the person is'. In other words, the truth claim has slipped from the telling to the told. No longer is the emphasis on the process of narrativisation and the agency of the narrator, but the truth claim clearly sits upon the content of the tale.

A sleight of hand has occurred in the argument. A slippage of truth claim has been effected, it seems to me, in the problematic truth claim introduced with the notion of identity. Identity is positioned as a construct, closely aligned with the life story as noted above, and thus, like the life story, initially makes a minimal truth claim. However, this is a somewhat counter-intuitive position. The intuitive position, the subjective truth as we experience it, is that identity is simply *there*, it is *who we are*. The argument implicitly taps into this subjective experiential knowledge by invoking the first person plural, 'we know or discover ourselves', and it works because it is experientially, subjectively, intuitively true. As a result, the implicit truth claim of identity is sustained, and subsequently acts as a truth anchor for the life story.

Consequently, in Shamir and associates case study analysis, life stories occupy a somewhat paradoxical position. They are presented simultaneously as constructs, and are also mined for the truths they reveal. Further, despite the claim that the life stories are viewed as 'texts that operate at the time of their telling' (Shamir et al. 16), the study explicitly excludes a consideration of 'specific individuals in their particular context', aiming instead to 'transcend particular contexts' (18). The study does not consider the individual lives, but the texts as stand alone artefacts, out of any spatiotemporal context. This effectively excludes the possibility of drawing any conclusions about authorial agency, a point so vividly delineated earlier (other than the representation of it in the tale). Instead, the study focuses on identifying 'self-concepts, values, traits and behaviors' (24) as they are depicted, in other words, at face value. From these a 'taxonomy' of 'proto-stories' is produced, based upon the major themes found (19).

In the final analysis it is the story which is attributed with the agency; it is the 'stories that enable leaders to lead and exert influence on followers' (24). This demonstrates a final slippage of the truth claim. Ironically, the carefully argued and supported explicit claim to truth, that of authorial agency in the act of the telling, is used to cut the story free from its author and its context. The effect is a potent example of the power of implicit truth claims. The disconnection of the story from its grounding effects a generalisation of the story; it is now a story from which can be drawn universal truths.

Thus the narrative of the life-stories approach is founded upon, and promulgates, a confusion between the explicit truth claims in the presented argument, and the implicit truth claims of the first-person narrative. Through this confusion it becomes enmeshed within the narratological problematic as identified by Kreiswirth, unable to adequately distinguish between the tale and the telling.

From truth claim to truth value

[I]gnorance of the distinctions between the different functions that are achieved by this form, distinctions between the truth value and truth claim of narrative knowledge, is an issue that has consistently plagued the recent narrativist turn in the human sciences. (Kreiswirth 314)

It is not enough to consider only the truth claims made by the text (or narrator), whether they be claims to referential accuracy, causal coherence, or even to the production of subjective experiential meaning. Truth value and the commitment to it, Kreiswirth argues, also need to be considered. This section argues that the most significant slippage which occurs in the life-stories approach is the shift in commitment to truth value. This shift becomes evident only when the site of reception is considered. The life-stories approach itself anticipates a striking contrast between the site of production and that of reception, but leaves this difference undiscussed.

Truth value is a measure of the accuracy of the truth claims made by the text against the commitment to truth value of that particular discourse, while taking into account the operation of that discourse within the particular context of reception. The commitment to truth value is based upon 'convention, contract, and context as these are inferred from the discourse and played out in the world' (Kreiswrirth 313–14). In other words, the commitment to truth value varies from discourse to discourse and audiences make assumptions about the commitment to truth value of a particular text as an instantiation of a particular discourse. Further, narrators play on these assumptions by using discursive techniques which invoke one discourse or another, and sometimes several. Only when such a commitment is determined can the truth value be determined. So, while truth claims are made by the text, truth value is determined by the audience. This determination necessarily occurs within a particular context of reception, the time and place of the particular communication of the story to that particular audience. Truth value is therefore a tricky and variable thing, as the reception of a text can change, and depends upon the particular uses to which the text is being put in any particular instance.

For Shamir and associates in the life-stories approach the commitment to truth value of the life story is heavily modified by the explicit claim to the constructedness of the narratives, a position supported by first-person subjective perspective (as noted above) and further compromised, legitimately in their view, by the strategic purpose of the life story: 'the self as narrator not only recounts but justifies' (Shamir et al. 17), both to the self and to others. The assumption is that leaders' life stories provide the leader with 'a self-concept from which he or she can lead' (13). The argument runs thus:

> to lead, people need to justify to themselves, as well as to others, not only their social position, but also their sense of self-confidence and self-efficacy, and knowing better than others where to go or what to do. (Shamir et al. 15)

The life story can be used to develop such a self-concept, indeed those who aspire to be leaders 'need to find or construct' (15) a life story that is appropriate to these desired goals.

In terms of its referential accuracy the commitment to truth value is therefore minimal. This potentially affects the truth value assigned to the story, as any truth claims made by the story are compromised by the low commitment to truth value. This position is consistent with the high level of commitment to truth value in the process of narrativisation of the life story, in the constructedness of the story and the agency of the narrator. The truth value of the claim to narratorial agency is, therefore, potentially high.

There is, however, one more question that needs to be asked before any truth value can be determined in relation to these life stories. According to Kreiswirth's formulation, in the final analysis, it is the audience who evaluates truth value. The self as audience has already been considered above. The audience as those third parties who are in receipt of the life story, or more precisely, the followers who are constructed by the life-story of the leader, remain to be considered. As noted above, the truth value is determined against the commitment to truth value inferred by the audience, with reference to the particular context of reception. In other words, it is not only the putative functions the text performs that are relevant, but the effects the text has on the audience in the real world. The actual effects on the audience cannot be retrieved and discussed here, but the commitment to truth value of the life stories from the audiences' point of view is anticipated by Shamir and associates' study.

Shamir and associates present four arguments to support their proposal that 'life stories play an important role in the leadership process' (Shamir et al. 14). Two of these relate to the effects that the story can have on followers. The first is when the leader is not personally known to the followers. In this case, the leader's life story can provide 'indirect sources of information' (14) upon which the followers may base their knowledge of the leader. Second, even when the followers do come to know the leader personally, their initial expectations may be formed by preceding knowledge which 'often includes parts of the leader's life story' (14). The life story in both of these cases is presented as a repository of 'information' (13, 14, 16), particularly about the leader's 'beliefs', 'traits', 'behaviors', and 'values' (13, 14, 15, 16, 24). Such initial expectations may even 'constrain or bias' subsequent perceptions, becoming 'self-fulfilling prophecies' (14). This 'indirect knowledge' from the life stories is therefore given a higher status by individuals than even their own subsequent personal observation. In this way Shamir and associates position the reception of the life stories as within a discursive space which has a high commitment to truth value. Moreover, they assume that the audience will grant the life stories a high truth value, even to the extent that the belief in the stories will override any discrepancy the audience might personally perceive. This commitment to truth value is quite specifically related to the referential accuracy of the text of the life story itself.

There is, therefore, a fundamental disconnection between the commitment to truth value in the discursive location of the production of the life story, and that assumed in the discursive context of reception. This is a significant issue, particularly in relation to the claims of authenticity that the life-stories approach seeks to make. Gardner et al. argue that 'authentic relations' are an essential component of authentic leadership, and authentic relations are characterised by, among other things, 'transparency, openness, and trust' (Gardner et al. 345). An argument for authentic relationships would be difficult to sustain alongside an awareness of the disjunction in the commitment to truth value.

It seems to me that the life stories approach is unaware of its own processes of narrativisation. While on the one hand it embraces a narrative method, on the other hand the only narrative it recognises is the life story. It seems blind to the story the approach itself actually tells. As a result the story of the life story approach becomes paradoxical, in that it is driven by conflicting impulses. It wants the process of the telling to matter as much as the tale itself, but gives so much licence to the narrator that the potential truth value of the tale is undercut. At the same time, the life stories approach eschews the narrator, relegates the process of telling, and decontextualises the tale in the taxonomic project of proto-stories.

Another conflicting impulse can be found in the troubled question of context. The dismissal of context as a relevant consideration is a dismissal of the importance of discursive location. Different claims are made, however, of the context of production and the context of reception, particularly in relation to the commitment to truth value. This lack of self-reflexivity is evident in the claim of a generalised ambiguity in the truth value of life stories, that leaders' life stories 'partially reflect social reality and partially create social reality both for the leader and for others' (Shamir 499). This statement implies that the relationship between reflection and creation is somewhat arbitrary and variable, effectively glossing over very different truth claims that are made for each of the narrator and the audience, and most particularly the different commitments to truth value of each discursive location.

Kreiswirth notes that the 'received notions of narrative' in the human sciences make it very difficult for even the most careful researchers to avoid such slippages. The only way to overcome them is to embrace the narrative *of narrative*, to be aware of one's own processes of narrativisation. The narrativist turn has been based upon the premise that narrative is ubiquitous, that narrative is 'present in every age, in every place, in every society', it is 'international, transhistorical, transcultural', 'it is simply there, like life itself' (Barthes 79). If this is so, then it is operating in and through us. As much as we might sit back and observe it elsewhere, we are producing it every day. As such, we need to be aware of what kinds of narratives we are producing, of what kinds of uses we are putting them to, and how they are received in the world. We need to be aware of what kinds of truths we are telling, not only through our work, but about that work. In other words, we need to be aware that when we begin to write, no matter on what subject matter or in what genre, we are beginning to spin a tale. And on reflection, it might be good to know just as much about the process of spinning as about the tale itself.

Works Cited

Abbott, H. Porter. *The Cambridge Introduction to Narrative.* Cambridge University Press: Cambridge, 2002

Alvesson, Mats, and Stefan Sveningsson. 'Good Visions, Bad Micro-management and Ugly Ambiguity: Contradictions of (Non-)Leadership in a Knowledge-Intensive Organization'. *Organization Studies* 24:6 (2003): 961–988

———, and Hugh Willmott. 'Identity Regulation as Organizational Control: Producing the Appropriate Individual'. *Journal of Management Studies* 39:5 (2002): 619–644

Barthes, Roland. *Image, Music, Text.* Trans. Stephen Heath. Hill and Wang: New York, 1977

Boje, David M. Narrative Methods for Organizational & Communication Research. London, Thousand Oaks, New Delhi: Sage, 2001

Collinson, David L. 'Identities and Insecurities: Selves at Work'. *Organization*, 10:3 (2003): 527–547

Gardner, William L., Bruce J. Avolio, Fred Luthans, Douglas R. May, and Fred Walumbwa. '"Can you see the real me?" A self-based model of authentic leader and follower development'. *The Leadership Quarterly*, 16 (2005): 343–372

Giddens, A. *Modernity and Self-Identity.* Cambridge: Polity, 1991

Knights, David, and Hugh Willmott. 'Power and Subjectivity at Work: From Degradation to Subjugation in Social Relations'. *Sociology* 23:4 (1989): 535–558

Kreiswirth, Martin. 'Merely Telling Stories? Narrative and Knowledge in the Human Sciences'. *Poetics Today* 21:2 (2000): 293–318

Rhodes, Carl, and Andrew D. Brown. 'Narrative, organizations and research'. *International Journal of Management Reviews,* 7:3 (2005): 167–188

Shamir, Boas. 'Leaders' Life Stories *Are* Social Reality: A Rejoinder to Gronn'. *Leadership* 1:4 (2005): 491–500.

———, Hava Dayan-Horesh, and Dalya Adler. 'Leading by Biography: Towards a Life-story Approach to the Study of Leadership'. *Leadership* 1:1 (2005): 13–29

———, and G. Eilam. '"What's your story?" A life-stories approach to authentic leadership development'. *The Leadership Quarterly* 16 (2005): 395–417

Shaw, J. 'Papering the cracks with discourse: the narrative identity of the authentic leader'. *Leadership* 6:1 (2010): 89–108

Sparrowe, Raymond T. 'Authentic Leadership and the Narrative Self.' *The Leadership Quarterly* 16.3 (2005): 419–439

Sveningsson, Stefan & Mats Alvesson. 'Managing managerial identities: Organizational fragmentation, discourse and identity struggle'. *Human Relations* 56:10 (2003): 1163–1193

———, and Magnus Larsson. 'Fantasies of Leadership: Identity Work'. *Leadership*, 2:2 (2006): 203–224

Chapter 3

A Critical Politics of the Human: Judith Butler and Gilles Deleuze

Hannah Stark
University of Adelaide

My interest in this chapter is in the legacy of Hegel in contemporary critical theory. In particular, my concern is with how the contested inheritance of Hegelian theory illuminates particular questions about the 'human' for speculative political discussions. Two philosophers who demonstrate the polarities of this debate are Judith Butler and Gilles Deleuze precisely because they offer divergent readings of Hegel.[1] Butler's rejection of Deleuze is well documented (*Subjects* 205–17; *Undoing* 198), and the reasons for this rejection become evident when the differences in their readings of Hegel are brought into relief. I believe Butler's work is foundationally Hegelian. Her first monograph, *Subjects of Desire*, is concerned with Hegel's place in twentieth-century French thought; and when re-releasing it in 1999 she defended the Hegelian model of subjectivity which informs her enduring interest in a politics of recognition.[2] Alternatively, Deleuze developed the central concept of his work, difference, through his critique and eventual abandonment of Hegel's dialectic. This is evident in his work on Bergson, Nietzsche and Spinoza during the 1960s and culminates in *Difference and Repetition*. Butler's defence of Hegel is deeply nuanced and the Hegel that she offers is different to the Hegel that Deleuze critiques. Consequently, although both use Hegel strategically, they read him so differently that their conclusions are incommensurable. I do not endeavour to create artificial communication between these interpretations but rather to examine how they engender very different kinds of politics.

Butler's writings on Hegel are concerned with his model of subjectivity and its implications for politics. Of her many explications of the Hegelian subject, I will focus only on her rendering of it (in both *Subjects of Desire* and some of her more recent publications) as etymologically 'ec-static.'[3] This subject is always outside of itself because it can find itself only through its external relations (*Subjects* 48). It becomes self-conscious in this state because its identity is mediated by the reflexivity that being outside of itself allows. As Butler acknowledges, Hegel's subject is paradoxical. Isolated in its pursuit of an autonomous self-consciousness, it also and necessarily discovers its identity by relating to others (*Subjects* 4). In her later work, Butler resolves this tension through rejecting autonomy to emphasise the binding of the subject to others. Because this results in a more nuanced articulation of identity and difference, her conception of the subject evades a common criticism of Hegel's subject, that it simply turns difference into identity. Rather, Butler's subject realises, at the moment its identity would cohere, that it cannot return to its prior state. The foundational moment of identity thus entails self-loss, and reveals a 'subject that cannot remain bounded in the face of the world' ('Preface' xv). This process of non-return determines the subject's 'ec-static' nature. Because 'becoming is being outside of self', Jean-Luc Nancy argues, such 'exposition' (*exposition*, a placing outside of) 'is the very being of the subject' (57).

Butler's subject is surrounded by alterity and it relates to its surroundings through a Hegelian process of recognition and negation. Politically, this is important to Butler, who regards the embodied sociality of intersubjectivity as 'fundamental' (*Undoing* 22). This subject achieves recognition partly by finding itself reflected in the world and partly through being recognised by others. Positioning this desire for recognition as a condition of existence, Butler aligns it with Spinoza's *conatus*. To persist in one's own being, she argues, is to be recognised: an unrecognisable being lacks the status of possibility, and possible beings are the only ones capable of persistence (*Undoing* 31).

Central to Butler's reading of this dialectic process is the role of the negative. This is a slippery concept in her work because, she concedes, negation 'constantly undermines our own knowingness' ('Preface' xi). In

Subjects of Desire, Butler writes that the appeal of negation is that it allows for constant renewal (*Subjects* 62) and, in her work, it is also what ensures that the subject can neither remain self-identical nor arrive at absolute knowledge of the world. By opening the self to the world, the negative makes problematic the separation of interior from exterior. As Hegel argues in his *Phenomenology*, although initially it may appear that the negative is *external* to the subject (because it is excluded), its constitutive function in the formation of the subject makes it, on the contrary, *internal* (21). This process of self-constitution against this negative situates the subject on the cusp of differing from itself. Fundamentally unsatisfied, this subject can only ever be a subject-in-process (*Subjects* 13). In *Frames of War*, Butler explains that this subject is inextricably linked to others because 'the subject that I am is bound to the subject I am not' (*Frames* 43).

Butler explicitly acknowledges intersubjective relations in 'Beside Oneself: On the Limits of Sexual Autonomy', in which she writes that the subject is 'impressed upon by others, impressing them as well' (*Undoing* 21). Read literally, 'impression' foregrounds not only the corporeal dimension of existing in a community but also the incorporeal aspect of our ties to one another, both of which impact on negotiations of subjectivity and embodiment. This subject is never autonomous but is always 'given over' to others in ways that it may not always perceive or control (*Undoing* 22). While conceding that political struggle by minority groups for bodily autonomy is both necessary and important, Butler cautions that it would be a mistake to limit definitions of who we are to legal frameworks which make this independence ontological, because they 'fail to do justice to the passion and grief and rage, all of which tear us from ourselves, bind us to others, transport us, undo us, and implicate us in lives which are not our own, sometimes fatally, irreversibly' (*Undoing* 20). Butler theorises the states of rage, grief and desire, in order to re-posit the ecstatic nature of subjectivity through the cleaving of the subject from itself in affective experience.[4] What is exposed at these moments is the 'constitutive sociality of the self' which forms 'a basis for thinking a political community of a complex order' (*Undoing* 19).

The appeal to community that runs through Butler's work asks how the recognition in our intersubjective relations creates and polices the category of the human and the inhuman. Focus on the human is a central element of Kojève's influential interpretation of Hegel in which he refuses his appeal to ontological unity. He examines what recognition means for the human, writing, '[i]t is only by being "recognized" by another, by many others, or – in the extreme – by all others, that a human being is really human, for himself as well as for others' (9). This formulation is evident as a critical imperative in Butler's work on recognition. She concludes, however, that the Hegelian tradition ignores how the category of the human is an exclusionary mechanism which confers humanness on some while depriving others of its status (*Undoing* 2). In *Frames of War*, Butler describes the human as a 'differential norm' (*Frames* 76). The strong influence of Foucault is evident here as she theorises recognition as a site of power through which the regulatory operation of norms enable such categories to be produced and undone (*Undoing* 31–2).[5] To be possible in this context is to be recognisable, which means that existence is subject to norms which are pre-existing. This subject is therefore constituted as human by external norms, putting it outside of itself and reminding us of its ecstatic nature. Consequently, she writes, '*the ec-static character of our existence is essential to the possibility of persisting as human*' (*Undoing* 33; emphasis in original).

Butler's political project is to expand those 'grids of intelligibility' which designate the recognisably human (*Undoing* 35). In her most recent monograph she draws attention to challenging and shifting the frameworks themselves rather than diversifying the category of who is endowed with recognition (*Frames* 6). She asks if new frameworks of recognition might be possible which could allocate recognition on a more egalitarian basis (*Frames* 6). Politically, this would entail not only struggling against the epistemological systems which govern reality but also acknowledging that the project is endless (Butler 'Agencies' 35–6). 'What might it mean,' she asks, 'to feel the surety of one's epistemological and ontological anchor go, but to be willing, in the name of the human, to allow the human to become something other than what it is traditionally assumed to be' (*Undoing* 35).

Butler's focus on ontology is important here because she gives our binding to others – that is, our ecstatic nature – ontological priority. Constituted by our ties to each other, this means that ontologically 'the forming and un-forming of such bonds is prior to any question of the subject and is, in fact, the social and affective condition of subjectivity' (Butler *Frames* 182–3). This is why she speaks only of the '*social* ontology of the subject' (*Frames* 147 emphasis added). The subject, then, *is* this process of inter-relation and the ontological ecstasy it presupposes. Political engagement does not inhere in the subject but is located instead in those spaces where it negotiates the unknown, and where binding and unbinding take place (*Giving* 21). There the subject encounters those alterities which, by constantly displacing it from itself, make it ecstatic. It is at this point, when the subject is undone by the relationship to alterity, that Butler suggests is a space where the categories of human and inhuman are negotiated and it is therefore the site of 'our chance of becoming human' (*Giving* 136).[6] Theorised in this way, the category of the human is a regulatory matrix, subject to shifting norms. While contributing to the physical manifestation of the world, it exists always in a state of perpetual crisis on account of what Nancy describes as the 'restlessness' of the negative (5).

Although, Deleuze shares Butler's interest in the politics of difference, his reading of the place of negation in Hegel's philosophy differs radically from hers. While for Butler it is the negative which ensures the dialectical movement of difference, for Deleuze it is when negation is given a foundational role in ontology that the potential for difference is limited.[7] In his work he attempts to eradicate the negative and assert a notion of being which is purely positive. Although Deleuze developed his critique of Hegel while working on Spinoza as well as on Bergson and Nietzsche, I will focus here only on the latter two because he extrapolates from them his notion of the inhuman.[8] While Butler and Deleuze are both interested in asserting an ontological concept of difference and both do so, in part, through their engagement with Hegel, for Butler this is examined through its relevance for theorising subjectivity and embodiment, while Deleuze is interested in the manifestation of substance. This focus on substance is described by Hardt as an engagement with 'questions of the lowest order, questions of the nature of being' (xiii) and is consistent with Deleuze's refusal to prioritise the human.

In *Difference and Repetition* Deleuze argues that Hegel conceives of difference as infinitely large by figuring it dialectically as contradiction which positions it at its absolute maximum (*Difference* 44). For Deleuze, a model of difference which exists only at the extremities of contradiction, and enables self-constitution only through negation is a 'logical monster' in the service of identity (*Difference* 49). Deleuze discovered in Bergson a viable alternative to Hegelian difference that would sustain all of his subsequent work, because, as Elizabeth Grosz insists, 'Deleuzian difference *is* Bergsonian' ('Bergson' 5; emphasis in original). Bergson's notion of difference is described by Deleuze as 'more profound' ('Bergson's' 53) than the type of difference which could be accommodated by Hegel's system. Inevitably, Deleuze observes, Bergsonian difference loses its complexity when processed by Hegel's dialectical structure because it creates artificial polarisation, therefore eclipsing the intricacies of difference (*Bergsonism* 44). Deleuze agrees with Bergson that this is not only a false solution to a false problem. It is, 'something more profound: an illusion that carries us along, or in which we are immersed, inseparable from our condition' (*Bergsonism* 20).

In Deleuze's reading of Hegel's dialectic, the process of negation ensures that things contain what they are not as part of their essence (*Difference* 45–6). Within this structure, there is an endless process which allows for the encounter with difference but this encounter is always aimed squarely at the horizon of identity (which it will never reach). 'Hegel's circle is not the eternal return,' Deleuze writes 'only the infinite circulation of the identical by means of negativity' (*Difference* 50). For Deleuze, Bergson's critique of Hegel's dialectic hinges on his analysis of the place of the negative in the determination of being. For Bergson the negative is irrelevant to the manifestation of being because things differ from themselves immediately, not requiring the mediation of an external cause. In conceptualising the category of difference, Bergson dissociates a spatial difference-in-kind from a temporal difference-in-degree (*Bergsonism* 23). To illustrate this distinction, Deleuze cites Bergson's description of waiting for sugar to dissolve in a glass of water. Thought of in terms of difference in degree, sugar in this situation can be examined in relation to its difference from anything else. However, this process is over reliant on negativity because it defines things in terms of what they are not. Considered temporally, on the other hand, when sugar dissolves in water it differs from other things, but 'first and formally' it differs from itself (*Bergsonism* 31–2).

The essential contrast to Hegel which Deleuze finds in Bergson's work is evident here in the positioning of difference. For while Hegelian difference emphasises exterior difference (which makes the subject realise that it too is exterior to itself), Bergsonian difference is an interior property which unfolds itself over time. This has broader significance, Deleuze insists, because it indicates that, 'my own duration, such that I live it in the impatience of waiting, for example, serves to reveal other durations that beat to other rhythms, that differ in kind from mine' (*Bergsonism* 32). Difference-as-duration is important to Deleuze because it enables him to submerge the human in the temporality of all other durations.

The same imperative to contextualise the human with the inhuman can be seen in Deleuze's work on Nietzsche. In turning to Nietzsche, Deleuze finds an affirmation of difference which is rooted in his concept of the world as a composition of competing forces. These forces are not goal oriented but are engaged in ensuring their own expansion. Nietzsche categorises these constantly shifting hierarchical forces as active and reactive (Deleuze *Nietzsche* 40). Deleuze's sympathy with Nietzsche's anti-humanistic world-view gives him another reason to reject the negativity of Hegel's dialectic. By comparison with Nietzsche's Will to Power – which wills only its own difference, because that is what makes it joyous – the Hegelian dialectic is an exhausted force incapable of affirmation, and thereby irremediably reactive (Deleuze *Nietzsche* 9). Instead of thinking of the world in terms of subject and object, we should figure it as a never-ending process of shifting hierarchies and temporary alignments. In this context, the subject is not the stable entity it is often taken to be but a series of momentary crystallisations of competing forces.

The notion of the inhuman impinges on Deleuze's ontology because Bergson and Nietzsche persuaded him to minimise the importance of the human subject as an isolated and coherent entity. To think of forces rather than subjects in this context involves radically questioning traditional conceptions of the human. 'Force', Grosz writes,

needs to be understood in its full subhuman and superhuman
resonances: as *the inhuman* which both makes the human possible and
at the same time positions the human within a world where force works
in spite of and around the human, within and as the human. (*Time* 187;
emphasis in original)

Like Butler, Deleuze prioritises the subject's relation to alterity as
both constant and constitutive. However, this never contributes to the
negotiation of recognisable identities because in his work identity is only
ever a momentary illusion in a world of active and reactive forces. Because
of his rejection of recognition, Deleuze could never affirm the human as a
regulatory (albeit flexible) category on which to base politics. There is no place
in the ontological reality of incessant and uncontainable difference for the
illusions of identity that strive to subvert it. Deleuze aligns recognition with
both good sense and common sense, which are not only reductive because
they support established *doxa* (*Difference* 134), but also (Simon Lumsden
suggests) epistemologically 'homogenizing' in presupposing that all thinking
beings manifest a universal subjectivity (147). In this way, Lumsden observes,
'[r]ecognition as such comes to define the very meaning of what it is to think'
(148). The reason for Deleuze's critique of the assumption of commonality
in this Image of thought is that it contributes to abstract universals such as
the self. Deleuze's project is to reconceptualise thought in ways which require
neither recognition nor any representation to which recognition contributes
and which does not require a recognisable subject.[9] For Deleuze, recognition
is unable to perceive the new because it can only process what it knows
already. He writes,

> For the new – in other words, difference – calls forth forces in thought
> which are not the forces of recognition, today or tomorrow, but
> the powers of a completely other model, from an unrecognised and
> unrecognisable *terra incognita*. (*Difference* 136)

Deleuze insists on an image of thought which has access to the flux of
difference to which it is always immanent. While actual difference emerges

from a seething mass of virtual difference, it is always in the instant of differing from itself. What compels us to think, he maintains, is not recognition (which never perturbs thought) but encounters with what is strange and unfamiliar, or what he calls the 'imperceptible' (*Difference* 140).[10]

The role of the imperceptible, for Deleuze, destabilises both the recognisable subject and the recognisably human. 'The recognised "I" ', Baugh points out,

> is only the everyone of 'everyone knows' or 'everyone recognises', that is, the person who conforms to the status quo, and the 'We' is only the social consensus surrounding current values: this identity of the conformist with the social consensus is the outcome of the struggle for recognition. (136)

The political place at which Deleuze arrives is thus vastly different from the one reached by Butler. There is no potential for an identity politics in Deleuze's work, or even for the very complex politics of recognition which Butler develops from Hegel. He offers instead what Grosz calls 'a politics of imperceptibility' ('Politics' 470). This politics is a 'politics of acts, not identities' ('Politics' 470), prioritising not *who* is behind the actions but the actions themselves, in alignments and assemblages which refuse finality and also obstruct political teleology.

The requirement for this politics is to be open to the 'mobile cusp' (*Difference* 304) of difference, manifesting as the imperceptible. Described by Grosz as 'that which the inhuman musters' ('Politics' 471), the imperceptible cannot engender a politics based on either human agency or regulation. Ontological reality, as Deleuze understands it, is composed only of the kind of difference which is always on the instant of differing from itself. Difference is sustained, for him, not by the cycle driven by negation but through openness to forces which are beyond the human. In this respect, Deleuze's description of Bergson's philosophical project is equally applicable to his own: '[t]o open us up to the inhuman and the superhuman (*durations* which are inferior or superior to our own), to go beyond the human condition' (*Bergsonism* 28; emphasis in original).

Neither Butler nor Deleuze locates politics in the interior of the subject. By privileging exteriority instead, they demonstrate the need to ground politics in the spaces that connect all of us to one another and to the world we inhabit. To conceive of a politics which focuses only on these connective spaces is perhaps to find resources in places which have been considered the negative space of absence or vacancy. There are, however, significant limitations to both these approaches, and looking to theorise politics exacerbates these limitations. For instance, should we continue to base politics on 'the human' if we know that by doing so we will endlessly subjugate those who fall beyond the category? Or should we look to found politics on what is beyond our frameworks of perception? Although Butler's work is strategically valuable for thinking about how non-normative actions and modes of being are regulated by the process of recognition, it may not deal adequately with the complexities Grosz evokes when rejecting the political use of identity. Those problems with Hegel's philosophy that Deleuze draws attention to can be recycled, to an extent, in the critique of Butler's politics of recognition. A politics of imperceptibility, however, may be a less adequate way of dealing with the intricate specificities of community. When reviewing Grosz's *Time Travels* and *The Nick of Time*, Dorothea Olkowski commented that '[t]he explanatory power of this theory is enormous but its implications for any improvement to human life are devastating' (220). While this is undoubtedly too strong a critique, the question remains: is imperceptibility adequate to our political realities?

Works Cited

Baugh, Bruce. 'G. W. F. Hegel.' *Deleuze's Philosophical Lineage*. Eds. Graham Jones and Jonathan Roffe. Edinburgh: Edinburgh University Press, 2009. 130–46

Butler, Judith. Subjects of Desire: Hegelian Reflections in Twentieth-Century France. New York: Columbia University Press, 1987

———. 'Preface to the Paperback Edition.' Subjects of Desire. New York: Columbia University Press, 1999. Vii–xvii

———. 'Agencies of Style for a Liminal Subject.' Without Guarantees: In Honour of Stuart Hall. Eds. Paul Gilroy, Lawrence Grossberg and Angela McRobbie. London and Brooklyn: Verso, 2000. 30–38

———. Undoing Gender. New York and London: Routledge, 2004

———. Giving an Account of Oneself. New York: Fordham University Press, 2005

———. Frames of War: When is Life Grievable? London and New York: Verso, 2009

Cohen, Jeffrey J., and Todd R. Ramlow. 'Pink vectors of Deleuze: Queer theory and inhumanism.' Rhizomes 12 (2006): n.p. pp. 2/03/09 <http://www.rhizomes.net/issue11/cohenramlow.html>

Deleuze, Gilles. Bergsonism. 1966. Trans. Hugh Tomlinson and Barbara Habberjam. New York: Zone Books, 1991

———. Difference and Repetition. 1968. Trans. Paul Patton. Columbia: Columbia University Press, 1994

———. 'Bergson's Conception of Difference.' Trans. Melissa McMahon and Peligia Goulimari. The New Bergson. 1956. Ed. John Mullarky. Manchester: Manchester University Press, 2000. 42–65

———. Nietzsche and Philosophy. 1962. Trans. Hugh Tomlinson. New York: Columbia University Press, 2006

Grosz, Elizabeth. 'A Politics of Imperceptibility: A Response to 'Anti-racism, Multiculturalism and the Ethics of Identification'.' Philosophy and Social Criticism 28.4 (2002): 463–72

———. 'Bergson, Deleuze, and the Becoming of Unbecoming.' parallax 11.2 (2005): 4–13

———. Time Travels: Feminism, Nature, Power. Crows Nest: Allen and Unwin, 2005

Hardt, Michael. Gilles Deleuze: An Apprenticeship in Philosophy. Minneapolis and London: University of Minnesota Press, 1993

Hegel, G. W Phenomenology of Spirit. 1807. Trans. A. V. Miller. Oxford: Claredon, 1977

Hickey-Moody, Anna, and Mary Lou Rasmussen. 'The Sexed Subject in-between Deleuze and Butler.' Deleuze and Queer Theory. Eds. Merl Storr and Chrysanthi Nigianni. Edinburgh: Edinburgh University Press, 2009. 37–53

Holland, Eugene W. 'On Some Implications of Schizoanalysis.' Strategies 15.1 (2002): 27–40

Kojève, Alexandre. Introduction to the Reading of Hegel. Trans. James H. Nichols. New York and London: Basic Books, 1969

Lumsden, Simon. 'Deleuze, Hegel and the Transformation of Subjectivity.' The Philosophical Forum 33.2 (2002): 143–58

Nancy, Jean-Luc. Hegel: The Restlessness of the Negative. Trans. Jason Smith and Steven Miller. Minneapolis: University of Minnesota Press, 2002

Olkowski, Dorothea. 'Rev. of The Nick of Time: Politics, Evolution, and the Untimely and Time Travels: Feminism, Nature, Power. By Elizabeth Grosz.' Hypatia 21.4 (2006): 212–21

Notes

1   The correlation of these philosophers is not without precedent. This is perhaps due to their mutual interest in the concepts of difference and repetition and is particularly evident in scholarship on gender, sexuality and kinship. See for example Hickey-Moody and Rasmussen 2009, Cohen and Ramlow 2006, and Holland 2002.

2   Butler writes that her work is interested in the question: '[w]hat is the relation between desire and recognition, and how is it that the constitution of the subject entails a radical and constitutive relation to alterity?' ('Preface' xiv).

3   Although Butler refers to *Subjects of Desire* as her 'juvenilia' ('Preface' viii), there is no doubt that the germination of themes central to her oeuvre can be found in this early work and I therefore defend its usefulness for Butler scholarship. Butler's rendering of Hegelian subjectivity is complex because it takes this subject as an historical trajectory to which the work of Hegel and his interpreters (particularly Kojève and Hyppolite) contribute.

4   Butler's rejection of the autonomous subject is a continuation of themes central to her work in the 1990s, as for her the subject has never possessed an interior agency but has

always found itself in the external structures of language, discourse and power which it
then internalises.

5   These norms are not static but are brought into crisis through the failure of recognition,
causing them to exist in a state of perpetual remaking (Butler, *Giving,* 24).

6   It is significant that the 'our' which is appealed to here appears to be outside the
designated category. Butler has commented on Donna Haraway's use of this strategy,
suggesting that it brings the finality of the category into question and I read this
quotation in that light (*Frames* 76).

7   Bruce Baugh writes that Deleuze's reading of Hegel is 'almost unrelentingly negative'
(130) which Baugh finds significant in the context of Deleuze's work on the history of
philosophy which is generally concerned with affirmation.

8   For a detailed discussion of Deleuze's rejection of Hegel in his works on these
philosophers, see Hardt 1993. The problem with resistance to Hegel, both Butler and
Hardt assert, is that being situated in opposition to his work is to assume a structural
position which confirms the dialectic (Hardt xi; Butler *Subjects* 184). Deleuze's work is
not simply an opposition to the dialectic but rather, as Hardt writes, 'Deleuze's strategy
of developing a total opposition to the dialectic is accompanied by another strategy: to
move away from the dialectic, to forget the dialectic' (53).

9   It might appear that Deleuze is embracing a level of extreme abstraction here, but,
because he theorises the I and the self as abstract universals, the point of their
replacement is to address more adequately the concrete difference which composes the
world (*Difference* 258).

10 It is imperceptible because it cannot be recognised (Deleuze, *Difference,* 140).

Chapter 4

Not Quite Human:
Traversing the Uncanny Valley

Kathy Cleland
University of Sydney

From the earliest automata to contemporary robots and digital animation, human beings have always been fascinated by life-like human simulations. With advances in computer graphics, robotic technologies and artificial intelligence programming, robots and animated digital characters are becoming increasingly human-like in both appearance and behaviour. However, there are a number of difficulties for roboticists and artists who want to create believable robots and animations that have human-like appearance, behaviour and emotions. It is not easy to achieve the 'holy grail' of the perfect human simulation. Simulating human appearance, particularly facial expressions and fluid physical movements, and creating believable and appropriate social behaviour are proving to be far more difficult challenges to conquer than simulating logical human intelligence. Artificial Intelligence (AI) programs such as IBM's Deep Blue can beat even the best human chess players but no one has yet created a robot or a digital animation that can pass as human. And the real problem is not only that these near-human creations fail to pass as human, but that they often generate decidedly uncanny responses in audiences.

The uncanniness of human-like simulations is not a new phenomenon. Sigmund Freud's 1919 *The Uncanny* describes the inherent uncanniness of waxwork figures, life-like dolls and automata, and includes a lengthy discussion of E.T.A. Hoffman's 1816 story 'The Sandman' where a young man becomes infatuated with an uncanny life-like doll. But what exactly is it about these 'almost human' simulations that arouse feelings of uncanniness?

Why do they disturb us? Both Freud and Ernst Jentsch (whose 1906 'On the Psychology of the Uncanny' Freud references extensively) suggest that uncanniness is generated by our sense of unease when the boundary between living and non-living is put in question. According to Jentsch, uncanny feelings are awakened 'when there is intellectual uncertainty whether an object is alive or not, and when an inanimate object becomes too much like an animate one' (Jentsch cited in Freud 135).

Looking at simulated humanoid entities makes us reflect on the boundary conditions of exactly what it means to be human and the qualities that characterise human appearance and behaviour. The more human our humanoid creations look, the more we expect from them. When humanoid robots or virtual characters fail to look and behave as we expect humans to behave, whether this is a result of technical limitations or programming glitches, they typically come across as being unconvincing, stupid, socially inept and even downright creepy. Technical problems lead to social problems.

Feelings of uncanniness are also generated by humans who appear inhuman or out of control of their mental or physical faculties. Freud quotes Jentsch's discussion of the uncanny effect 'produced by epileptic fits and the manifestations of insanity, because these arouse in the onlooker vague notions of automatic – mechanical – processes that may lie hidden behind the familiar image of a living person.' Freud also links this sense of uncanny unease to primitive fears of demonic possession (135). Unhealthy, possessed and lacking agency – these are the uncanny qualities that are evoked by robots and digital animations that look almost (but not quite) human.

Freud's ideas about the uncanny have been taken up more recently by Japanese roboticist Masahiro Mori in his essay about 'bukimi no tani,' translated as the uncanny valley. Mori arrived at his hypothesis of the uncanny valley while conducting psychological experiments where he measured human responses to robots that incorporated varying degrees of anthropomorphism; and his ideas have also been applied in the film and animation industries. Mori argued that positive human responses to human-like entities increase as those entities become more realistically humanoid in their appearance and behaviour up until a certain point when these entities become almost human. It appears we are quite willing to suspend our sense of disbelief when human-like characteristics are displayed in entities that behave in human-like ways but are clearly non-human, for example, cartoon-like entities such as Bart Simpson or robots like *Star Wars'* R2-D2 and C-3PO. We are happy to fill in the gaps and project features and qualities into these abstract humanoid representations. However, when those gaps are filled in for us by simulations that try to be more realistically humanoid but don't quite get it right, our responses are far less positive. Rather than generating feelings of engagement and empathy, these simulations generate feelings of disquiet and repulsion.

At this point, Mori argues, it is the non-human characteristics that tend to stand out, we start to notice the 'not-quite-right' facial expressions, the flat skin tone, the strangely lifeless eyes and the disjointed movements. These 'almost human' entities appear more like animated corpses or zombies than the healthy human beings they are supposed to resemble. At this point human responses dip from feelings of empathy into the disquiet of the uncanny valley. Creating a healthy looking human simulation remains the ultimate challenge in beating the uncanny valley.

The disturbing and alienating effects of the uncanny discussed by Freud, Jentsch and Mori can be clearly seen in contemporary audience responses to humanoid robots and digital animations. Japanese roboticist Hiroshi Ishiguro, based at Osaka University, has created a number of ultra life-like humanoid robots including one modelled on his young daughter. The goal of Ishiguro and his team at Osaka University is to create a perfect humanoid robot that overcomes the uncanny valley. However, Ishiguro's creations, while impressive, still come across as more than a little creepy. Repliee 1, the android twin of his young daughter, which he calls 'my daughter's copy' reportedly made his daughter cry. 'My daughter didn't like my daughter's copy,' Ishiguro told a journalist over the phone. 'Its movement was very like a zombie' (Tucker 5). His more recent creations including Repliee Q2, based on a female Japanese television presenter, and his new Geminoid, a tele-operated robot copy of Ishiguro himself, have more life-like skin textures and movements but they have still not fully emerged from the uncanny valley. Even more unsettling is the giant robot baby CB2 which is 130cm tall, weighs 33kg, and is covered in a strange greyish putty-like silicon. CB2 has been designed to learn from its environment and its human interactors and YouTube footage shows the robot baby blinking and looking around with strangely blank, black eyes as it responds to human touch and its uncoordinated body flops around as it tries to learn to stand. Rather than evoking the strong feelings of protective care and empathy that we would normally feel for a human baby, CB2 is a bizarre creation, and its strange vocalisations, appearance and freakish size make it the poster child for the robotic uncanny.

Similar feelings of uncanniness are provoked by human simulations in digital animation. In an article in *Wired* magazine, journalist Paula Parisi calls a resurrected digital clone of Marilyn Monroe a 'digital Frankenstein' commenting that in her reanimated form, the digital Marilyn has 'a propensity to slip at a moment's notice from strikingly beautiful to alarmingly grotesque' (Parisi, sect. 3, par. 3). Similarly, animator Ward Jenkins describes Robert Zemeckis' digitally animated film *The Polar Express* as a: 'living-dead land' with 'freakish half-dead soulless children' and characters that look 'bizarre' and 'unconvincing' (Jenkins, par. 7).

What is most uncanny about these 'nearly human' simulations is that they resemble unhealthy humans, or humans who are not truly alive. As Mori states in his essay on the uncanny, it is the appearance of the healthy human that is the goal to be strived for in trying to beat the uncanny valley. The uncanniness of today's robots and digital animations is that they look like sick humans, or humans who are not in full control of their mental functions or physical movement – they resemble mechanically possessed zombies, or dead things digitally animated. As Freud and Jentsch point out, unhealthy humans and humans that appear possessed or in some way mechanical, call into question their status as fully human and provoke strong feelings of intellectual uncertainty, disquiet and anxiety.

It is also possible that there is a neurological basis underpinning these feelings of uncanniness that goes deeper than intellectual uncertainty about whether something is human or non-human, living or dead. We react on a subconscious neurological level to signs that something is 'not quite right' when we watch human movement, facial expressions and body language. Our reactions are based on thousands of years of human interaction where human physical agility and being able to correctly read human facial expressions and interpret emotions and intentions have been vital evolutionary survival skills. We use these same skills to read and evaluate humanoid robots and digital simulations.

Indeed, in *The Media Equation* (1996) Byron Reeves and Clifford Nass argue that there is no essential or functional difference in how the brain responds to 'real' people in the physical world, and how it responds to media images and artificial entities. According to Reeves and Nass our 'old brains' have not yet caught up with our new media technologies and they do not have the sophistication to distinguish between a real physical object in the world and a media image or robotic simulation. Their research suggests that humans are neurologically 'hardwired' to respond to computer images and robots in the same way that they respond to real life people and places. This does not mean that we can't tell the difference on a rational conscious level, but rather that people tend to unconsciously respond in essentially the same way to screen images of a person or a virtual computer persona as they would to a real person. Ingrained physiological responses (such as reacting to facial expressions and emotions) and social responses (such as a tendency to be polite) are carried over from the physical world into our interaction with virtual characters and robots.

Drawing on Reeves and Nass's thesis that our 'old brains' respond to human simulations as if they were human, it is not surprising that when those humanoid simulations don't look quite right, rather than putting the disturbance down to a mere technical issues, we respond in the same way as we would to a human that looked unhealthy, sick or zombie-like – we feel uneasy and disturbed. Roboticist David Hanson speculates that the experience of the uncanny valley phenomenon can be traced to a hardwired neurological response – a neurological 'emergency alarm' – as our brains respond uneasily to images of humans who look sick, unhealthy or zombie-like ('Interpreting the Neural Basis' 1).

Even if the uncanny valley can be overcome in terms of appearance and movement, creating robots and digital animations that display appropriate social responses and emotions will continue to be challenging. Researchers and theorists such as Rosalind Picard from the Affective Computing Group at MIT suggest that the development of believable, life-like robots and virtual characters also depends on creating humanoid simulations with an emotional, affective dimension that incorporates appropriate interpersonal behaviours and social responses. The more human-looking a virtual character or robotic entity is, the more audiences will expect them to act and behave and communicate in a human-like manner.

This is a tough job. Even without visual cues, getting a humanoid simulation to engage in a believable conversational exchange with a human has proved to be a very difficult task as is evidenced in the so-called Turing Test. Alan Turing set out his famous test for computer intelligence in his influential 1950 essay 'Computing Machinery and Intelligence' where he describes the scenario for an 'imitation game' to test whether a computer can successfully imitate a human being. The test is based on an earlier imitation game where an interrogator tries to guess the gender of two participants (one male and one female) by asking them questions and assessing their typewritten replies (the participants are hidden from view). In Turing's version of the game, he replaces one of the human participants with a computer and suggests that if the interrogator cannot tell the difference between the human and the computer purely from their answers, then the computer can be said to be intelligent. So far, no computer has successfully fooled a human interrogator over a lengthy period of interaction.

Once visual cues are added to the purely textual responses of the Turing Test, things are even more complex. In humans, emotion is displayed by facial expression, vocal intonation, gesture and body language. Humans learn to understand these affective cues as infants long before they learn to understand spoken words and to form rational thought processes. However, while emotion and affect are natural and integral components of social relationships and communication for humans, giving digital simulations the ability to recognise and display emotion is a very complex problem. It is much easier to program computers to process higher level cognitive skills such as rational thinking and complex mathematical computation than to create fluid movements, believable facial expressions, emotions and appropriate social responses.

Avoiding the uncanny valley

So, how can artists, animators and roboticists avoid the uncanny valley? The most obvious solution is for them to make their creations more abstract and less naturalistically human in appearance and behaviour. Mori recommends designing aesthetically pleasing robots with human appearance and human-like movements, but still maintaining a clear degree of visible artificiality. Another strategy is to play up the alien and non-human aspects of humanoid simulations, for example the Gollum character in Peter Jackson's *The Lord of the Rings* and the humanoid Na'vi race in James Cameron's *Avatar*. The advantage of incorporating clearly artificial non-human elements is that audiences will be more accepting of non-human movements and other behavioural lapses.

It is also possible that the uncanniness we experience in response to robots and digital animations may just be a transitional phase in our cultural evolution. New technologies and media forms, particularly when they are still in their glitchy developmental phase, are far more likely to generate responses of uncanniness than technologies that we have become habituated to. Film theorist Tom Gunning argues that when a new media technology is experienced for the first time, it evokes a sense of wonder and awe which is often equated with the magical and the uncanny. In his essay 'Re-Newing Old Technologies: Astonishment, Second Nature, and the Uncanny in Technology from the Previous Turn of the Century,' Gunning links the early 'cinema of attractions' with the magic tricks and illusions of variety theatre and with the display of scientific curiosities and marvels in science fairs and expositions. Just as contemporary audiences today marvel at new digital special effects in films, games and technology fairs, so too were early cinema audiences intrigued and delighted by the uncanny magic of still images coming to life and early stop motion animation and special effects.

Robotics and digital animation are still relatively new technologies. In the current cultural moment we have a heightened awareness of the unique new qualities and modalities of these emerging new digital technologies and the images and artefacts they create. We are still watching their development, marvelling over new technological accomplishments and keenly discussing future possibilities and limitations. While these new technologies are in this transitional state, the attention of audiences will continue to be drawn to technical aspects, both the 'wow' features of technical virtuosity and the failures of technological limitations such as the uncanny valley.

However, as Gunning argues, the introduction of new technologies is an evolution from 'the spectacular and astonishing' to 'the convenient and unremarkable' (39). As new media become old media, they become part of the fabric of our reality and start to be taken for granted as a 'second nature.' Media theorist Marshall McLuhan makes a similar argument in his essay 'The Gadget Lover: Narcissus as Narcosis' in *Understanding Media*, where he suggests that as media technologies are domesticated and we become familiar with their different modalities, we become increasingly anaesthetised to them (41-47). So it is likely that the uncanny valley will increasingly become less of an issue as technological advances in robotics and animation lead to more life-like and realistic human simulations and we become increasingly inured to small technical glitches and anomalies. Our hardwired primitive brains may still perceive anomalies but we will cease to be so strongly affected by them. Digital animation and robots will pass into the terrain of everyday 21st-century experience, and become increasingly familiar and unremarkable, as perhaps they already are for a younger generation of 'digital natives' (Tapscott; Prensky) who have never known a world without computers, the internet and video games.

The pleasures of the uncanny: fantasy, suspension of disbelief and the magic circle

While it is perhaps more common to focus on the problems associated with the uncanny, it is important to point out that there are also positive aspects associated with the experience of uncanniness. Although uncanny objects and experiences typically generate uncomfortable and negative emotions, human beings also appear to be strangely drawn to them and fascinated by them. Why is this? There is no doubt that uncanny entities are interesting and compelling—they represent an intriguing challenge for the human brain because they are difficult to categorise and they blur the boundaries between different types of entities. Is it alive or not? Is it human or not? Does it think? Does it feel? Uncanny objects generate intensely ambivalent feelings – disquiet and uncanniness go hand in hand with interest and fascination. Our brains and emotions go on high alert as we try to work out what we are dealing with. Are they threats or opportunities? Potentially dangerous or friendly? The uncanny makes us think, and it makes us feel. It generates a seductive frisson, a delicious shiver down the spine.

The ambivalent feelings and responses generated by uncanny objects make them highly ambiguous and emotionally charged entities. Rather than seeing this ambivalence and ambiguity as negative, I would argue that this is precisely what makes the uncanny so fascinating. This is particularly true in art and literature where the experience of ambiguity is a valued characteristic, and multiple and unstable meanings are viewed in a positive rather than a negative light. As the English Romantic poet John Keats argues, intellectual uncertainties don't necessarily need to be resolved, there is a fertile creative potential in what he calls the 'negative capability' of the artwork, a 'capability of being in uncertainties, Mysteries, doubts without any irritable reaching after fact & reason' (Keats cited in Wu 1351). We derive pleasure from novelty and unpredictability. The human brain likes a bit of cognitive friction and uncertainty and this experience can be very productive and creative.

The experience of the uncanny in the artistic domain can also be productively related to the idea of 'making the familiar strange and the strange familiar.' This function of art was first suggested by the German poet Novalis and was taken up by the Romantic movement (Rosen 174). Art makes us look at things with fresh eyes and to re-evaluate familiar assumptions and preconceptions.[1] Marcel Duchamp makes the familiar strange by putting a urinal in a gallery and making us view it as a sculptural object. Mari Velonaki makes the strange familiar by putting two robotic wheelchairs in a gallery and encouraging audiences to view them as sympathetic characters in a love story.[2] It is remarkable how little time it takes for audiences to get over their surprise at the fact the wheelchairs move autonomously around the gallery space and to start responding to their written text messages as if the wheelchairs were living, sentient and emotional entities.

The context of how we experience potentially uncanny objects is clearly a very important factor in determining whether those experiences will be positive or negative. In *The Uncanny*, Freud relates feelings of uncanniness to a blurring of the boundary between fantasy and reality—magical practices and something imaginary becoming real can both be sources of the uncanny (150). However, as Freud points out, these experiences are only uncanny when they occur in the real world. Inanimate objects coming to life in myths or in fantasy narratives (e.g. Pygmalion and Hans Christian Anderson fairytales) are not necessarily perceived as disturbing or uncanny, '…many things that would be uncanny if they occurred in real life are not uncanny in literature, and…in literature there are many opportunities to achieve uncanny effects that are absent in real life' (155–156). In the world of fantasy the usual rules of reality and everyday experience do not apply, we experience what Samuel Taylor Coleridge famously called a 'suspension of disbelief' where elements of fantasy and the supernatural are readily accepted by readers and audiences within the context of artistic scenarios.

Also relevant to the idea of fantasy and the suspension of disbelief is the concept of the magic circle that is used in theories of play and game analysis (Huizinga 10; Salen and Zimmerman 95). Johan Huizinga uses the term magic circle to describe zones of cultural interaction where the realities and rules of the everyday world may be temporarily suspended:

> All play moves and has its being within a playground marked off beforehand materially or ideally, deliberately or as a matter of course… The arena, the card-table, the magic circle, the temple, the stage, the screen, the tennis court, the court of justice, etc., are all in form and function play-grounds, i.e., forbidden spots, isolated, hedged round, hallowed, within which special rules obtain. All are temporary worlds within the ordinary world, dedicated to the performance of an act apart (10).

Many zones within society can act as magic circles including game environments, theatrical performances, films, galleries and even technology fairs. Strange 'magical' things can happen in these spaces without necessarily triggering feelings of uncanniness. Or perhaps it is more accurate to say that these spaces allow us to experience and maximise the pleasures of the uncanny while minimising its more disturbing aspects. When the uncanny is experienced within the safe confines (the 'magic circle') of a film, novel, gallery or science fair, we are free to explore the pleasures of the uncanny without any real threat. Audiences can have physically, intellectually and emotionally 'risky' experiences without the 'real' risk or threat that might accompany that experience in everyday life.

This is clearly demonstrated in David Hanson's exit poll of visitor responses to his realistic android head of Philip K. Dick at a science expo. As Hanson comments, despite the fact that the back of the robot's head was missing so that audiences could see the uncanny robotic interior behind its artificial human-like 'frubber' skin,

> people who interacted with the robot appeared entertained, not disturbed or afraid. The robot held people's attention in conversation for many minutes and even hours. People held the android's hand while talking with it, and even spontaneously hugged the android at the end of the conversation. In the exit interviews, 71% said the robot was 'not eerie,' and 89% 'enjoyed' interacting with the robot. ('Exploring the Aesthetic Range' sect. 3, par. 4)

Clearly the context of the encounter and the audience's expectations are very important in determining whether an encounter will be experienced as uncanny or not. Hanson's example above shows that audiences can quickly get over initial feelings of uncanniness if they become sufficiently intrigued and engaged by the interactive encounter. It is also likely that the lack of uncanny responses to Hanson' robot head is due to the fact that the audience clearly knew that the head was robotic from the start of the encounter.

Clearly foregrounding the non-human nature of a humanoid simulation provides a strong measure of inoculation against uncanniness. Uncanny responses are far more likely to be provoked when something that was thought to be human is unexpectedly revealed to be non-human. As Freud points out, the uncanny involves a revelation, a moment of unexpected and shocking awareness as 'something that was secret or hidden away com[es] into the open' (132). Because of this, Hanson's exposed robot head is not as uncanny or disturbing as the scene in Steven Spielberg's film *Artificial Intelligence: AI* where a robot that perfectly simulates a young woman is suddenly turned off before her head is opened to reveal the inner workings of her robotic interior, or the scene in *Terminator 2: Judgement Day* where Arnold Schwarzenegger's terminator character peels back the human-looking skin on his arm to reveal a bloody but non-human mechanical interior to his horrified audience. Here, the perfect human simulation is revealed to be an inhuman machine, the display of the interior machinic workings inside the human exterior opens up the uncanny gap between the strange and the familiar, the human and the non-human.

The uncanniness of the technological double

Another possible reason why we find robots and other humanoid simulations uncanny is due to a fear that these technological doubles may end up competing with and even replacing us. Perhaps, after all, this is the true source of the uncanniness that robots and digital simulations provoke in us. It is not the failure of our technological creations to be human that disturbs us so much as our fear that they will surpass and destroy us—a narrative that has been played out in countless Western science fiction narratives from Mary Shelley's *Frankenstein* and Karel Capek's *R.U.R. (Rossum's Universal Robots)*, to more recent narratives such as *Bladerunner, The Terminator* and *The Matrix*.[3]

In *The Uncanny*, Freud links the idea of the double (as seen in mirror images, shadows and other representational images) with ghosts, tracing the origin of the double to the evolution of the idea of the soul as a response to the fear of death. Freud speculates that the existence of a double is at first seen as a protection from death, 'an insurance against the extinction of the self,' but then 'the meaning of the 'double' changes: having once been an assurance of immortality, it becomes the uncanny harbinger of death' (142).

Today's humanoid doubles are being created through robotic technologies, digital animation, artificial intelligence and genetic cloning. While these new technologies may promise a life beyond the grave (for example, human brains transplanted into robotic bodies, virtual avatars and physical clones), they also represent a threat to traditional religious and humanistic notions of the human. Optimistically, these technological doubles can be seen as prosthetic extensions of the human leading us to a post-human future, but, for some, there is a threat that what is human may be lost in this transition to the post-human, or that the post-human future may even leave the human behind entirely.

Jean Baudrillard, the 20th century's leading commentator on and critic of simulation technologies, writes of the uncanny fear generated by the double and the clone, particularly when they are materialised as separate and autonomous entities. In his essay 'Clone Story' published in *Simulacra and Simulations*, Baudrillard writes:

> Of all the prostheses that mark the history of the body, the double is doubtless the oldest. But the double is precisely not a prosthesis: it is an imaginary figure, which, just like the soul, the shadow, the mirror image, haunts the subject like his other, which makes it so that the subject is simultaneously itself and never resembles itself again, which haunts the subject like a subtle and always averted death. This is not always the case, however: when the double materializes, when it becomes visible, it signifies imminent death. (95)

In the entertainment industry, digital imaging and animation techniques are already being used to create virtual actors that can act on behalf of or replace their human counterparts. The computer gaming industry is at the forefront in this arena, developing increasingly realistic digital characters based on living actors and other public figures. In video games, the images of actors, sports stars and other celebrities are routinely scanned and then digitally animated as interactive characters, and it is becoming increasingly common for actors and sports stars to negotiate the use of their images in game titles such as HBO's *The Sopranos: Road to Respect* and EA Sport's games such as *NFL Tour* and *Tiger Woods PGA Tour*.

Dead movie stars like Marilyn Monroe, Humphrey Bogart and Marlene Dietrich have also been brought back to life and reanimated using digital compositing and animation techniques so that their virtual clones can perform in new contexts. Virtual actors may come to compete with or even supersede living human actors entirely. In *Media Matrix*, Barbara Creed comments that:

> A digitised film star is a studio's dream – capable of performing any tasks, continuously available, cost effective and causing no scandals, unless of course, the digital star is given an off-screen life in order to keep alive other areas of the film-star industry such as fan magazines, merchandising and promotions. (161)

Creed quotes Hollywood actor Tom Hanks as being 'very troubled' about this idea of digital actors replacing human actors. Hanks comments 'it's coming down, man. It's going to happen. And I'm not sure what actors can do about it' (Hanks quoted in Creed 160).

This scenario of a virtual star replacing a human actor is played out in *S1m0ne* (2002) directed by Andrew Niccol. In the film, Hollywood director Viktor Taransky (Al Pacino), becomes so frustrated with the behaviour of his female star (played by Winona Ryder) that he creates his own virtual star 'Simone' (short for 'simulation one') to replace her. In Simone, Viktor creates his idea of the perfect actress—and the perfect woman—a digital composite morphed together from the digital files of famous actresses such as Meryl Streep and Lauren Bacall. Simone quickly becomes a global star and, despite the fact that she never appears in person, her many fans never doubt for a moment that she is as human as she appears to be. Simone is the perfect fake, Tom Hanks' fear come to life.

However, the hype around virtual stars has largely remained just that, hype – novelty gimmicks that have failed to live up to either the promises of their creators or the fears of their technophobic critics. Today's human simulations are a pale reflection of the real thing. From the audience's point of view it is also questionable whether these digitally created performances can ever have the same emotional depth and impact as an original human performance. Jim Rygiel, the Oscar-winning visual-effects supervisor of *The Lord of the Rings* trilogy comments:

> There's talk in my field about creating Bogart and Marilyn Monroe and making movies with them again. But you'll never really be able to do it

because you can't capture their souls in a computer. You'll never know how Bogart would've played a scene. And ultimately that's what people pay to see. (quoted in Gordon 3)

The central irony in *S1mOne* is that the digital actor Simone is in fact played by a human actor (the uncredited actor Rachel Roberts)—Hollywood couldn't deliver on its own premise. We are not yet at the point where an animated digital character can pass what we could call the 'Virtual Human' Turing Test, that is, when the viewer can't tell whether the image they're watching is a virtual human simulation or a real human actor.

And, as Rygiel observes, even if virtual actors do become visually indistinguishable from human actors, they will still differ from human actors in their lack of emotional history and psychological depth. While they may have a human appearance they have no life history and have to make do with emotional repertoires borrowed from their human creators. As Creed comments:

> The cyberstar is not subject to the same experiences as the living star—
> experiences such as birth, mothering, separation, loss, ecstasy, desire and
> death. The cyberstar has not been through a process of being civilised,
> of learning to repress anti-social behaviour or taboo wishes. In short, the
> synthespian does not have a conscious or an unconscious mind. It is the
> latter—the unconscious—which is crucial in the formation of the self, and
> which binds us together as human beings. (167)

'More human than human' ... or the birth of the new?

Creating a perfect human simulation is the holy grail of digital animation and robotics. 'More human than human' is the slogan of the Tyrell Corporation that makes the humanoid Nexus replicants in *Blade Runner*. But why this obsession with the human? Why do we want our new digital creations to replicate the human? Why limit them? Why should they be human? Isn't the birth of the new more intriguing than the replication of the old?

Perhaps the uncanniness we feel when we look at robots and digital simulations is a problem of 'first contact.' Perhaps we should think of robots and digital animations as 'alien lifeforms' presaging an alien digital future. In *The Language of New Media*, Lev Manovich tells us that the '[s]ynthetic computer-generated image is not an inferior representation of our reality, but a realistic representation of a different reality,' the reality of the cyborg. Manovich argues that we should not see these digital images as imperfect copies of the human body but as a new reality, a 'perfectly realistic representation of a cyborg body yet to come' (202–203).

In the faces of Asian anime-styled virtual characters and robots we see the emerging image of a new life-form whose features bear an eerie similarity to those of an alien species—a large head with large eyes and residual nose and mouth. These same characteristics are also typical of neonates. The combination of alien otherness with neonatal cuteness signifies a potent amalgamation of the alien with the neonate, appropriate signifiers for the birth of an alien technological species.

Conclusion

Our humanoid technological 'others' reveal a lot about what we believe is important to the notion of the human. They are technological reflections held up as mirrors that both affirm and challenge our humanity. In the 21st century humanoid robots and digital animations are set to become an increasingly familiar part of our everyday lives. While it is unlikely they will ever be able to fully pass as human, nevertheless, with improved technology and greater ubiquity, it is inevitable that they will become more familiar and less uncanny. We will learn to live with our part-humanoid and part-alien others.

Works Cited

Baudrillard, Jean. *Simulacra and Simulation*. 1981 (in French). Trans. Sheila Faria Glaser. Ann Arbor: University of Michigan Press, 1994

Creed, Barbara. *Media Matrix: Sexing the New Reality*. Crows Nest, NSW: Allen & Unwin, 2003

Freud, Sigmund. *The Uncanny*. 1919. Trans. Hugh Haughton. London: Penguin, 2003.

Gordon, Devin. 'Polar Expedition.' *Newsweek* (25 October 2004). <URL: http://www.newsweek.com/id/55375> Accessed 6 October 2006

Gunning, Tom. 'Re-Newing Old Technologies: Astonishment, Second Nature, and the

Uncanny in Technology from the Previous Turn of the Century.' *Rethinking Media Change: The Aesthetics of Transition*. Eds. David Thorburn, Henry Jenkins and Brad Seawell. Cambridge, Mass.: MIT Press, 2003. 39–60

Hanson, David. 'Interpreting the Neural Basis of The "Uncanny Valley." ' (6 October 2003). <URL: http://sites.google.com/site/elenapasquinelli/Hanson2003.pdf > Accessed 2 February 2006

———. 'Exploring the Aesthetic Range for Humanoid Robots.' *Toward Social Mechanisms of Android Science: an ICCS/CogSci–2006 Long Symposium*. Vancouver, Canada, 2006. 16–20

Huizinga, Johan. *Homo Ludens: A Study of the Play-Element in Culture*. Boston: Beacon Press, 1955

Jenkins, Ward. 'The Polar Express: A Virtual Train Wreck.' (5 December 2004). blog. Accessed 14 December 2006. <URL: http://wardomatic.blogspot.com/2004/12/polar-express-virtual-train-wreck.html>

Manovich, Lev. *The Language of New Media*. Leonardo. Cambridge, Mass. ; London: MIT Press, 2001

McLuhan, Marshall. *Understanding Media: The Extensions of Man*. 1st Sphere ed. London: Sphere Books, 1967

Mori, Masahiro. 'Bukimi No Tani (the Uncanny Valley).' *Energy* 7.4 (1970): 33–35

Parisi, Paula. 'The New Hollywood'. *Wired* 3.12 (1995). Accessed 5 November 2006. <URL: http://www.wired.com/wired/archive/3.12/new.hollywood_pr.html>

Picard, Rosalind W. *Affective Computing*. Cambridge, Mass.: MIT Press, 1997

Prensky, Marc. 'Digital Natives, Digital Immigrants.' *On the Horizon* 9.5 (2001): 1–2

Reeves, Byron, and Clifford Ivar Nass. *The Media Equation: How People Treat Computers, Television, and New Media Like Real People and Places*. Stanford, Calif., New York: CSLI Publications, Cambridge University Press, 1996

Rosen, Charles. *The Romantic Generation*. Cambridge, Mass.: Harvard University Press, 1995

Salen, Katie, and Eric Zimmerman. *Rules of Play: Game Design Fundamentals*. Cambridge, Mass.: MIT Press, 2004

Sone, Yuji. 'Realism of the Unreal: The Japanese Robot and the Performance of Representation.' *Visual Communication* 7.3 (2008): 345–62

Tapscott, Don. *Growing up Digital: The Rise of the Net Generation*. New York: McGraw-Hill, 1998

Tucker, Abigail. 'Robot Babies.' *Smithsonian Magazine* (July 2009). Accessed 10 November 2009. <URL: http://www.smithsonianmag.com/science-nature/Birth-of-a-Robot.html>

Turing, Alan. 'Computing Machinery and Intelligence.' *Mind* 59 (1950): 433–60.

Wu, Duncan (ed.). *Romanticism: An Anthology*. 3rd ed, Malden MA: Blackwell Publishing, 2006

Notes

1   Freud himself suggests that the 'familiar made strange' is key trigger for the uncanny or *unheimlich* (un-homely): 'the uncanny is that species of the frightening that goes back to what was once well known and had long been familiar' (124), for example, something that appears to be human is revealed to be an automaton, or an inanimate object suddenly displays signs of movement and life-like properties.

2   See http://mvstudio.org/work/fish-bird-cicle-b-movement-b/ .

3   These typically dystopian representations of robots in Western culture contrast strongly with the more positive depiction of robots in Japanese popular culture (e.g. Astroboy) and this cultural difference is reflected in the general popularity of humanoid robots in Japanese culture. This positive attitude towards robots has been linked to the Japanese tradition of animism that blurs distinctions between organic beings and inanimate objects (Sone 351–7).

Chapter 5

Diffused Reflection of Body Imageries: Dolls as Humans and Humans as Dolls

Mio Bryce
Macquarie University

Introduction

What does it mean to be human now? Yōrō Takeshi,[1] a prominent Japanese anatomist and critic, warns of the invisibility of integral humans with body and soul/mind, in today's 'brain-orientated' society (脳化社会) where the presence of Nature (e.g. the corporeality, mortality and perishability of human bodies) is obliterated and imageries and rhetoric may project a stronger sense of reality than real things. (Yōrō 1996, 1997).

The image of a human being as a solid, integrated and unique entity is fragmented with the increasing significance of performativity through advanced information technology. Our bodies are manipulated to a profound extent, medically, theatrically and otherwise, to project desired self–images: plastic surgery, biological and artificial organ transplants and implants, and designer babies are just a few examples. Playfulness has also intensified in our media and everyday life, in which exaggerated theatricality, or even fakeness, has gained public acceptance as 'performance', exemplified by 'cosplays' (costume plays), maid and Goth-Loli (Gothic Lolita) fashions; and by the virtual representation of self within telecommunication networks using pseudonymous handle names and avatars. Figuratively, human beings are becoming dolls or play dolls (Kotani; Winge). Likewise, dolls may appear to become humans or play humans, as seen in the emergence of virtual girlfriends.

This chapter explores kaleidoscopic and often unsettling imageries of dolls in Japan. Doll in Japanese is 人形 (*ningyō* or *hitogata*), literally 'human shape'. Depending on the occupier and the viewer, a doll represents the Other and/or the human self. They are thus involved in the dialogical formation of subjectivity (McCallum 1999). Napier (2006) sees dolls as 'transitional objects' (by Donald Winnicott) as they function both by being a mythic Other to give freedom and guidance to the other world, whilst offering a site of self-identification. Dolls engage or reflect human emotions such as love and hatred (Masubuchi 1982). Thus the analysis of dolls involves analysis of human interactions, an essential element in being human.

Artefacts in a human shape such as dolls, sculptures and robots, have been continuously created since ancient times in many parts of the world. Made of varied materials and for differing purposes, they express universal as well as culturally specific aspects of human being. These objects, either in solid forms or imageries, are diverse and abundant in artistic works, reflecting our desires and concerns.

Dolls in narratives embody the ambiguous relationship between bodies and *kokoro* (mind and soul) and the crossing of the border between the natural / intrinsic and the artificial / purpose-built. Many dolls are mass-produced commodities and easily replaced by other identical ones. Nevertheless, when loved, a doll can become a unique individual. They are analogues of our reality – being unique individuals in our personal relationships but replaceable labour in the workforce. Through dolls in historical, cultural and artistic contexts in Japan, we will look at what they represent, how they relate to humans and how they offer a liminal space through which alienated, suffocated, solipsistic humans may be able to (re)gain their sense of self and an altruistic view of life and the world.

Dolls in Japan

What are dolls and what do they signify? Dolls in Japan were initially created as ritual artefacts as exemplified by ancient terracotta dolls (*dogū* and *haniwa*).

In Japanese, dolls are referred to by various terms such as *hitogata*, *ningyō* and *hina*. Distinguished from the more recent term, *ningyō* (mostly toys and ornaments), *hitogata* has been used to imply religious/magical significance, however, it has resurfaced in popular culture, especially in cyborg narratives, as typified by *Ghost in the Shell 2: Innocence* (Oshii, *Innocence*). *Karakuri* is also used for mechanical dolls and *kugutsu* for puppets. Western-style dolls are often referred as 'doll', 'puppet' and 'marionette,' written in *katakana* (Japanese phonetic letters in angular shapes) or alphabet.

The essence of dolls is 'human shaped', as evident in the fact that *hitogata* and then *ningyō* are both written using the same *kanji* (Chinese characters): 人形 (human + shape). A doll's emptiness is essential, to accommodate a soul or represent it. *Hitogata* could be very simple: for example, a piece of wood with a round head or a symmetrical piece of paper cut with a circle for a head, arms, and possibly legs, with or without clothes. They could embody a specific person. They are used to protect the person, by wiping the body with it or breathing on it, in order to transfer his/her sin and misfortune, so that they can carry it away when they are burnt in fires or floated on streams or seas.

However, dolls made of wood or straw were also used to curse. For example, a wooden *hitogata* with nails through the eyes and heart was found in the excavation site of the ancient capital Heijō-kyō (710–784). Yumemakura Baku's story which became Yōjirō Takita's film *Onmyōji* ('The Yin and Yang Master') (2001), set in the Heian period (794–1185), shows the imperial consort Suke-hime placing a curse on her enemy by visiting a shrine at midnight to nail a straw doll onto a sacred tree.

Many aesthetic customs and artefacts existing in present-day Japan were accomplished in the Heian noble culture. Dolls provide one such example. *The Tale of Genji* (written around the turn of the eleventh century by a female author known as Murasaki Shikibu) distinguishes religious dolls as *hitogata* and toy dolls as *hina*. *Hitogata* are used for Prince Genji's purification rituals and the doll, placed in a boat and floated away on the sea, appears to be of human size. *Hina* refers to dolls, which a girl protagonist, Murasaki, plays and enacts stories with (e.g., Genji's visit to the palace), using beautiful costumes and sets of furniture.

The term *ningyō* came into use by 1477 (in *Oyudono no ue no nikki*, a diary written by ladies-in-waiting serving emperors between 1477 and 1826). A doll was made for an imperial purification ceremony of Chinese origin, the same as Prince Genji's, and discarded afterwards. The diary, however, shows that even religious dolls became fondling objects, when adorned with beautiful clothing (Masubuchi 1982).

The Edo period (1603–1868) was epoch-making with the mechanical *karakuri* and puppet theatres, *ningyō jōruri*, which were developed and performed in parallel to *kabuki*. Both puppet and *kabuki* theatres are characterised by their stylised aesthetics from costumes, make-up, poses, actions, speech and scripts, to the appreciation of the audiences. In a sense, *kabuki* actors are dolls. It may reflect the period's ambience with strong pressure for conformity and a rigid and meticulous social class system (samurai, farmer, artisan and merchant) and inter-surveillance which made people like dolls.

Hina too became an important cultural commodity in the Edo period, and today the term is almost exclusively used for dolls for *hina matsuri* (the doll festival) on 3 March, derived from the aforementioned imperial purification ritual for protecting girls. Although there are still some customs such as *nagashi-bina* (floating dolls), most *hina* are owned and cherished for a long time. The dolls are in pairs and attired in traditional style. They are characterised as an emperor and empress, hence formal and rigid. A full set includes this pair and their retainers on a seven-tiered stand which is covered with a red cloth and decorated with miniature furniture symbolising the palace. With the significance of being a pair, the loss of one is considered ominous. Moreover, in Japanese animistic belief, human attachment to dolls, especially *hina*, can give them life, therefore, their disposal requires funeral-like ceremonies to avoid their resentment.[2] Today, *hina* are generally bought by a girl's grandparents to celebrate her birth. The price varies widely, with a pair of expensive dolls possibly costing over ¥1,000,000. Although rather commercialised, a superstitious connotation pertains to *hina* so they are only displayed from late February to early March.

Humans need interaction, either real or imagined. A doll 'comes alive' and is personalised with a human's gaze and emotional commitment. In Hori

Hiroshi's *ningyō–mai* (doll dance),[3] his doll (like from *The Tale of Genji*) of near his size is instilled with life by being gracefully embraced by him and danced with. Atae Yūki's realistic and nostalgic dolls[4] also poignantly inspire the viewer's emotions with their gentle facial expressions and gestures. These dolls' impressive yet somehow vague eyes and facial expressions are significant as they encourage the viewer to communicate with the doll, allowing their expression of feelings and interpretations. This is similar to women's masks in Nō plays which change in terms of emotional expressions through the actor's subtle gestures.[5]

Dolls are also made to be faithful partners of the dead, as seen in bride dolls for the deceased, a (folk) religious practice in places such as Tsugaru to console lonely souls who died in wars (Schattschneider 2001). They are young-looking female dolls in traditional bridal attire (a gorgeously embroidered kimono in white, or red and white). After the 'marriage', the doll and the photo of the man are placed in a glass case and kept in temples and periodically offered in commonly required Buddhist memorial ceremonies. The beauty of the dolls is essential as aesthetic values have often been equated with ethical values, such as goodness, purity and holiness, as typified by Heian noble culture (Morris). However, the dolls are preferably mass-produced and bought, rather than hand-made. This indicates their purpose to ensure the purity of the doll in becoming the only soul-mate of the deceased, and more importantly to isolate the potentially harmful deceased from the living. Doll 'marriage' uses the same logic as the enshrinement of revengeful ghosts and annual Buddhist memorial ceremonies for them (e.g., Gion Festival in Kyoto), which reflect the survivors' ambivalent feelings (affection, respect, fear and a sense of guilt) towards the deceased.

As Masubuchi Sōichi (1982) asserts, dolls are only complete when clothed, unlike sculptures. The fashioning of a doll is its individuation. Dolls are contextualised and personalised by the holders/viewers, unlike sculptures with solid bodies, fixed facial expressions and gestures. Fashioning dolls involves aesthetics that are often culturally specific. In Japan, a typical representation of dolls is *kawaii* (cute). Cuteness is an engaging and inviting, thus commercially successful, aesthetic code. Cuteness is embodied by the image of an angelic infant, possessing ambiguous qualities

– warmth, innocence and comical liveliness, as well as vulnerability, which secure the viewer's superiority. As discussed by many scholars (Kinsella; Masubuchi 1994; Ōtsuka; Shimamura; Yomota), the preference of cuteness has thoroughly penetrated Japanese society as a '"standard" aesthetic of everyday life' (McVeigh 135). It is exemplified by the popularity of eleven year-old Licca dolls over seventeen-year-old Barbie.[6] A Licca doll is often taken care of by Japanese girls as though she is their daughter, unlike Barbie who is perceived by western girls as their ideal of womanhood – sexy and independent (Masubuchi 1987). Their differences are also evident in the most popular dolls accompanying them, respectively: Licca's mother vs. Barbie's boyfriend, Ken.

Recent decades have seen a resurgence of interest in dolls in Japan, with an introduction of small, soft plastic figurines (e.g., by Kaiyōdō) and exquisite ball-jointed dolls (like bisque dolls), with mass produced ones (e.g., Super Dollfie) and artistic ones. Their cuteness is refined to increase aesthetic perfection and performance. Their bodies are agile and pose naturally, so that, like a diorama, they can be framed in a specific story with appropriate dress, postures, companion dolls and settings, and displayed in real or virtual exhibitions.

Plastic figurines are mostly anime characters (e.g., *Sailor Moon*, *Chobits* and *InuYasha*) and generally well detailed yet inexpensive (between ¥300 and ¥600). Unlike dolls like Licca, they come in parts in a small box, or a plastic capsule (e.g., *Gachapon*) from vending machines. Although they are mere plastic figures, seeing tiny body parts in a clear plastic capsule can be bizarre. The popularity of such products reflects a fundamental cultural shift in our perception of the body. This is not limited to Japan: some dolls for children, including Barbie and Bratz, come with additional body parts such as a head with a different hairstyle and feet in different shoes. Do such commodities promote the perception of the human body as an assembly of replaceable parts, rather than organic and integral?

Artistic, ball-jointed dolls exploit the body far more radically. Many artists (e.g., Yotsuya Simon and Koitsuki-hime) are directly or indirectly influenced by Hans Bellmer's surreal photographs of ball-jointed dolls and create gothic, anatomical or whimsical dolls. The incongruence between the cute dolls' calm faces and their distorted or dissected bodies is unsettling. Some works focus on the passivity of dolls and imply a sense of paedophilia, sadism and even necrophilia. Are they perceived simply as inert material or do they signify humans? Can their total submission be appreciated as their innocence and as an ideal human status, as Takahara Eiri (2006) suggests? Does the doll embody the 'Other' or the human self? 'Loving dolls is loving self,' says Yotsuya, who created dolls resembling himself (e.g., 'Pygmalionisme and Narcissisme'). Moreover, Mario A's photo work, *ma poupée japonaise*, comprises images of a doll and its dismantled body, 'performed' by a human actor, Hara Sachiko. Is a dissected doll non-human or human? Does she remain fragmented? Or, if reassembled, who is she?

Dolls in manga and anime

Dolls in manga and anime are 'excess', drawing on the aforementioned intrinsic dispositions of dolls (e.g., their vacancy, pliability and susceptibility), interacting with humans and revealing human ambivalences. Dolls may also refer to robots, clones, cyborgs and even humans. The representation of dolls is diverse and may be better described as a spectrum. As a human replica, they are often fragmented and deficient yet connect with, and violate, other imageries and concepts (e.g., humans and machines). They are exploited differently depending on the consumers' perspectives, desires and interpretations; as a rounded character or as mere data to construct another character. They are consumed endlessly and omnidirectionally, much the same as with other popular culture products, as Azuma Hiroki (2001) analyses, using the concept, 'database' culture.

Some dolls can mediate human interactions, by being emotionless objects and refusing a human's emotional alignment with them. Orbaugh argues that, '"Affect" refers to the emotions that arise from and are felt within human interiority, and also to how information about those emotions is conveyed to the body's surface, allowing others to "read" them and respond' (152). 'Maruichi' (which are totally mechanical robots for domestic assistance) in Yanahara Nozomi's *Maruichi-teki fūkei* (*Maruichi-like scenery*, 1995–2008) create 'genuine affect' (Orbaugh 153) and mediate human interactions, similar to the mechanical Halady in *L'Ève future* (*Future Eve*, by Jean-Marie Mathias Phillipe Auguste, comte de Villiers de l'Isle-Adam, 1886). Unlike the pre-programmed Halady with human-like appearance, however, Maruichi[7] are clearly characterised as mechanical and mute and require a user to act in front of them to register their behaviour. The lack of a Maruichi's own personality thus its invisibility as an individual is essential for them to act as the clients and express their personalities and emotions and inspire others' emotive responses. For example, after his estranged father's death, Arisaka Kōta realises his father's love for him through a Maruichi's particular gestures registered by his father.

Likewise, empty puppets are simply manoeuvred by their puppeteers, thereby conveying their personalities, emotions and even the unconscious. In Paul Gallico's *Love of Seven Dolls*, Michel's puppets represent his severe fragmentation, which is only cured by the acceptance of Mouche, an innocent girl who embodies Otherness (Kawai). In manga, Chigiri's dolls in Omi Ayako's *Ningyōshi* (*Doll Master*, 1987) possess her jealousy for her twin sister, Saira, and attack her, and via this, she fails to communicate with others as she is. Similarly, in *Kurosagi Shitai Takuhaibin* (*The Kurosagi Corpse Delivery Service*, Ōtsuka Eiji and Yamazaki Hōsui, 2000, vol.9), an obsessed, dead man controls dolls to play hide-and-seek with an idol who rejected his presents – the dolls.

Being empty, doll bodies are also able to console humans, by temporarily accommodating their souls to complete the deceased's unfinished business, thereby healing all involved in the deaths. 'Dolls are loved or hated, thereby fulfilling people's desire to heal,' says Genzō, an exocentric genius doll maker/puppeteer in Takada Yūzō's *Genzō hitogata kiwa* (*Demonic Stories of Genzō Dolls*, 1998– , vol.1, 26). Genzō creates a doll perfectly resembling his murdered fianceé, Saki, to die with her; however, when he is attacked by her brother, the doll Saki, with broken strings, comes between them to stop the fight. Imbued with his intense love for her, the doll body enables Saki to express her love, gratitude and farewell.

Tachibana Yutaka's *Ningyōshi no yoru* (*Doll Master's Nights*, 1996–) is a collection of stories, in which marionette-like dolls are lent to the deceased or those near-to-death for only a week or so, by a mysterious female doll master.

The door of her room is only found by someone with a pure heart. Thus dolls are generally used, either in their own shape or someone else's, to farewell with love and ease the grief of their beloved. A young girl's parents return and take care of her and in desperation, consider taking her with them, although eventually happily leave her with her great-grandmother. An old man also returns to rescue a discarded boy. Their actions involve people around them and change their lives positively, as represented by Misae's story. It begins when a disillusioned salaried man encounters a young boy, Wataru, playing alone in a park at night, and then finds his sister, Misae. He soon learns that Misae was engaged in prostitution to help them survive, but died a week ago and returned in a doll body to find Wataru's guardian. By then, Misae's legs begin to reveal inorganic matter, a doll's legs, but she is relieved when the man promises to look after Wataru. Besides her gratitude, she says, 'being beside you, I could be just an ordinary girl,' something that was impossible for her in life. As her doll legs show, the time limit is absolute for the use of dolls, but this in itself crystallises their communication as being true and eternal, healing Misae and the man so that they can regain themselves and trust in humans.

Fujita Kazuhiro's *Karakuri Circus* (1997–2006) is a lengthy story constructed as a doll play and depicts intricate battles amongst literal and figurative puppets and puppeteers, bloodthirsty automata, Shorogane (a group of automata destroyers, using marionettes), and dead and alive humans, some of which are puppeteers and some are puppets. Shorogane were humans but were conferred longevity by the 'water of life'. As exemplified by Eleanor (a young Shorogane), their life is thoroughly dictated by their role as automata destroyers. In a sense, they are more like dolls rather than humans, due to their total submission to the assigned role. In contrast, automata seek human blood to become 'complete'.

Dolls with (possible) subjective agencies are individuated through their given idiosyncrasies and circumstances, then developed through their interactions with others and the memories from such experiences. They provide multiple viewpoints on the human, which consist of conflicting yet interconnected notions including: nature and artificiality, tangibility and virtuality, body and soul/mind/memory, mortality and immortality, individuality and replaceability, and Self and Other. Incorporating inherent dichotomies (such as humanness and non-humanness) and moving between them, dolls frequently offer exaggerated visions of both, representing the continual process of fragmentation and reintegration of self.

Oshii Mamoru (director of the discrete anime *Ghost in the Shell* in 1995 and *Ghost in the Shell 2: Innocence* in 2004) explores the tangled notions of humans and dolls. His *Innocence* visualises the extreme ambiguity of humans and dolls (physical and virtual), and the fluid, continual, bidirectional border crossings. The protagonist, Kusanagi Motoko, is now bodiless, living in cyberspace and freely occupying cybernetic bodies as she wishes. The story evolves around the unthinkable murders and suicides of sexaroids. It eventually reveals that human girls are exploited to provide their 'ghosts' for sexaroids to animate.[9] It follows one girl's resentment and search for help. To save the girl, many androids are 'killed'. The explosive destruction of naked sexaroids is especially confrontational and expresses intense uncertainties about our corporeality. What is offered is an animistic vision of the world of chaotic diversity and continual transitions that encompass bodiless entities like Kusanagi (Oshii, *Innocence*; Napier).

Dolls can be vulnerable and exposed to the affectionate, inquisitive and/ or invasive gazes of their holders/viewers. As exemplified by Kusanagi's provocative attire, female dolls, robots and cyborgs, especially in stories for male audiences, are excessively sexualised. This does not necessarily mean such characters are depicted as submissive to dominant male characters. Many love comedies depict love between a nice but unconfident human boy and his ideal non-human girlfriend, privileging intersubjective love over physical desire, as evident in Katsura Masakazu's *Video Girl Ai* (1990–1992) and CLAMP's *Chobits* (2001–2002) (Stephens and Bryce). Nevertheless, currently popular maid narratives tend to focus playfully yet blatantly on submissive female characters in overtly erotic maid attire, who are often bound by debt, as seen in Mattsū and Tsubaki Asu's *Kore ga watashi no goshujin-sasma* (*He is my Master*, 2002–2008). In such narratives for female readers, such playfulness can be complicated: for example, Mihara Mitsukazu's *Dolls* (1998–2002) depicts totally subservient dolls in Goth-Loli fashion, who lack subjective agency and thus, self defence. Takahara argues that readers can align with both the arrogant humans (masters) and the passive, beautiful dolls. In playful disguise, however, these narratives can critically undermine human integrity and equality, by commodifying humans in patriarchal, class-conscious, and thus fatalistic, contexts.

The dolls' vulnerability is intensified when exposed to voyeuristic, necrophilic gazes. A mad anatomist Okada in Takahashi Akira's *Kugutsu* (1999) and a pervert hairdresser and embalmer Tsutsui in *Kurosagi shitai takuhaibin* murder girls to acquire parts to create perfect bodies, justifying their grotesque acts as artistic accomplishment to preserve human beauty (like plastination). In their views, humans are objectified as mere parts. For the extremely solipsistic Tsutsui, it is also a form of doll-playing, to escape from, and take revenge on, his demanding customers. Moreover, some dolls are made of their own dead bodies but are used as tools and expected not to have their own wills and desires, as exemplified by Teteu (an unborn baby who was killed within his raped mother's body) in Takahashi's *Kugutsui*, and Kana in his *Kugutsugi: Kuǐlěi Xì* (2001–).

Humans may willingly regress to a doll state to protect themselves. Mizushiro Setona names her story *Shōjo ningyō* (*Girl Doll*, 1999) to suggest the character Aoi's recovery of humanness. Aoi has been constantly sexually abused by the employer of herself and her father from the age of 13 and is only able to bear the situation by 'becoming a doll', so that she neither needs to feel pain nor hate and hurt others.

Kawahara Yumiko's *Kan'yō shōjo: Plants Doll* (1995–1999)[10] is a collection of ingenious stories of exquisite, bisque, doll-like 'living' beings of child size: the fantastic hybrid of doll, human and plant. It offers a poignant story of a young girl being mistakenly discarded as a doll, by her father. This is one of those stories in which dolls expose human flaws (Barber). The girl lost her speech and emotional expressions after her mother's suicide, but being with her potpourri doll, she smiles again and allows her father's new partner to interact with her and her doll, as evident in their sharing of the doll's aroma by taking scent balls. The fragrance, however, maddens her father as he smells it as the unbearable stench of the pulsating city, which reminds him of his wife's adultery with a man from there, followed by her failed apology and suicide. In a rage, he knocks his partner down, causing one of the girls (human or doll) to scream almost mechanically, exactly as his daughter did beside her mother's body. The doll could be the girl's 'transitional object' enabling her to express herself ventriloquially, however, with her thorough assimilation with the doll, their roles are reversed: the doll screams whilst she remains frozen like a doll and is handed to the shop. His vocalised and inner speech, full of harsh rejections, is written around his silent daughter's stunned eyes, showing her resignation. It is the damage caused by his solipsistic 'brain-orientated' projection to make his wife and daughter ornamental dolls in his artificial place – where he dominates and moulds others as he wishes, depriving them of human warmth and communication.

A warning for those humans who become dolls is ironically expressed by a girl android, Riru, in Takao Shigeru's *Ningyō shibai* (*Doll Play*, 1996). Riru urges Satoru (her human sibling) not to discard his human abilities such as creativity, in contrast to Satoru's mother who compels him to be like Riru, to confirm social norms, thereby making him a fake robot with encyclopaedic knowledge. Satoru and Riru are both written in the same *kanji* 流里, thus they can be interpreted as complementary, integral parts of a human, rather than two individuals.

Doll narratives also explore the significance of memory and experience as core elements of a unique and autonomous individual. In this regard, dolls are compared to some clones, such as Addy in Hagio Moto's *A-A* (*A, A Prime*) (1981) and Ayamami Rei in Anno Hideaki/Gainax's *Shinseiki Evangelion* (*Neon Genesis Evangelion*, 1995–), whose multiple bodies are waiting to be activated, when the current one dies, through the transferring of memories. Similarly, in CLAMP's *Chobits*, a super-persocom (robot) Elda is reborn as Chii with no previous memory yet some essential disposition when reactivated by Hideki, and redevelops her personality through her interaction with him and the outside world. Conversely, in *Ningyō shibai*, Maria, an extensively damaged android, refuses to be reset and instead, requests to be sold as a collectable item so that she can help out a man who treats her warmly as an individual, whilst she can remain as Maria in his memory.

In terms of the transfer of a soul and memory from one body to another, Takahashi Rumiko's *InuYasha* depicts Kikyō's separation of soul and body, by her soul being reincarnated in Kagome, and her body being recreated from her bones and grave soil, activated by injection into Kagome's soul. Kikyō soon loses the majority of the soul, thus having to live as the 'living dead' with her memory and personality. The plot somewhat resembles James Cameron's *Avatar* (2009) in which genetically engineered bodies, imitating the Na'vi (the native people of Pandora), need human souls to animate them. Cameron's story follows the protagonist Jake who goes back and forth between two bodies; his paraplegic body and that of an agile humanoid-like Na'vi, ending with the spiritual transfer of his soul into the latter, which he feels has become his 'real' body.

Likewise, Kamata Yukimi's *Yomi ningyō* (*Yomi's Dolls*, 1993–) depicts dolls made from human remains and a drop of blood by a mysterious woman, Yomie. Her residence is 'Yomoji-an' (lit. 'hermitage on a pathway to the world of death'). 'Yomi' in her name and 'Yomoji' are homonyms and identify her as a gatekeeper of the pathway. She can capture wandering souls before crossing the river of Sanzu (the border between this world and the other in Buddhism). She enables bodies to complete their unfinished work, for instance, a woman who was killed by a car and returns in a doll body to nurse her terminally ill husband.

The bodies of Yomi dolls are inorganic and they cannot die with physical damage, however, when alive, their bodies function like living human bodies – warm and agile. The dolls' identities are determined by the drop of blood, which gives 'life' to them. If a doll is awakened with his/her own blood, the person is fully resurrected. If it is with someone else's, they are possessed by the blood-giver, possibly without the memory and personality of the person. The doll's body therefore becomes a site of tense relations between humanness and non-humanness, autonomy and heteronomy, the possessing and the possessed. With his own will, Tsukiya becomes Yomie's doll and lover with her blood; however, the creation of dolls is often initiated by the clients' (selfish) desires in relation to the deceased. For example, a man and a woman who died in a car accident are made into dolls with Yomie's blood, by request of their respective partners, however, they refuse to 'relive', confessing that their death was a double suicide. Similarly, a boy doll pretends to be broken, then asks Yomie to let him go, in order to save his father's life. He is stabbed by his father's partner, who sees his return as putting his father into 'a living death' (quitting his job, refusing her and indulging himself in playing with his regained son). Human greed also motivates clients. Uika's mother kills her to make her an obedient and ever young bride for a rich, old paedophile, so that she can live in luxury. Pitying the girl, Yomie uses Uika's own blood, against her mother's request to use hers. This makes it hard for Uika to bear the sexual abuse because of her remaining sense of herself, although she can finally have revenge on her mother after her husband's death.[11]

Doll narratives align readers empathetically with both the dolls and the human participants and their intersubjective developments. One of the plants dolls chooses a desperate, young jobless man with a terminal illness and becomes his exclusive girlfriend when she gently touches his cheek, exactly when he recalls his childhood wish for a girl to do so. Following the shopkeeper's suggestion, he 'steals' her. Her acquisition gives him a new zest for life – someone needs him. When their happy yet short cohabitation ends with his death, she is returned in inexpensive clothes, but her increased beauty manifests the utmost love she had received. Similarly, a speechless android, Minto, in *Ningyō shibai* attaches himself to his kidnapper, Teru, who treats Minto as he is. They develop a warm relationship which heals them both. Minto is traumatised because after the death of his human sibling, Akira, his mother sees Minto as Akira, then becomes devastated when she realises he is not. Minto's acute sensitivity – his loneliness and longing for affection – is touchingly visualised through his face and gestures, magnifying the vulnerability of humans and their hope for true relationships.

Ningyō shibai contains episodes of dedicated, child-type dolls (androids) created by twin boy androids, Shizuka (tranquilness) and Arashi (storm), demonstrating the ambivalent positioning of dolls as affectionate tools, which is shared by Tezuka Osamu's *Astro Boy*. The androids are customised to meet clients' orders (e.g., as a sibling of a child because having siblings is prohibited due to overpopulation). They are made to 'love' the human they are assigned to assist and, with their learning ability, develop individual personalities intersubjectively with their owners. In order to maximise their capacity to help, they are even equipped with human senses, including feeling pain, similar to Ai in *Video Girl Ai*. Such senses enhance their human quality and effectively engage the sympathetic alignment of fictional human characters and readers alike to share their feelings. The androids hence have an inevitable conflict: they are selfless, affectionate, expressive, and endowed with 'excessive' human goodness, but also are an efficient tool that is eventually disposed of.[12] This story is light-hearted and often comical. However, a quiet pathos is present throughout the story, within the shadow of Isaac Asimov's Three Laws of Robotics, which order robots' absolute submission to humans.

The power relationship between human and doll characters is ambiguous and unstable in some stories. For example, in Peach-Pit's *Rozen Maiden*, Shinku and other dolls treat Sakurada Jun as their caretaker (servant). Likewise, Plants Dolls are proud and demanding, whilst fully depending on their owners. Nevertheless, in utilising dolls, instead of human characters, doll narratives imagine affectionate yet somewhat unequal relationships between two individuals: the giver and the taker. This reveals our fear of fragmentation and our (unattainable) desire for gaining integrity of self through total acceptance by others, even including a desire for regression to a mother's uterus. Beneath such depiction is therefore what Doi Takeo (1971) defined as *amae*, a Japanese empathetic interdependence typically found between an infant and its mother.

Conclusion

Doll fantasies offer readers/audiences multi-faceted experiences of being human. The analogue between dolls and humans signifies our ambivalence as unique individuals for those close to us, but as replaceable units for unrelated others. Human desire for love and full acceptance is depicted through relationships between lonely humans and their devoted, self-sacrificing dolls, that enable them to (re)form or rehabilitate a sense of self. Nevertheless, their relationships are based on unequal standing (as human and non-human), hence implying the solipsistic nature of being. The popularity of doll fantasies, especially those with cute, devoted dolls, may indicate ironically our bleak realisation of the schizophrenic complexity and ambivalence of being human, and the unattainability of full integrity of Self and genuine, equal and lasting relationships.

Works Cited

Azuma, Hiroki. *Dōbutsuka-suru postmodern: otaku kara mita Nihon shakai* Tokyo: Kōdansha / *Otaku: Japan's database animals* (2001). Trans by Jonathan E. Abel and Shion Kono. Minneapolis: University of Minnesota Press, 2009

Barber, Christie. '"Living" dolls: Finding humanity in Japanese manga.' Unpublished paper presented at AULLA Congress at the University of Sydney, 4–6 February 2009

Doi, Takeo. *'Amae' no kōzō*. Tokyo: Kōbundō, 1971. Trans by John Bester, *The Anatomy of Dependence*. Tokyo: Kodansha International, 1973.

Kawai, Harao. *Fantasy o yomu*. Tokyo: Nire Shuppan, 1991

Kinsella, Sharon. 'Cuties in Japan.' In *Women, Media and Consumption in Japan*. Edited by L. Skove and B. Moeran. University of Hawai'i Press, 1995. Pp. 220–254

Kotani, Mari. 'Doll Beauties and Cosplay.' Trans by Thomas Lamarre. In *Mechademia 2: Networks of Desire*. Edited by Frenchy Lunning. Minnesota & London: University of Minnesota Press, 2007. Pp. 49–62

McCallum, Robyn. *Ideologies of Identity in Adolescent Fiction: The Dialogic Construction of Subjectivity*. New York: Garland, 1999

McVeigh, Brian J. 'How Hello Kitty Commodifies the Cute, Cool and Camp: Consumutopia versus Control in Japan.' *Journal of Material Culture* 5:2 (2000): 225–245

———. *Wearing Ideology: State, Schooling and Self-Presentation In Japan*, Oxford: Berg, 2000

Masubuchi, Sōichi. *Ningyō no jōnen*. Tokyo: Keisō shobō, 1982

———. *Licca-chan no shōjo fushigi-gaku*. Tokyo: Shinchosha, 1987

———. *Kawaii shōkōgun*. Tokyo: Nihon hōsō shuppan kyōkai, 1994

Morris, Ivan. *The World of the Shining Prince: Court Life in Ancient Japan*. 1964; rpt. New York, Tokyo and London: Kodansha International, 1994

Napier, Susan J. 'Lost in transition: sekai no owari no ningyōtachi.' In *Jinzō bijo wa kanō ka?* Edited by Takayuki Tatsumi and Ogino Anna. Tokyo: Keiō gijuku daigaku shuppankai, 2006. Pp.270–309

Orbaugh, Sharalyn. 'Emotional Infectivity: Cyborg Affect and the Limits of the Human.' In *Mechademia 3: Limits of the Human*. Edited by Frenchy Lunning. Minnesota & London: University of Minnesota Press, 2008. Pp. 150–188

Oshii, Mamoru. *Subete no eiga wa anime ni naru*. Tokyo: Tokuma shoten, 2004

———. *Innocence sōsaku note: Ningyō, kenchiku, shintai no tabi + taidan*. Tokyo: Tokuma shoten Studio Ghibli jigyō honbu, 2004

Ōtsuka, Eiji. '"Kawaii" no tanjō.' In *Shōjo zassi ron*. Edited by Ōtsuka Eiji. Tokyo: Tokyo shoseki, 1991. Pp. 85-102

Pate, Alan S. *Ningyō: The Art of the Japanese Doll*. Boston: Tuttle, 2005

Schattschneider, Ellen. '"Buy Me a Bride": Death and Exchange in Northern Japanese Bride-Doll Marriage.' *American Ethnologist* 28:4 (Nov. 2001): 854–880

Shimamura, Mari. *Fancy no kenkyū: 'kawaii' ga hito, mono, kane o shihai-suru*. Tokyo: Nesco, 1991

Stephens, John, and Mio Bryce. '"Nothing dirty about turning on a machine": Loving your Mechanoid in Contemporary Manga.' *Papers: Explorations Into Children's Literature* 14:2 (2004): 44–52

Takahara, Eiri. 'Gothic no isō kara.' In *Jinzō bijo wa kanō ka?* Edited by Takayuki Tatsumi and Anna Ogino. Tokyo: Keiō gijuku daigaku shuppankai, 2006. Pp.178–204

Winge, Theresa. 'Undressing and Dressing Loli: A Search for the Identity of the Japanese Lolita.' In *Mechademia 3: Limits of the Human*. Edited by Frenchy Lunning. University of Minnesota Press, 2008. Pp.47–66

Yomota, Inuhiko. *'Kawaii' ron*. Tokyo: Chikuma shobō, 2006

Yōrō, Takeshi. *Nihonjin no shintaikan no rekishi*. Tokyo: Hōzōkan, 1996

———. *Shintai no bungaku-shi*. Tokyo: Shinchōsha, 1997

Notes

1 In Japanese names, the surname is followed by the given name.

2 The word *Ningyō* is also used in compound words for special dolls, for example, *hina ningyō* for the doll festival, *gosho ningyō* for child-shaped dolls appreciated by adult aristocrats as a symbol of youth, *bunraku ningyō* for *ningyō jōruri* (the Japanese puppet theatre from the Edo period, 1603-1868), and *karakuri ningyō* for mechanical dolls, also developed in the Edo period (see Pate).

3 Dolls may be brought to temples and shrines for special memorial services. This is related to the animistic belief that lifeless things (even needles and utensils) can gain 'life' through lengthy, intimate relationships with humans. This is particularly true for dolls with their close spiritual proximity to humans.

4 See <http://www.jump.co.jp/bs-i/chojin/archive/055.html>

5 Atae Yūki's dolls are seen in Kawaguchi-ko Muse-kan (http://www.musekan.net/index.php)

6 The popularity of Sanrio's Hello Kitty among mature women also lies in her extremely simple and vague face, which effectively reflects human emotions (Brian, 'Hello Kitty').

7 The fondness of cute dolls is so strong in Japan that even Mattel had to produce a Japanese version of Barbie modified by Takara between 1982 and 1986, with this doll later becoming 'Jenny'.

8 The Maruichi trade name comprises *maru* (round and zero) and *ichi* (one) which represent their computerised disposition, completeness and simplicity; as well as humanness (soft and round) and technology (angular and numerical), that indicate the Maruichi's role as a mediator of human communication via technology. The extreme simplicity of the Maruichi's features also urges the user's personalisation.

9 A similar plot is also used in *Paracite Dolls* (2003), directed by Nakazawa Kazuto and Yoshinaga Naoyuki.

10 The title is pronounced as *Plants Doll* as written in *katakana*, although different in *kanji*: 観用少女 (*Kan'yō shōjo*), which was coined from 観葉植物 (*kanyō shokubutsu*), ornamental leafy plants. The title means ornamental girls or girls for visual pleasure, like foliage plants. The dolls are expensive and need special care and love. They have a sense of non-humanness and affectionate and intuitive child-likeness. They are waiting 'asleep' (like inert dolls) for their future owner (usually male) to come along. Once awakened, they attach themselves to their chosen owners so exclusively that sometimes the shopkeeper has to sell them cheaply to avoid their wilting. Their relationships with their owners are thus essentially mostly non-verbal, as they interact through their emotive facial expressions (e.g., beaming smiles).

11 Uika then 'sleeps' like an inert doll until Yomie finds a man for her. The man is haunted by his late partner, who killed herself to possess him as a ghost. Uika uses her mythical power as a doll and defends him from the dead, then lives happily as his partner.

12 This is why they are programmed to return to Shizuka and Arashi upon the accomplishment of their missions. As Arashi explains, this is to rescue the dolls from their unbearable loneliness, after their human partner has grown up or passed away. The returned androids are lulled to sleep by Shizuka's flute, until awakened by Arashi's, as a new android.

Chapter 6

Human and Superhuman in Contemporary Japanese Girls' Manga

Rebecca Suter
University of Sydney

Introduction: posthuman beauties

The question of what it means to be human has a central theme in Japanese comics and animation for a long time. In recent years, these media have been increasingly active in challenging conventional definitions of human nature, playing a pivotal role in the surge of academic interest in so-called 'posthuman criticism.' As Christopher Bolton notes in his introduction to the third issue of *Mechademia*, aptly entitled 'Limits of the Human,' with their focus on the 'trio par excellence of nonhuman others,' i.e. the machine, the monster/animal, and the network, Japanese comics and animation have gone far in exploring, challenging, and transgressing the boundaries of the human, and a significant corpus of scholarship on the topic has developed concurrently. (Bolton xi)

An important part of such scholarship has dealt with the genre of *mecha* anime, science fictional animation revolving around the encroachment of technology upon the human body, often in combination with the themes of artificial intelligence and virtual networks. Blurring of gender conventions, a staple of posthuman theory since Donna Haraway's famous analysis of the subversive power of biotechnology in her 'Cyborg Manifesto,' is also a central feature of *mecha*. One of the most interesting figures of *mecha* in this respect is the so-called *sentô bishôjo*, or 'battling beauty,' a female warrior-like figure endowed with a mechanically enhanced body.[1] Detached from biological constraints thanks to technology, battling beauties are reminiscent of the cyborg as a symbol of women's liberation celebrated by Haraway.

At the same time, in *mecha* such apparent emancipation is often accompanied by a high degree of sexualization of the characters according to conventional patriarchal stereotypes of femininity. As Kotani argues in her study of the series *Revolutionary Girl Utena*, while the battling woman of *mecha* appropriates conventionally masculine prerogatives such as physical strength and fighting spirit, she is also invariably 'a beauty, which configures her in relation to boys' desires' (Kotani 166). Her nature as a 'beauty' frames the *sentô bishôjo* through a male gaze, an effect that is paradoxically only reinforced by the superhuman powers the authors provide her with. The *sentô bishôjo*'s muscular cyberbody is endowed with large breasts, shapely legs, a pretty face; to better show her cyborgian qualities, she is generally naked or scantily dressed, resulting in a wide display of so-called 'fan service,' i.e. sexual material designed to amuse/arouse the (generally male) audience. Empowered through mechanical devices in the diegesis, on the level of representation the battling beauty is thus reified for the benefit of the male viewer. Tellingly, this figure is more common in *shônen manga*, or comics aimed at an audience of boys, though not exclusive to them.

Shôjo manga, comics aimed at a female readership, on the other hand, present us with a more complex vision of gender and sexuality. Possibly because girls' manga tend to prefer the mode of fantasy to that of science fiction, few scholars have approached them through the framework of posthuman studies. However, the genre is equally if not more interesting in terms of its reflection on human nature. In this essay, I therefore propose to analyse *shôjo*'s approach to the question of 'what was the human,' with particular focus on its treatment of gender and history. As a premise, I will focus on a classic feature of *shôjo*: the combination of gender/sexual blurring and fantahistory to question social and cultural conventions. I will then concentrate on a text that applies these strategies to a rewriting of Christian legends, Akaishi Michiyo's *Amakusa 1637* (2002), in order to examine in greater detail the concrete articulations of these dynamics and to reflect on their broader significance in terms of theories of the human and posthuman.

Girl knights and boys' love

A paramount example of the different conception of human and posthuman in girls' and boy's *manga* is the *shôjo* equivalent of the *sentô bishôjo*, which I define as the 'girl knight' trope. As the name suggests, this figure presents similarities with the 'battling beauty,' particularly its combination of gender bending and empowerment, yet it is also different in some crucial respects. Rather than relying on biotechnology, girl knight stories challenge gender and societal conventions through a combination of cross-dressing and a rewriting of history. This results in a very different, and highly intriguing, approach to the question of what constitutes the human.

The 'girl knight' trope has been highly popular in *shôjo manga* since its inception. The first appearance of this figure dates back to one of the founding works of the genre, Osamu Tezuka's *Ribon no kishi* (*Ribbon Knight*, 1953–6 *manga*, 1963–6 *anime*). Sapphire, the protagonist of the series, is a princess in a fictional medieval kingdom, biologically female but endowed with two hearts, a boy's and a girl's. Cross-dressing as a knight, Sapphire passes as a male in order to inherit her father's throne. According to Frederick Schodt, the series set the main features of contemporary *shôjo manga*: 'a love story, a foreign setting, and a heroine with large eyes and a somewhat bisexual personality' (Schodt 96).

Arguably the most famous instance of this trope appears in Ikeda Riyoko's *Berusayu no bara* (*The Rose of Versailles*, *manga* 1972; *anime* 1979–80). Set during the French Revolution, the series was originally a biography of Marie Antoinette, but adjusting to the audience's response it soon shifted its focus on a secondary, fictional character, Oscar François de Jarjayes. Oscar is the youngest daughter of a French aristocrat who desired a male heir so strongly that, when his eighth daughter was born, he gave her a male name and raised her as a boy. Oscar's performance as a boy is both successful and tragic: she pursues a military career, becomes the captain of the Royal Guard, then shifts sides and joins the revolutionaries, and finally dies on the barricades.

Alongside the revolution drama, the story features a number of romantic subplots involving queen Marie Antoinette, the queen's lover, Count Axel Von Fersen, a girl from the underclass, Rosalie Lamorière, and André, the son of Oscar's housemaid. Struggling with his/her gender identity, Oscar refuses both homosexual and heterosexual romances throughout the series, and finally settles for her childhood sweetheart and military companion, André, the only character who does not seem to threaten either her/his male or female self.[2]

Vastly popular both in its time and to this day, *The Rose of Versailles* was a foundational text of the renaissance of girls' comics in the 1970s, spurred on by the so-called *24nengumi*, or '49 group.' The term refers to a number of female authors, all born in or around the year 24 of the Shôwa era (1949 in the Western calendar), who aimed to revolutionize *shôjo manga* and re-appropriate its production, at the time dominated by male authors such as Tezuka Osamu and his heirs, while also claiming the right for women to write in different genres. Spanning from science fiction and horror to historical drama, the *24nengumi*'s works challenged both genre and gender conventions. Cross-dressing was a staple of the genre, and it played an important role in its formal and ideological experiments.

More generally, an interest in clothes, hairstyle and makeup as identity markers was a central feature of *shôjo manga* of the time. As Frederik Schodt notes in his discussion of girls' manga of the 1970s:

> Characters become fashion models. The clothes they wear conform to the seasons in which the stories are drawn and, to please young readers, may be changed on every other page. If their faces are so stylized that they all look the same, as is often the case, characters may be distinguished by their hairstyles. (Schodt 90)[3]

Such focus on fashion ultimately drew attention to the clothes' function of covering the body and reshaping it into an arbitrary, constructed figure, denaturalizing conventional definitions of human subjectivity. For the protagonists of these stories, dressing up was a way to acquire an identity, and at the same time to show its staged quality. Cross-dressing further complicated the picture, offering a critique of conventional notions of femininity and masculinity. Presenting uniforms, rather than biological features, as the markers of gender, 'girl knight' stories highlighted its performative quality.

The genre remains very popular to this day, and presents a vast range of variations and settings, as different as the hundred-year war in Miuchi Suzue's *Shirayuri no kishi* (*The White Lily Knight*, 1975) and the rise of the Hittite Empire in Shinohara Chie's *Sora wa akai kawa no hotori: Anatolia story* (*The sky next to the Red River: Anatolia Story*, 1995 –2002).

An analogous mechanism can be found in another subgenre of *shôjo* that was central to the *24nengumi* revolution, namely *shônen ai*, or 'boy's love' (hereafter *BL*). The terms refer to stories written by women authors, aimed mostly at a female readership, centering on male homosexual romance. The genre was inaugurated by Hagio Moto and Takemiya Keiko, the founding members of the group, with two comics both centering on romance between boys at a European boarding school, *Jûichigatsu no jimunajiumu (The gymnasium of November*, 1971*)*, and *Kaze to ki no uta (A song of wind and trees*, 1976), respectively. Typical features of *shônen ai* include a foreign setting and effeminate, beautiful young male protagonists, as well as a markedly erotic tone, often tinged with sado-masochism. The texts feature a combination of escapist and subversive strategies to address the question of gender and sexual normativity that are reminiscent of those displayed in 'girl knight' stories.

Similar to girl knight tales, *BL* stories became highly popular among female readers and gave rise to a vast and varied production throughout the years. During the 1990s, as it became increasingly popular among female fans, the genre of *BL* drew sharp criticism from the male gay community in Japan, which accused the authors of objectifying and misrepresenting male gay identity, ultimately harming the already difficult position of homosexual men in Japan. This spurred a long debate between *BL* authors and fans, gay activists, and feminists, which is too complex to summarise here (for a brilliant and concise overview see Vincent 69 –77). What is most relevant to my argument, though, is the response of *BL* fans and authors such as *mangaka* Takamatsu Hisako and *manga* critic Fujimoto Yukari, who laid claim to their male gay love fantasy arguing that it offered them an invaluable refuge from the patriarchal society they were immersed in. In a culture in which girls and women could only be constructed as the object of a male gaze, they argued, *BL* offered a unique opportunity to invert this mechanism.

Interestingly, another element that *BL* and 'girl knight' stories have in common is the use of exoticised foreign and/or historical settings. As I discussed elsewhere in relation to Miuchi Suzue's rewriting of the legend of Joan of Arc as a girl knight tale, it is my contention that such use of history has a similar function to the blurring of gender and sexual norms: while on one hand it caters to the readers' taste for exotica, it also increases critical distance, allowing authors and readers alike to reflect on societal conventions from the vantage point of a different time and space, and to reflect on their arbitrary nature (Suter 2009). In this respect, the comics are reminiscent of what Linda Hutcheon defines as postmodernist 'historiographic metafiction,' comprising works that 'are both intensely self-reflexive and yet paradoxically also lay claim to historical events and personages' and whose 'theoretical self-awareness of history and fiction as human constructs (historio*graphic* *meta*fiction) is made the grounds for its rethinking and reworking of the forms and contents of the past' (Hutcheon 5). Similar to novels such as John Fowles' *The French Lieutenant's Woman* (1969) or Salman Rushdie's *Midnight's Children* (1980), in *shôjo manga* the use of fantahistory becomes both a source of creativity and a political gesture.

This use of fantahistory is therefore an ambiguous operation, difficult to categorize as either escapist or subversive. While constituting a compensatory fantasy, it also provides a space for a critique of normative representations of gender and sexuality. If *mecha* relies on science fiction and technology to celebrate the advent of the 'posthuman,' girl knight and *BL* stories concentrate on gender bending and fantahistory to explore conventional definitions of the 'human' and challenge them from within. In the remaining part of the essay, I will look at the specific articulation of these mechanisms in one *shôjo manga*, Akaishi Michiyo's *Amakusa 1637* (2002).[4]

Revolutionary girl Shirô

Amakusa 1637, a 12-volume series published by Shôgakukan in 2002, features all of the elements I have just mentioned: a girl knight tale, a *BL* theme, and a creative rewriting of history, specifically the so-called Shimabara rebellion of 1637, a popular revolt against excessive taxes which relied on Christian symbols, and was brutally repressed by the Tokugawa government, marking the definitive ban on Christian religion. The comic tells the story of Hayumi Natsuki, a Japanese teenage girl who is shipwrecked during a school trip and time-travels along with five classmates to medieval Japan, a few months before the beginning of the upheaval.

Due to an uncanny physical resemblance, Natsuki is mistaken for Masuda Shirô Tokisada, a young low-rank *samurai* from Amakusa and the future leader of the revolt. A survivor of the January 1995 Kôbe earthquake, Natsuki is highly troubled by the thought of the impending bloodbath, and resolves to take advantage of her newly acquired identity to try to prevent the massacre. She enacts her plan through two main strategies: first, traveling around Kyûshû to persuade the local lords to help the cause of the oppressed Shimabara people, or at least promise that they will abstain from intervening once the uprising begins and the Tokugawa government orders the local lords to crush it, and second, winning the favour of the population in order to become the leader of the revolt and bring it to a peaceful end.

Centering on revolution, cross-dressing, and gender ambiguity, the *manga* reads in many respects like a tribute to *The Rose of Versailles*. In both comics, the heroines pass as males by donning military attire, the French Royal Guard uniform for Oscar and a samurai outfit for Natsuki; they occasionally secretly revert to a female identity by wearing elegant, frilly women's clothes, eighteenth-century evening dresses for the former, *kimono* for the latter. Like Oscar, Natsuki is extremely skilled with the sword, coming from a family of renowned *iaidô* champions. Similar to her French counterpart, Natsuki/ Shirô is an object of desire for a number of male and female characters, but is indifferent to all except for the main love interest, Miyamoto, a childhood friend and martial arts classmate who in 1637 Kyûshû acquires the identity of the legendary *samurai* Miyamoto Musashi. The Natsuki/Miyamoto couple parallels the Oscar/Andre one in a number of ways, especially on the visual level: they have very similar features and wear similar clothes, one is blonde the other dark, they are often shown riding horses or fighting enemies together, and so forth.

The comic also features a number of *BL* subplots, some centering on one of the modern-day protagonists, Yatsuka, and some between various historical characters, the most significant of which is the tormented love affair between the third *shôgun* Tokugawa Iemitsu and the renowned swordsman Yagyû Jûbei. Through the story of Yatsuka, who in seventeenth-century Kyûshû is finally able to embrace his gay identity and live his sexuality freely, the *manga* exposes both the constructed nature of heteronormative sexuality (showing that there is nothing 'natural' about the taboo on homosexuality that constrained Yatsuka in present-day Japan) and its pervasiveness (it is only in a displaced, fantastical setting that it is possible to overcome that taboo). A similar mechanism applies to gender, as shown in the story of Natsuki herself, who in present-day Japan had to see her younger brother inherit the leadership of the family's *iaidô* school despite her own superiority in swordsmanship, but performing as a man in medieval Japan is acclaimed as a political and spiritual leader. At the same time, in both cases the space of Amakusa in 1637 offers readers a standpoint to reflect on social conventions and an occasion to experiment with non-normative gender and sexual patterns, to rethink/rewrite themselves outside those conventions.

Interestingly, while Yatsuka's homosexuality is portrayed as part of his 'human nature,' lesbian identity is presented through a more conservative framework, as a 'phase' that girls need to outgrow. This is evident in the development of the character of Eri, a female classmate who is in love with Natsuki since their schooldays in modern-day Japan. As the story progresses and her emotional attachment to Natsuki grows stronger, a number of characters tell Eri that, while her devotion to her friend is admirable, she needs to overcome her infatuation. The message of the *manga* could not be clearer: all her friends consistently advise Eri to renounce her lesbian love, and ultimately events force her to follow their advice. At the peak of the Shimabara battle, through another time slip, Eri is separated from the group and magically sent back to the year 2000, thus having to renounce her romantic dream forever.

After the high degree of ambiguity and excitement that Akaishi presented us with over the course of the twelve volumes, the final pages of *Amakusa 1637* are rather underwhelming in terms of gender and sexual politics. At the end of the last volume, we flash-forward to the 2020s, and once again through the point of view of Eri, now turned into a famous history professor, we learn that Amakusa no Shirô mysteriously disappeared after the battle of Shimabara, while Miyamoto Musashi became the leader of Southern Japan, after marrying 'a certain Natsuki.' Both Natsuki and Eri are thus apparently reinscribed into a normative framework: the former has to relinquish her role as a revolutionary leader to become a samurai's wife, while the latter is forced to renounce her lesbian infatuation to 'go back to reality.' However, Eri's return to the future also lends itself to a more nuanced interpretation.

First of all, Eri, who throughout the series acts as a sort of stand-in for the reader in the text, a reflector from whose point of view the story of Natsuki is presented, is the character readers are most likely to identify with. Thus, her return to modern-time Japan can be read as an indication of the *manga*'s choice to reconnect to reality after its plunge into a fantasy world, and its use of alternative history as platform to reflect critically on the present, rather than escape from it. Furthermore, Eri becomes a successful academic and a renowned historian of Japan, and is entrusted with the task of preserving the memory of her classmates' adventure.

The text therefore ends on an assertion of the importance of historical knowledge within the relativised, fantastical context that it had constructed over the course of the series. This need to reconnect with the 'real' had been foreshadowed in the text by the insistence, especially on the level of graphic representation, on the dreadful realities of the revolt and its gruesome repression. While foregrounding the textual, constructed quality of historiography, the *manga* also acknowledges the need to engage the 'reality' of the past, of the fact that, as Jameson famously put it, 'history is what hurts' (Jameson 102). The comic's treatment of history is in fact one of its most distinctive features.

The queer Messiah

One major aspect in which *Amakusa 1637* departs from its ostensible model, *The Rose of Versailles*, is the protagonist's role in history. While Oscar is involved in the political turbulence of her time, first as a member of the Royal Guard and later as one of the revolutionaries, her role is arguably quite marginal. Natsuki, on the other hand, does not simply join a revolution.

Rather, she becomes its leader, bringing the revolt to a peaceful conclusion and, in the process, changing the course of Japanese history. Interestingly, Natsuki/Shirô's ascent to power is accompanied by a clear shift from military to cultural means, from 'hard' to 'soft' power. In the first part of the series, the protagonist relies mainly on her extraordinary sword skills to achieve her objectives, but as the story unfolds, she gradually becomes less of a warrior and more of a spiritual leader, and achieves her final victory by symbolically deposing her *katana* at her enemies' feet. Such transition from military means to religious/ideological persuasion is accompanied by increasing gender blurring. While initially Natsuki simply passes as a *samurai*, straightforwardly acquiring traditional Japanese male military characteristics, in the course of the series she gradually transforms into a more gender-ambiguous figure.[5]

Natsuki's spiritual leadership is thus explicitly related to her androgynous nature: characters constantly connect the impossibility of categorising him/her as a man or a woman to her being 'a creature from another world,' 'an angel,' and 'a deity.' The character's gender ambivalence is a source of attraction for both men and women, from the future and from the past, including the aforementioned Yatsuka, who is in love with him as a man, and Eri, who is attracted to her as a female. Various prominent figures in Tokugawa history, including the Kyûshû aristocrat Hosokawa Mitsutoshi and the same Yagyû Jûbei who is represented as Iemitsu's lover, are captivated by his unique combination of weakness and strength, femininity and masculinity. On her part, Natsuki exploits the charm of her androgyny for political and humanitarian purposes, in order to win over the daimyô of Kyûshû to the cause of the oppressed people of the Amakusa and Shimabara areas.

To this rather canonical *shôjo* format, half girl-knight adventure and half gay romance, Akaishi adds a new element: religion. Besides her androgyny, the other main source of Natsuki/Shirô's power lies in a combination of military might, technology and Christianity. These are represented on the visual level by the objects that the character always carries with her: a sword, a mobile phone, and a cross, blatant symbols of traditional martial power, modern machinery, and a foreign religion (Figure 1). Initially mistaken for a Jesuit convert because of her Catholic school uniform, Natsuki soon becomes known as 'Deusu no tsukai,' literally 'the messenger of God' (from

Figure 1: Natsuki/Shirô holding the symbols of her power: Japanese daggers, a mobile phone, and a cross

the Japanese transliteration of the Portuguese *Deus*, the term used by the Jesuit missionaries and the Japanese converts of the time).

The shift from hard to soft power is thus accompanied by a three-stage transformation from schoolgirl to *samurai* to priest. This is reflected on the graphic level in the evolution of the protagonist's clothes. Initially, Natsuki wears her 'sailor suit' school uniform top with a *hakama*, traditional trousers used, among other things, in martial arts, which is how she happened

Figure 2: Natsuki/Shirô in her half-samurai, half-schoolgirl outfit

to be dressed during the shipwreck, as she was getting ready for a *iaidô* demonstration. (Figure 2) She then switches to fully Japanese attire, wearing a kimono top above her *hakama* (Figure 3). Finally, in volume 7, she starts to wear a white cape, which makes him/her look like a bishop (Figure 4). Accordingly, as the story progresses, Shirô/Natsuki acquires more and more priestly prerogatives; in the second half of the story, we see him/her officiate weddings, perform funeral rites, and baptize children. In the end, it is mainly

Figure 3: Natsuki/Shirô transitioning to a fully Japanese outfit

thanks to the position of spiritual authority s/he has reached that Natsuki is able to reject the Shogunal army without a direct military confrontation and avoid the Shimabara massacre. Christianity is thus another central component of Natsuki's 'soft power' strategies, together with gender and sexual ambiguity. Religion is not only connected to gender in the diegesis but it is framed in a very similar way, i.e. as performative and hybridized.

Although the story features a number of fantastic elements, such as time-travel, Natsuki's uncanny ability to perceive 'killing will' around her, and

Figure 4: Natsuki/Shirô turning into a priest-like figure

a sky unnaturally turned red that makes mobile phones work without any antenna, religion itself is framed through a rational perspective. The 'miracles' performed by Natsuki/Shirô are clearly faked: like her samurai identity, her priestly persona is based on a conscious performance. Christianity is presented as a moral system, emphasizing notions of equality and social justice, and as a staged form of magic, enacted through a number of modern-day devices rescued from the shipwreck, which enable Natsuki to perform 'miracles' and convince the crowds that s/he possesses supernatural powers.

Building a float with pet bottles rescued from the shipwreck, s/he fools the people of Kyûshû into believing that she can walk on water; s/he revives children dying of starvation using 'calorie mate' energy bars; s/he convinces people that s/he is a clairvoyant by communicating with her friends via mobile phones; s/he fakes the presence of angels by playing Händel's 'Hallelujah' on a mobile phone, and so forth. Framing the supernatural through a humanistic approach, the story foregrounds the staged character of the protagonist's superhuman qualities. While the performance is ultimately successful, the comic is far from celebratory of this deception. Throughout the series, Natsuki constantly fears that her lies may be exposed and her female identity revealed, fatally undermining her authority as the leader of the rebels. Foregrounding the protagonist's awareness that only by passing as a male and as a semi-divine figure will she be able to achieve her objectives, the comic once again highlights both the arbitrariness and the pervasiveness of social norms.

The Japanization of Christianity

Furthermore, both religion and technology in the story are constructed as hybrid, a mixture of traditional and modern, Japanese and Western elements. Christian symbols are introduced via their modern-day Japanese versions, such as the school uniforms of Natsuki's catholic school or her friends' memories of 'Kôbe no luminarie,' the light festival held in the city of Kôbe at Christmas time since the 1990s, which the students try to reproduce for the people of Amakusa with candles and torches. Similarly, modern technology appears in the form of instances of 'Japanized modernity,' such as stereotypically Japanese mobile phones complete with Harajuku-style straps, or *calorie mate* tablets, a popular brand of energy bars produced by Otsuka pharmaceuticals since the 1980s. Military technique too is introduced through the frame of a modernized martial art such as *iaidô*, blurring the boundary between the modern and the traditional.

Another example of this syncretism can be found in the use of language: in a number of scenes, the characters utter 'Japanized' English words such as 'sankyuu' (thank you) or 'asupirin' (aspirin), transliterated into *katakana*, the syllabary used to transcribe foreign words, while their uncomprehending interlocutors from the Edo period repeat the words in *hiragana*, the syllabary used for Japanese words. The defamiliarising effect emphasizes the foreign origin of these words, but also reminds us that they have become an integral part of contemporary Japanese culture.

Hybridity and performance are thus crucial to the comic's rewriting of history and religion. Tellingly, the parallel-universe Japan that we are shown in the last pages of the comic has become a utopian society because it developed from a 'Southern shogunate' that did not close contacts with the world, and instead engaged foreign influence and subjected it to what I have elsewhere defined as a 'Japanization of modernity' (Suter 2008). In this respect, the comic reads like an intriguing twist on the development of Japan's modern nationalism.

As recent scholarship has pointed out, anti-Christian discourse played a pivotal role in the formation of modern Japanese state ideology, particularly in the late Tokugawa and early Meiji periods. In his study of Christianity and ideology in Japan, Kiri Paramore notes that anti-Christian literature in the Tokugawa period centered on the danger of the foreign religion's appeal to the masses and its challenge to feudal loyalty and Confucian social relations. In the nineteenth century, however, while still rejecting Christianity, Japanese intellectuals also started advocating an appropriation of this obviously successful technology of power. As Bob Wakabayashi argues in his study of Aizawa Seishisai's so-called *New Theses* of 1825, in the Bakumatsu ('End of Shogunate') period scholars began to see Christianity as a highly efficient form of social control that was at the roots of European power on the national and international level. Seishisai saw this as both a threat and a model to emulate. His response was the formulation of two future pillars of the modern Japanese state, which functioned as ideological tools to appeal to the masses, namely *kokutai* ('national polity') and state Shintô.

A similar simultaneous rejection and imitation of Christianity as a system of social control was central to the nationalist ideology formulated in the Meiji period, particularly Emperor worship. In his study of anti-Christian discourse of the 1880s, Kiri Paramore argues that '*tennôsei* ideology, the emperor-centric ideology of modern Japan, was formed in reaction to a perceived model of the ideological role of Christianity in Europe.' (Paramore 131) Similar to Aizawa's formulation of *kokutai*, this construction of a native alternative to the European 'opium for the people' was accompanied by a surge of anti-Christian populist works that presented it as foreign, superstitious, and dangerously egalitarian, in contrast with Shintô notions of cultural integrity and Confucian ideals of rationality and hierarchical order.

Through the portrayal of Natsuki's career as a religious revolutionary leader, *Amakusa 1637* both appropriates and subverts this mechanism. Like Bakumatsu and Meiji intellectuals, Natsuki/Shirô sees religion as a powerful sham that can be exploited for political purposes, and readily takes advantage of it to reach her political goals; these, however, are not nationalist and authoritarian, but egalitarian and revolutionary. Furthermore, rather than emphasizing Christianity's foreignness, the comic presents it as completely Japanized. The comic thus performs a parallel and inverse operation to that of the late Tokugawa and early Meiji ideologues. While they denounced its superstition and its foreignness to uphold national spirit and reinforce authoritarian policies, Akaishi's text embraces performance and hybridity for their revolutionary potential.

Conclusion

Amakusa 1637 reads as a fairly conventional *shôjo manga* in many respects. The addition of the element of 'Japanized Christianity,' however, allows the comic to deepen its enquiry into human nature in two ways. First, the text presents the supernatural as ultimately human-made, a clever sham created with the tools of Japanized modernity, a performance and a construct. In so doing, it simultaneously questions societal norms and highlights their pervasiveness and durability. Unlike the cyborg, Haraway's 'creature in a post-gender world' (Haraway 150), Akaishi's 'girl knight' is anything but superhuman: she is very much of this world, and subject to its constraints and limitations. Rather than pretending that gender divisions have been overcome in the posthuman world, the comic reveals the arbitrary, but also persistent, nature of gender and societal conventions, and chooses to question them from within, in the realm of the human.

Furthermore, both in its treatment of gender and in its portrayal of religion, the *manga* shows that hybridity, both cross-gender and cross-cultural, is a key factor in subversive appropriation. I read this mechanism as a *mise en abyme* of the ideological operation performed by the comic itself, and more broadly by *shôjo manga*: it is by incorporating and 'queering' Japanese and Western culture, past and present, tradition and modernity, and recombining them into a new hybrid product, that girls' comics offer a platform for a critical reflection on, and a rethinking of, 'what was the human.'

Works Cited

Bolton, Christopher. 'Introduction.' In *Mechademia 3: Limits of the Human*. Minneapolis: University of Minnesota Press, 2008. Pp. xi–xvi

Haraway, Donna. 'A Cyborg Manifesto: Science, Technology, and Socialist–Feminism in the Late Twentieth Century.' In her *Simians, Cyborgs and Women: The Reinvention of Nature*. London and New York: Routledge, 1991. Pp. 149–81

Hutcheon, Linda. *A Poetics of Postmodernism*. London and New York: Routledge, 1988.

Jameson, Fredric. *The Political Unconscious: Narrative as a Socially Symbolic Act*. Ithaca: Cornell University Press, 1981

Kotani Mari. 'Metamorphosis of the Japanese Girl: the Girl, the Hyper-Girl, and the Battling Beauty.' In *Mechademia 1: Emerging Worlds of Anime and Manga*. Minneapolis: University of Minnesota Press, 2006. Pp. 162–70

Paramore, Kiri. *Ideology and Christianity in Japan*. London and New York: Routledge, 2009

Saitô Tamaki. *Sentô bishôjo no seishin bunseki*. Tokyo: Ôta Shuppan, 2001

Schodt, Frederik. *Manga! Manga! The World of Japanese Comics*. Tokyo and New York: Kodansha International, 1983

Shamoon, Deborah. 'Revolutionary Romance: *The Rose of Versailles* and the Transformation of Shojo Manga.' In *Mechademia 2: Networks of Desire*. Minneapolis: University of Minnesota Press, 2007. Pp. 3–17

Suter, Rebecca. *The Japanization of Modernity: Murakami Haruki between Japan and the United States*. Harvard University Press East Asia Series, 2008

———. 'From Jusuheru to Jannu: Creative Misreadings of Christianity in the works of Miuchi Suzue.' In *Mechademia 4*. Minneapolis: University of Minnesota Press, 2009. Pp. 241–56

Vincent, Keith. 'A Japanese Electra and her Queer Progeny.' In *Mechademia 2: Networks of Desire*. Minneapolis: University of Minnesota Press, 2007. Pp. 64–79

Wakabayashi, Bob. *Anti-foreignism and Western Learning in Early-Modern Japan: the New Theses of 1825*. Harvard University Press East Asia Series, 1986

Notes

1 For a discussion of the notion of *sentô bishôjo* in the English language, see Kotani 167; in Japanese, see also Saitô Tamaki.

2 According to Deborah Shamoon, this is one of the main reasons behind the astounding

success of the series: 'Oscar remains popular among girl readers even thirty years after the story's initial publication not only because she displays masculine strength and agency without sacrificing her feminine beauty and empathy but because she finds true love without losing her identity to her partner' (Shamoon 12).

3   The focus on clothes was influenced by, and had an impact on, the drawing style and narrative structure of these comics. A typical feature of the genre was the insertion on one side of the page of a fashionably dressed character, in full figure, an image completely unrelated to the diegesis. This was in line with girls' *manga's* peculiar combination of visual and verbal elements and its experimental graphic style, the way in which the comics broke the margins of frames, merged dialogue and images, and centered on emotional impact more than on linear narrative.

4   In the essay, I will follow the Japanese convention for writing names, with the family name preceding the first name.

5   In the remaining part of the paper, I will alternately refer to the protagonist as Natsuki, Shirô, or Natsuki/Shirô, and as she, he, or s/he, depending on the relative positioning of the character as female, male, or both, in different episodes and contexts.

Part Two
Spaces for the Human: Personal and Political Frontiers

Chapter 7

Frontiers of Life and Death: The Human, New Wars and World Literary Sensibilities

Debjani Ganguly
Humanities Research Centre
Australian National University

On the eve of the 2003 Iraq War, Henry Perowne, the neurosurgeon protagonist of Ian McEwan's novel *Saturday*, ponders the pervading sense of anxiety and vulnerability across the world, a feeling aggravated by incessant exposure to electronic images of violent global flashpoints:

> He takes a step towards the CD player, then changes his mind for he's feeling the pull, like gravity, of the approaching TV news. It's *the condition of the times, this compulsion to hear how it stands with the world*, and be joined to a generality, to a community of anxiety ... a different scale of news value has been set by monstrous and spectacular scenes ... the television networks stand ready to deliver, and their audiences wait. (McEwan 176, italics added).

Saturday is a symptomatic case study for this essay on the predicament of being human in our times, a *zeitgeist* marked by our voyeuristic *compulsion* to be world-oriented in the aftermath of the Cold War and the geopolitics of violence that has ensued. This spectatorial, world-making sensibility, mediated by electronic images that iconicize terror-inducing devastation as a sign of our times is what informs the literary works I propose to examine.

What is the Human?

Drawing on a larger study of world Anglophone fiction on post-Cold War geopolitical deathworlds – Kosovo, Rwanda, Iraq, Palestine, Afghanistan, and the United States – this essay makes a case for a new configuration of the 'human' through a contemporary form of literary globalism, one mediated by World English. This global literary space, I argue, has emerged at the intersection of post-1989 geographies of violence, hyperconnectivity through advances in information technology, and the emergence of a new humanitarian sensibility in a context where suffering has a presence in everyday life through the immediacy of digital images. The rationale for linking the 'human' to the 'global' and to literature at large may appear, at one level, as plain commonsense. Isn't the human a universal category? Doesn't the universality of the idea of 'human' always already imply the extension of the global as its concrete sphere of actualization? Further, isn't literature all about our human condition, our frailties and our vanities, our commonness and difference, our violent predilections, our loves, hopes and disappointments? Why undertake such a study then? What is it about our contemporary moment of literary worlding that compels us to think anew about the 'human' as a category? Does the genre of the novel itself configure the human in ways we are no longer attuned too? These are some questions that animate what follows.

There are three parts to this essay. In the first, I provide a geopolitical and disciplinary context for the global fiction I propose to study. In the second, I historicize the emergence of the global fictional form and its world-oriented sensibility by taking us to a narrative grammar of the human informed by two concepts, Sympathy and Sovereignty, that constituted the foundations of the novel in the eighteenth century. This allows me to make a case in the concluding section of the essay for the evolution of contemporary global fiction as the apotheosis of the novel form's configuration of the human since the eighteenth century. Here I contend that the contemporary global confluence of literary voices enables us to address the interplay between two conflicting conceptualizations of the 'human': one based on a liberal world view of the human as the possibility of freedom and transcendence, and the concomitant alienation produced by barriers to achieving its full potential; and the other of the 'human' as immanent in the inhuman, the human as the product effects of the brutal instrumentalities of global capital and its political coordinates that transmogrify into 'war machines', a state that Achille Mbembe calls 'Necropolitics'(2003). In this last, the calculus of life passes through death, and sovereignty is embedded not so much in the idea of freedom and individual autonomy but in the will and capacity to incarcerate, maim, humiliate and kill in order to live.

Literary Worlds after 1989

In recent years the idea of World literature has acquired new purchase as the site of transaction between theories of globalization and comparative literature. Literary globalism for our age is envisioned in two ways: as a *field* of transnational production, circulation and reception of literary texts in a world radically transformed by a high-velocity interconnectivity, itself a qualitative innovation that gives this new century its identity; and as a *discipline* that demands new theoretical and methodological approaches that go beyond the Eurocentric underpinnings of the comparative literature discipline and Nation/Empire literary studies models of the last century. These developments take cognizance of post-War and especially post-Cold War realignments of the global capitalist order and transformations they have wrought on cultures of the world through unprecedented levels of migration and accelerated information flows, by reconfigured territorial alignments in a post-Soviet era, and the emergence of multiple war zones and new ethnic and religious conflicts in the new century.

My choice of literary world-making after 1989 as an object of study is informed as much by these developments as by a broad consensus among political analysts and cultural historians that with the end of the Cold War, the world had entered a new phase of international politics, and economic and cultural exchange. The post-1989 period has been labelled the era of intense globalization via a technologically advanced capitalist expansion and the age of unprecedented transnational networks of migrancy, violence and terrorism. In the wake of the collapse of the bipolar antagonism of the Cold War, the world has seen the emergence of a collaborative network of global capital with the U.S.A. as a politically central node. This neoliberal world order has had to contend with radical political imaginaries such as those of the Al-Qaeda and other extremist/fundamentalist networks around the globe in ways that continue to have grim implications not only for governance, but for human sociality as a whole. Especially pertinent to my analysis here is the emergence in this period of what Mary Kaldor has called 'New Wars' (2006), transnational forms of violence that occur at the interface of conventional warfare between sovereign states, organized crime and state-sponsored violations of human rights through population displacement and genocide. Predominantly fuelled by fragmented ethnic and identity politics as opposed to the bipolar ideological divide of the Cold War, the 'new' wars have the globe as their battle ground and are peopled with mercenary troops and diasporic volunteers adept at using insurgency techniques aimed at mass scale destabilization, generation of fear and perpetuation of a state of emergency. More than any other kind of war in human history, civilians are the largest casualty in these new wars. These transformations in the nature of political violence have in turn amplified the scale of operation of a global humanitarian industry made up of media reporters, NGO workers and international human rights networks. Advances in communication and information technology have further transformed the nature of wars in this era, both in terms of their execution and impact (Baudrillard; Singer; Virilio and Lotringer).

In the last decade and a half, a critical mass of literary works from across the Anglophone world have creatively captured and transfigured shifts in sensibility triggered by these momentous transformations. Some the novels that are distinct products of the post-1989 world include: Ian McEwan's *Saturday*, Andrew Miller's *The Optimists*, Tom Keneally's *The Tyrant's Novel*, Salman Rushdie's *Shalimar the Clown*, David Mitchell's *Ghostwritten*, John Murray, *A Few Short Notes on Tropical Butterflies*, Gil Courtemanche's *Sunday at the Pool in Kigali*, Richard Flanagan's *The Unknown Terrorist*, John Updike's *The Terrorist*, Janet Turner Hospital's *Orpheus Lost,* Don De Lillo's *Falling Man*, Khalid Hosseini's *The Kite Runner* and Mohsin Hamid's *The Reluctant Fundamentalist*. Each of these novels is inflected with an acknowledgement of crisis - the mass of stateless people, the plight of refugees, the experience of war and terror, genocidal reprisals – and seeks urgent strategies of affiliation.

Written at the cusp of what has been a horrific century of wars and ethnic carnage and a new millennium that does not augur much better, such works appear to express a new kind of humanitarian ethic, a new 'internationalism' built on a shared dread of human capacity for evil coupled with a deep awareness of the ambiguities of sharing grief across large expanses of devastated humanscapes

This literary capture of a new humanitarian internationalism is completely at odds with the narratives of 'muscular' or 'military' humanitarianism of the neoliberal regime and its many 'interventions' in the name of order, democracy, justice and peace in parts of the non-Anglophone world, such as Kosovo, Afghanistan and Iraq (Orford; Chomsky). In an analysis of intervention narratives of the post-Cold War era, Anne Orford identifies a teleological pattern ending with the victory of the 'good' invading forces over the 'evils' of disorder, violence and powerlessness of the invaded dysfunctional polities. The narratives begin with a frightening inventory of threats to the established world order:

> The world is entering a period of great instability, characterized by long-standing international rivalries and resentments, intense ethnic and religious turmoil, a vast flow of arms and military technology, domestic disintegration, poverty and deep economic inequalities, instantaneous communication throughout the world, population pressures, natural and ecological disasters, the scarcity of vital resources, and huge movements of population (Urquhart 11)

The narratives are populated by a composite of 'knights in white armour', heroic characters who embody the international values of democracy, peace, security, order and freedom. These are usually the UN Security Council, the NATO forces, the large contingent of humanitarian foot soldiers and, of course, the US. They progress from crisis to resolution through the 'punishment, sacrifice and salvation of the target state' (Orford 699), the liberation of abject victims and the reestablishment of the international order. Security or intervention texts regularly produce images of the people in states targeted for intervention/occupation as starving, powerless, suffering, abused or helpless victims, often women and children in need of rescue or salvation.

The novels of this period, on the other hand, are trenchant critiques of the 'redemption' projects of the international community. As the serial post-Cold War security crises reveal repeatedly, such redemption is always carried out over the bodies of others. Further, the massive civilian casualties caused by aerial bombings and targeted infrastructural warfare of the 'knights' are dismissed in such texts as collateral damage, inevitable, if unfortunate, side effects of the noble project of restoring order. Incessant media projections of such strategic justification of unlawful wars and military occupations enable the latter to enter into the domain of everyday commonsense. The world is in constant danger of seeing the dictum of 'just war' naturalized as ordinary wisdom. The power of the literary works mentioned above lies precisely in their ability to tear through this dangerous fabric of received political truth. The humanitarian imagination of the post-1989 literary texts is also, of course, inescapably mediatized as we saw with Ian McEwan's *Saturday* at the start of this essay. But far from being image brokers of the dominant neoliberal narrative of powerful international do-gooders and right-less victims, these novels function as sites of capture of an emerging humanitarian sensibility honed through witnessing the shock and horror of instantaneous spectacles of war, violence and suffering in electronic media, spectacles that leave deep traces on the sensibility of its viewers well beyond their immediate impact. These novels constitute deep time repositories of such traumatic traces; narratives that preserve for history a radical transformation of sensibilities, an expansion of the moral imagination, due to instant and incessant electronic exposure to distant suffering. The relationship I invoke here between the novel, distant suffering, technologies of mediation and the emergence of a humanitarian sensibility has an interesting intellectual genealogy to which I now turn.

The Novel and the In/Human: A Genealogy

In literary history one finds close links between the emergence of the novel and a certain narrative grammar of the human. Two aspects of this narrative grammar are integral to the rise of the novel form, and are particularly significant to my study of post-1989 literary globalism: one emerges from the theory of sensibility and moral sentiments that has an intellectual history going back to the eighteenth century with the works of the Scottish Enlightenment philosophers, Adam Smith and David Hume. The second is the 'Rights of Man' discourse that eventually informed the idea of Human Rights in the post-War period. I use the terms, 'Sympathy' and 'Sovereignty' respectively as shorthand to mark the two. Book-ended by these two categories, this narrative grammar of the human accounted for the rise of the novel as a genre manifesting a capacity to respond sympathetically to distant suffering due to the technologies and conventions of moral responsibility generated by the rise of capitalism. The historian Thomas Haskell, in his essay, 'Capitalism and the Origins of Humanitarian Sensibility' (1985), argued that the ability of the human to feel the suffering of others remote and distant – the humanitarian sensibility as we now call it – did not just exist in a timeless, transcendental domain of moral choice, but could be historically accounted for by the emergence of certain forms of life, certain changes in cognitive and social styles wrought by the demands of the market during the era of capitalism. These by no means determined the emergence of the humanitarian sensibility, but they constituted its enabling preconditions. One of these was the relation of technology to distance, so that the more technology covered distance the less remote the rest of the world seemed. Accordingly the threshold of responsibility towards others shifted too. Two others included 'promise keeping as a form of life' – for markets could not function without the contractual imperative – and responsibility for the remote consequences of one's actions, for as Haskell notes, in the market one is a node in a 'long chain of wills' (Haskell 551–52). These together created certain conventions of moral responsibility that coalesced to give momentum to the anti-slavery movement during the latter half of the eighteenth century. As literary scholars and historians have noted, it is not a coincidence that the rise of the sentimental novel in the eighteenth century occurred in tandem with the emergence of the idea of humanitarian sensibility that culminated in the rise of Abolitionism in America and England (Cohen, 1999; Chandler; Hunt).[1] The narrative code of the eighteenth century sentimental novel, like that of humanitarian sensibility, begins with one primal scene: 'a spectacle of suffering that solicits the spectator's sympathy' (Cohen, 2002, 108).

Likewise the narrative code of the *Bildungsroman* tracks the emergence of the sovereign self from pre-given relations based on status, custom or tradition, and the right to make its own destiny, albeit within a framework of incorporation into an emerging capitalist world order. This 'self' as a free and fully developed person is but an abstraction of 'common modalities of the human being's extension into the civil and social order' (Slaughter 17), and is intrinsically linked to what Lynn Festa has referred to as 'the affective work of the sentimental novel in the eighteenth century (Festa 73). For only such a self could recognize that a distant subject of suffering was also a subject with full rights despite vast cultural and political differences.

The questions I pose in the context of the discussion above are: How are the foundational categories of 'sympathy' and 'sovereignty', which marked the human in the era of industrial capitalism, reconfigured in the world literary archive of the post-1989 era where the locus of narration has moved from Europe to encompass the globe as such?

How does one theorize the power with which they continue to resonate with representations of the 'human' and the human condition in literary texts that are more than two hundred and fifty years removed from the emergence of the first successfully recognized sentimental novel, Samuel Richardson's *Pamela* (1740)? I'll take up this last question first and address the other in the concluding section of this essay.

Sympathy, or more specifically the notion of 'humanitarian sensibility' as theorized by Thomas Haskell in the context of eighteenth century capitalism, is transformed in our era by the emergence of a late modern moral imagination mediated by further advances in technology. When 'distant suffering' is visually and instantly vivified, it radically shifts the ground on which conventions of moral responsibility are erected. Instant televisual and internet images of extreme duress amplify the possibilities of moral relations between strangers in ways that early capitalism could not. This is not to suggest that an electronic internationalism and the possibility of a new humanitarian sensibility I am invoking here necessarily leads to more ameliorative action on a global scale. But they certainly create a precondition for greater global engagement with extreme human suffering – a new infrastructure of sympathy – that the world novels under study manifest in graphic ways.

It is not incidental, I argue, that though Britain and France produced some of the richest crop of sentimental novels in the eighteenth century, no author could write beyond the moral compass of their regional or national spaces. But now we have an Australian-Canadian author Janet Turner Hospital produce an international epistolary fiction, *Dear Amnesty* (2001) that breaks down conventional social, racial and geographical barriers to sympathy and solidarity by connecting globally dispersed letter writers in an imaginary collective of electronic epistles responding to escalating human rights violations around the world. Here we can see the makings of a world literary imagination that is immanently global in that the writing is generated and informed by political, cultural and linguistic forces not limited to any single nation or region. Another illustration of such global fiction is John Murray's collection of short stories, *A Few Short Notes on Tropical Butterflies* (2003). Murray is an Australian citizen who has worked as a medical researcher for many years in the US and then as a doctor in countries like India and Rwanda among others. Within the covers of this single collection we find cross-hatched stories of stranger care and hospitality in situations of suffering in late modern societies in India, Central Africa, the UK, the US and Australia. Authors like Turner-Hospital and Murray bring the globe inside the text. Such works herald a new literary globalism at the confluence of immanent violence, heightened mobility/connectivity through technological advancement, and the consequently shifting frontiers of our humanitarian imagination. In the concluding section of my essay I examine two other works from the period under study – Ian McEwan's *Saturday* and Gil Courtemanche's *A Sunday at the Pool in Kigali* – that foreground the limits and challenges to the sympathy-sovereignty dyad of the novelistic human grammar outlined above.

The Human in World Fiction

In recent expositions on the limits of thinking the human, cultural theorists, Achille Mbembe and Pheng Cheah, contend that in late modernity it is harder and harder to theorize the 'human' in transcendental terms as the realm of reason, imagination, dignity and freedom, as a project that needs to be actualized, in a temporality that is essentially futural (Mbembe; Cheah). It is as futile, they argue, to see the 'inhuman' as humanity's alienation from itself, whether through commodification or technology or totalitarianism, and something that can be overcome through collective socio-political regulation. It is futile, in other words, to argue that the inhuman is the finite limit of the human, 'a defective feature of human existence that is not proper to the true end of man, but something that we have thus far failed to control'(Cheah 2). Rather for our epoch, they forcefully argue for the immanence of the 'human' in the 'inhuman', for a late modern production of the human in an inhuman force field of both global capitalism and its war machines.

Figures of sovereignty in these violent times, Achille Mbembe argues, often have as their central project not the struggle for autonomy, freedom, dignity, but the 'generalized instrumentalization of human existence and the material destruction of human bodies and populations' (Mbembe 14). More often than not, as is evident from the post-Cold War geographies of violence – Palestine, Kosovo, Rwanda, Iraq, Afghanistan – sovereignty is expressed predominantly as a 'right to kill', a right over life and death. This modality of politics as the work of death – necropolitics as Mbembe calls it – transforms fraught geopolitical spaces into states of exception with their own elaborate architectures of enmity. Pheng Cheah's distrust of cosmopolitan and human rights talk which are, as he says, two of the primary ways of figuring the global as 'human' in terms of freedom, dignity and transcendence, arises from a post-Marxist conceptual standpoint. He contends that both the discourses of cosmopolitanism and human rights tend not to pay attention to the 'inhuman' infrastructural and material foundations of the condition of being 'human' in this era of global capitalism:

There is, he suggests, a proscription of the inhuman instrumentalities or 'techne' of global capitalism in a human rights' approach that envisions amelioration purely in terms of an effort of human will, goodwill even, and the power of reasoning. The infrastructural coordinates of the making of this global 'human' subject are often not part of human rights discourses. For, more often than not, war and other brutalities constitute this infrastructure, and the intention very often is to ambush the enemy's life-support system, as we have seen so graphically in Kosovo and the most recent bombardment of Gaza in December 2008. In many parts of Africa, labour and minerals, two key resources, are often supplied by militarized non-state suppliers who are also purveyors of the brutal violence. Mbembe refers to this militarized network as War Machines. He notes: 'A war machine combines a plurality of functions. It has the features of a political organization and a mercantile company…. In order to fuel the extraction and the export of natural resources located in the territory they control war machines forge direct connections with transnational networks' (Mbembe 32–33). This rhizomic monstrosity of extreme capitalism wreaks havoc on global demographics by creating a multitude of war victims: child soldiers, fleeing refugees, raped women, mutilated yet living bodies. On display here is not the disciplinary power of the colonial and postcolonial regimes but biopolitical and necropolitical power of the post-Cold War era.

A character in Gil Courtemanche's novel on the Rwanda genocide, *A Sunday at the Pool in Kigali* asks the journalist narrator and, in effect, the rest of the watching world, 'While we die with you watching us all the time, you live, you thrive…. Don't you get a feeling, sometimes, that you're living off our death?' (32). How does sympathy in our technologically hyperconnected world manifest itself when confronted with the spectacle of deathworlds of such devastating magnitude? Our humanitarian imagination, I suggest, is tested to the extreme, and we are forced to confront the moment of *actualization* of a moral universal built on the idea of 'crime against humanity' where the interlocutor of the victim is a complete stranger and they both share a dread of the increasing globalization of large scale human suffering, no longer restricted, especially since 9/11, to the backwaters of the world. The 9/11 fireballs and falling bodies in the foreground of the collapsing Twin Towers, no doubt, fulfilled the attackers' desire to create a global *spectacle* of terror. But the monumental *stealth* of the attack by unconventional enemy combatants from the shadows of ominous caves thousands of miles away has given rise to an everyday fear of 'the evil of a malice knowing neither measure nor ground', as Derrida put it with such prescience years before the catastrophe (Derrida 83). This has temporalized fear less as a reaction to a past occurrence than to a future possibility, which in its turn has generated a newer form of state intervention that is proleptically violent. Pre-emptive war, detention without charge, torture, ticking-bomb scenarios, these are all manifestations of sovereign acts that 'militarize futurity and temporality' (Feldman 1709). To recognize the *global immanence* of human insecurity and dread amidst imminent terror is to acknowledge an important aspect of what Michael Hardt and Antonio Negri call 'life in common', the coming together of 'singularities' that are not 'incommunicable localities' in this era of global conflict (xi, 128). Both Courtemanche's *A Sunday at the Pool in Kigali* and McEwan's *Saturday* manifest the power and challenge of this 'life in common', the possibilities and limits of sympathy demanded by this idea of 'commons' in our era of global violence. They, however, differ in their respective configurations of the 'human'. While Courtemanche's novel brings to the fore the *immanence* of the inhuman in the human, McEwan's *Saturday* plays out the liberal fantasy of the transcendence of the inhuman through the exercise of a moral imagination grounded in reason, ethical care and respect for the other.

Genocide, Arthur Klinghoffer notes in his work on Rwanda, is the 'ultimate expression of absolute rightlessness' (132). Genocidal acts in particular create victims who are bereft of kinship and social networks. They, thus, make 'an ethic of universal moral obligation among strangers a necessity for future life on the planet' (Ignatieff 20). The ethic of hospitality from strangers due to a breakdown of more immediate filial and social networks is captured with a devastatingly visceral edge in Gil Courtemanche's docu-fictional novel, *A Sunday at the Pool in Kigali*. In the Rwanda of 1994 he writes of, no local inhabitant can take it for granted that he or she will not be hacked to death any moment by a relative or a friend or a neighbour. In Courtemanche's complex portrayal of Rwandan multi-ethnicity, the rhetoric of symbolically and semantically asserted Otherness – he's dark, squat and thick-lipped and so he's a Hutu, she's tall, slim and light-skinned, so she's a Tutsi – is by no means clearly demarcated either by spatial arrangements or by physiognomy. Only some stereotypes circulate with a myopic stubbornness that is lethal. Thus, Tutsis are cockroaches from which Rwanda needs to be cleansed. The only redeeming relationships seem to be between a few foreign aid workers/ journalists and their circle of friends from among the native population of

Kigali. The horrors of the genocide as also a shared sense of precariousness of life at the end of the millennium are narrated through conversations among them – virtual strangers bonded in both extreme fear and fragile hope. The novel is self-consciously marked as docu-fiction by the author, a Canadian journalist, who witnessed and reported on the genocide. Courtemanche was in Rwanda at the time to make a documentary on the HIV epidemic in Kigali which had affected almost one-third of the city's population. Tied to this harbinger of death were the rumblings of an ominous ethnic feud that waiting to manifest its fury. Courtemanche's razor-sharp yet deeply empathetic pen creatively transfigures this near-apocalyptic tableau of horror into a searing poetic document.

'We have come to the end of time, eaten away by two cancers, hatred and AIDS. We are a little like Earth's last children', says Raphael, one of Valcourt's Rwandan friends (10). The highlight of the novel is the juxtaposition of unsparing details of the genocide – too confronting, even pornographic at times, in its twin depiction of brutal rapes and the shameful might of machetes as they cut through flesh and bone – with a narrative of love, care and bonding between Valcourt and his hapless Rwandan friends. Kigali's mystique and menace are entwined in stunning metaphors: the stomach-churning sounds of the genocide outside the hotel precinct are described as 'a mortuary symphony against a picture postcard background' (144). Valcourt is entranced by the Kigali landscape, 'the hills sculpted by thousands of gardens, the mists caressing the valley floors' (18). But the deathwork of machetes at nightfall brings fear to the soul: 'The market's cheerful, noisy anarchy had ceased, the way the birds in a forest fall silent when a predator creeps near' (79). The morning after, 'life awakens as if a whole city was emerging from a coma, astonished to be alive even as it counts its dead' (41).

The tableau that endures for us in *A Sunday at the Pool in Kigali*, nevertheless, is that of the poignancy of uncanny, unpredictable affiliations between strangers in the midst of horrific human suffering induced by an absurd, colonially-engineered filiative ethnos and ethos.[2] The novel's poetic rendering of extreme human truths amidst a landscape of terror and beauty enhances rather than retracts from the moral power of such shared suffering. The narrator, Valcourt's prospective father-in-law, Jean Damascene, captures both the absurdity and poignancy of this tableau in his embrace of Valcourt, the French-Canadian in love with his Hutu-Tutsi daughter, Gentille, as his true son:

> My son, today we have closed the circle of history and absurdity. The head of the *interhamwes*, who have sworn to cut the throats of all Tutsis and send them all the way to Egypt by the Kagera river, is a Tutsi. He's an uncle of Gentille's. The Head of the Tutsi rebel army is a Hutu and he's also an uncle of Gentille's.... Both want to kill Gentille who doesn't belong to either side. Gentille is like the fruit of the red earth of this hill, a mysterious mix of all the seeds and all the toil of this country. Son you're going to marry a country they want to kill, one that could be simply Rwandan if it had the chance. (192–3)

In the apotheosis of Gentille as an aspired Rwanda, all-embracing in her numerous ethnic mixings and strange foreign affiliations, one finds an ethic of interconnectivity that transcends the current post-genocidal political rhetoric of Rwandan nationalism invested in an unlearning of ethnicity and an impossible embrace of the abstract 'human'. Humanism, the novel suggests, is not a commitment to abstract entities denuded of traces of belonging. Nor is it the triumphant assertion of the reasonable, right-bearing 'human' over forces of barbaric unreason. It is rather an acknowledgement of the enmeshment of human in his/her particular affiliations and a recognition of both the possibilities and dangers of such affiliations. It is this recognition of mutual vulnerability that is also the possibility of an ethic of caring and hospitality. Judith Butler gives it a name. She calls it our 'new humanism' of 'common corporeal vulnerability' (Butler 42). Contiguous with this notion of 'corporeality' is Michael Hardt and Antonio Negri's theorization of the 'common' as the 'flesh of the multitude' that links and expands social being, producing and performing it in 'excess of every traditional political-economic measure of value' (Hardt and Negri 192). This new social corporeality conceived in terms of a 'flesh-like' continuum rather than as racially and sexually marked difference is resistant to a logic of identity and segregation. It is the complete antithesis of the abstracted 'mass man' of totalitarianism so powerfully theorized by Hannah Arendt. It is, thus, a powerful and enabling conception for an ethics of nonviolent and transcultural relationality in an age of terror.

Ian McEwan's *Saturday*, while acknowledging the tremulous force of our intrinsic vulnerability in an era of globalized violence, affirms, at one level, a faith in the transcendence of the inhuman by the human, in the liberal power of a 'cognitive aesthetics' to manage our humanity. The term 'cognitive aesthetics' is Elaine Hadley's, a Victorian studies scholar who defines it as the power to generate images of beauty through a reflective self-consciousness 'in the face of a disorienting and alien external world that fundamentally challenged individual autonomy' (Hadley 94). *Saturday* depicts a traumatic experience, but its creative transmutation could not be more different from the confronting immanence of the 'inhuman' in the human, the necropolitical, life-in-the-face-of-death narrative of Courtemanche's fiction. Violence here, as we shall see, is anaesthetized by the knife of the neurosurgeon. The novel is set in London and depicts a series of events in the life of a single day of a neurosurgeon, Henry Perowne, on the eve of the Iraq War. This 2003 geopolitical crisis, along with 9/11 and the invasion of Afghanistan, has globalized the experience a very particular kind of post-Cold War terror and violence that is mediatized incessantly around the world. Due to such mediatization, terror now appears, as Derrida put it in an interview in *Philosophy in a Time of Terror*, 'less a past event than a future possibility' (Borradori xiii). This anticipatory temporality of terror is graphically evoked in *Saturday* which begins with Henry waking up before dawn and seeing a plane on fire descend in an ominous way in a part of London not known for aircraft landing. His first instinct is to read it as another 9/11 nightmare. But not hearing any declarations of an emergency, he reflects:

> It's already almost eighteen months since half the planet watched, and watched again the unseen captives driven through the sky to the slaughter, at which time there gathered round the innocent silhouette of any jet plane a novel association. Everyone agrees, airliners look different in the sky these days, predatory or doomed. (16)

The sense of an imminent catastrophe looms over the narrative as does the political ambivalence of a privileged, self-reflecting, liberal mindset that oscillates between giving in to this sense of dread and yet resisting it:

> How foolishly apocalyptic these apprehensions seem by daylight, when the self evident fact of the streets and the people on them are their own justification, their own insurance. The world has not fundamentally changed…. There are always crises, and Islamic terrorism will settle into place, alongside recent wars, climate change, the politics of international trade, land and fresh water shortages, hunger, poverty and the rest. (76)

When terror does ambush Henry Perowne's comfort zone, it comes not in an apocalyptic form, but in the figure of a deranged and angry resident of London, Baxter. A polymorphous depiction of the city's underclass, Baxter invades Perowne's home with a knife purportedly to take revenge for a car collision that morning, and allegorically of course, to tear into the privileged fabric of Henry's world. He threatens to rape Henry's daughter, Daisy, herself a poet and a vociferous opponent of the Iraq invasion, and kill the rest of the family. But how is he disarmed and made 'human'? Not apparently by the inhuman instrumentalities of a neoliberal world, but incredibly by the humanizing power of poetry. After stripping out of her clothes on Baxter's demand, Daisy begins reciting Matthew Arnold's 'Dover Beach' and Baxter is awestruck by its beauty even as he is Daisy's dupe, for he thinks she has written it. In a bizarre reprisal of a fantasy of agency of the Victorian liberal self and a belief in the capacity of art to humanize the Baxters of our day, the novel ends with Henry and his daughter deciding to attend with precision and care to Baxter's deranged corporeality. Daisy has now regained her composure and is full of sympathy for Baxter. Henry is no longer the vulnerable witness of unfolding terror, but the objective and brilliant neurosurgeon who diagnoses Baxter's condition as 'Huntington's disease' and offers to treat him. The final moments of the narrative are replete with images of Henry's domestic stasis, his grateful retreat into professional and marital fulfillment.

Elaine Hadley, as we saw earlier, marks this narrative conjuncture as the recuperation of a characteristically liberal aesthetic of the self: a combination of thought and thoughtfulness, 'a cognitive formalism that makes beautiful thought about humanity taken as a social whole' (Hadley, 95). In the light of our discussion about the narrative grammar of the human in the novel, *Saturday*, I would say, also appears to return to a configuration of sovereignty that is disciplinary in the liberal sense of restoring the rational order of things, recognizing individual autonomy and dignity per se; recognizing also the power of human will and consciousness to transfigure a threatening reality into a more humane one. At this level, the novel's shaping of human grammar could not be more different from Pheng Cheah's and Mbembe's reading of the inhuman and sovereignty as the right over life and death.

Yet, does not Henry Perowne's intervention with his surgical knife to take care of Baxter's brain disease parallel the surgical strike metaphor of the two Gulf Wars? The imminence of the Iraq War, after all, looms large in the backdrop of the novel. We are also only too familiar with the Pentagon's boast of its precision bombing techniques that, it claimed, would achieve the 'world' objective of freeing Iraq of tyranny with minimum battle scars. Can one, then, read this novel as a pro-Iraq War manifesto? Not, as we shall see, if one takes into consideration the subtlety with which McEwan distributes responses to the Iraq War in the novel. But *Saturday* can certainly be read as coding sovereignty as a site of tension between the fantasy of liberal agency that seeks to restore order and beauty of humanity, and the actualization of the same agency into a political force that makes decisions about the life and death of multitudes in 'disorderly' parts of the world. Henry's vacillations about the war capture this tension brilliantly. During his Saturday sojourn through London, Henry encounters protest marches against the war, and yet his bourgeois liberal mindset at first appears to support it. Better to rid the world of its tyrants, as he tells his irate daughter, Daisy, when she charges him with political naiveté and even conservatism. 'Here's a chance to turn one country around. Plant a seed. See if it flourishes and spreads,' he adds (192). His daughter retorts, 'You don't plant seeds with cruise missiles' (192). Daisy represents a more post-liberal mindset, one that has lost faith in the capacity of the state to restore order and that sees through the neoliberal rhetoric of 'just war'. 'You know very well', she rages at her father's obtuseness, 'these extremists, the Neo-cons, have taken over America. Cheney, Rumsfeld,

Wolfovitz (sic). Iraq was always their pet project. Nine eleven was their big
chance to talk Bush round … there's nothing linking Iraq to nine eleven, or
to Al-Qaeda generally, and no really scary evidence of WMD …. And doesn't
it ever occur to you that in attacking Iraq we're doing the very thing that the
New York bombers wanted us to do – lash out, make more enemies in Arab
countries and radicalize Islam' (190–91). After he counters her comeback
with an even more hawkish wager about a transformed democratic Iraq
in three months, he reflects bleakly on the truth of his vacillation about
this issue, on the luxury he has of taking different points of view about the
War with different interlocutors, 'a dove with Jay Strauss and a hawk with
his daughter', as he wryly muses (193). None of his conviction about the
rightness of the War persists as the novel progresses. The vacuous and timid
nature of his abstract desire to see the world freed of tyrants is exposed towards
the end of the novel when he acknowledges that his agency means nothing
in the larger scheme of things; that his liberal fantasy of sovereign agency can
only retreat further and further into gated communities in the face of the
necropolitical power unleashed by inhuman geopolitical instrumentalities:

> Perhaps a bomb in the cause of jihad will drive them out with all the
> other faint- hearts into the suburbs, or deeper into the country, or to the
> chateau – their Saturday will become a Sunday. (276)

There is, it appears, no real transcendence of the 'human' from inhuman
post-Cold War circuits of violence; only a timid retreat into an hypermediated
world-making sensibility that can but endlessly reflect on its incapacity to
bring some semblance of order to the world:

> Will he revive his hopes for firm action in the morning? All he feels now is
> fear. He's weak and ignorant, scared of the way consequences of an action
> leap away from your control and breed new events, new consequences,
> until you're led to a place you never dreamed of and would never choose –
> a knife at the throat. (277)

Works Cited

Baudrillard, Jean. *The Gulf War Did not Take Place*. Trans. Paul Patton. Bloomington: Indiana University Press, 1995

Borradori, Giovanna (ed.). *Philosophy in a Time of Terror: Dialogues with Jurgen Habermas and J. Derrida*. Chicago: University of Chicago Press, 2003

Butler, Judith. *Precarious Life: The Powers of Mourning and Violence*. London: Verso, 2004

Chandler, James. 'On the Face of the Case: Conrad, *Lord Jim* and the Sentimental Novel', *Critical Inquiry*, Special Issue, 'On the Case,' ed. Lauren Berlant. 33.4 (2007): 837–64

Cheah, Pheng. *Inhuman Conditions: On Cosmopolitanism and Human Rights*. Massachusetts: Harvard University Press, 2006

Chomsky, Noam. *The New Military Humanism: Lessons from Kosovo*. London: Pluto, 1999

Cohen, Margaret. 'Sentimental Communities', in *The Literary Channel: The Inter-National Invention of the Novel*. Eds. Margaret Cohen and Carolyn Dever. Princeton University Press, 2002

———. *The Sentimental Education of the Novel*, Princeton: Princeton University Press, 1999

Courtemanche, Gil. *A Sunday at the Pool in Kigali*. Melbourne: Text Publishing, 2003

Derrida, Jacques. *The Politics of Friendship*. Trans. George Collins. New York: Verso, 1997

Feldman, Allen. 'The Structuring Enemy and Archival War', *PMLA*, Special Topic, 'War.' Eds. Srinivas Aravamudan and Diana Taylor. 124.5 (October 2009): 1704–28

Festa, Lynn. 'Sentimental Bonds and Revolutionary Characters: Richardson's *Pamela* in England and France.' In *The Literary Channel: The Inter-National Invention of the Novel*. Edited by Margaret Cohen and Carolyn Dever. Princeton University Press, 2002. Pp 73–105

Hadley, Elaine. 'On a Darkling Plain: Victorian Liberalism and the Fantasy of Agency', *Victorian Studies*, 48.1 (2005): 92–102

Hardt, Michael and Antonio Negri. *Multitude: War and Democracy in the Age of Empire*. New York: Penguin Press, 2004

Haskell, Thomas. 'Capitalism and the Origins of the Humanitarian Sensibility', Part 1, *The American Historical Review* 90.2 (April 1985): 339-361; Part 2, *AHR* 90.3 (June 1985): 547–66

Hunt, Lynn. *Inventing Human Rights: A History*. New York: W.W Norton, 2007

Ignatieff, Michael. *The Warrior's Honor: Ethnic War and the Modern Conscience*. New York: Henry Holt and Company, 1997

Kaldor, Mary. *New Wars and Old Wars: Organized Violence in a Global Era*.Cambridge: Polity Press, 2006

Klinghoffer, Arthur. *The International Dimension of Genocide in Rwanda*. NYU Press, 1998

Mbembe, Achille. 'Necropolitics,' *Public Culture* 15.1 (2003): 11–40

McDougall, David. *The Corporeal Image: Film, Ethnography and the Senses*. New Jersey: Princeton University Press, 2005

McEwan, Ian, *Saturday*. London: Vintage, 2006

Orford, Anne, 'Muscular Humanitarianism: Reading the Narratives of the New Intervention.' *EJIL* 10.4 (1999): 679-711

Scherrer, Christian. *Genocide and Crisis in Central Africa*. London: Praeger, 2002

Singer, P.W.. *The Robotic Revolution and Conflict in the Twenty-first Century*. New York: Penguin, 2008

Slaughter, Joseph. *Human Rights Inc: The World Novel, Narrative Form and International Law*. NY: Fordham University Press, 2007

Taylor, Christopher. 'The Hamitic Hypothesis in Rwanda and Burundi.' In *Sacrifice as Terror: The Rwandan Genocide of 1994*. Oxford: Berg, 1999

Urquhart, Brian. 'Learning from the Gulf.' In *Whose New World Order? What Role for the United Nations.* Edited by M.R. Bustelo and P. Alston. Sydney: Federation Press, 1991

Virilio, Paul, and Sylvere Lotringer. *Pure War.* Trans. Mark Polizzotti. NY: Semiotext(e), 2008

Notes

1   See especially, Cohen, 1999, and Hunt. James Chandler, while not mentioning any explicit links with the abolitionist movement, notes that the term 'sentimental' in relation to the novel did not appear till the 1750s, and clearly demarcated a new narrative mode. He, however, establishes a connection between the emergence of the sentimental novel and the publication of Adam Smith's *The Theory of Moral Sentiments* in 1759: 'Thought Smith neither employs the term *sentimental* nor concerns himself at length with the novel, his arguments about the processes of character formation by way of sympathetic exchange of positions in modern commercial society do seem to resonate later in the first examples of the self-consciously identified sentimental novel. The connection seems especially strong in relation to the then-fashionable epistolary method of fiction, an exercise in the alternation of views, that, one might say, is very much at the centre of what Smith is describing' (Chandler 840, italics original).

2   For political and ethno-social details of how Belgian colonialists in Rwanda conceptually engineered a racial divide between Hutus and Tutsis, see Taylor; Klinghoffer; and Scherrer.

Chapter 8

Neurology is Destiny: Character and Consciousness in Ian McEwan's *Saturday*

Nicole Heber
University of Melbourne

On the opening page of Ian McEwan's *Saturday*, Henry Perowne, a neurosurgeon, wakes in the early hours of the morning to find himself in a strange, inexplicable state of euphoria. Moving to the window, Perowne is reflecting upon that 'brilliant invention,' (5) the city of London below, when his reverie is interrupted by the vision of a plane on fire, appearing to head for Heathrow airport. Anxious, but aware of his own incapacity to influence the outcome, Perowne considers the symbolic significance of the image: is it a sinister harbinger of catastrophe, 'an attack on our whole way of life,' (35) or a sign of nothing more than 'simple, secular mechanical failure' (18)? Here, in essence, is the dynamic that animates the novel: between the realm of the figurative, symbolic and subjective; and that of brute yet efficacious materiality. Thus, even as it eventually becomes clear that mere mechanical failure has been the cause of the accident, the figure of the burning plane continues to accrue symbolic charge. It quite literally inaugurates Perowne's own affective descent from euphoria to anxiety; parallels the catastrophic crash from healthy, untroubled consciousness into pathology and disease exemplified by the novel's numerous sufferers of neurological dysfunction; and prefigures the violent invasion of Perowne's home by one such figure, the Huntington's sufferer Baxter.

Upon closer inspection, however, the themes of terrorism and politics, and consciousness both healthy and diseased, sit somewhat uneasily with each other. What can be the political significance of a work of literature that attends so closely and so admiringly to a single, individual consciousness – a consciousness, moreover, that openly refutes the efficacy not only of literature, but of the entire symbolic realm? My own answer to this question has been formulated through an analysis of the novel's rather eclectic formal qualities, including the use of the omniscient perspective, and the employment of particular descriptive conventions in the construction of character. My argument is that it is through the adaptation and modulation of such formal qualities that McEwan attempts to bridge the novel's political themes and its unwavering focus upon the private, individual consciousness of the neurosurgeon Perowne.

Saturday is set on 15 February 2003, the day when hundreds of thousands of Londoners marched in protest against the war in Iraq. However, Perowne's encounter with this historical event is perfunctory – on his way to a squash game, the protest march causes him to become stuck in traffic. And yet, such quotidian activities – in addition to his squash game, *Saturday* describes Perowne shopping for dinner with his family that evening, visiting his mother, who has Alzheimer's, in a home, and watching his son's band rehearse – are belied by a genuinely sinister, potentially life-changing event. This aspect of the narrative centres upon Perowne's confrontation with a petty criminal named Baxter, an episode that begins when Perowne's car collides with Baxter's in a deserted alleyway. Baxter and two accomplices threaten and attempt to extort money from Perowne, and when he resists, Baxter assaults him. However, Perowne has meanwhile observed that Baxter exhibits the early symptoms of Huntington's, an inherited neurodegenerative disease. Perowne is able to distract Baxter with his diagnosis, then with deceptive promises of improved treatments, and even a cure. When Baxter's mood shifts again and he attempts to call back his accomplices, Perowne makes his escape. Perowne does not know that Baxter, realising he has been fooled and humiliated, has followed him home.

Later that evening, as the Perowne family gathers to celebrate the publication of Perowne's daughter Daisy's first book of poetry, Baxter and an accomplice enter the house armed with knives, and force Daisy to undress. Noticing the book of poetry, Baxter demands that she read a poem aloud. Perhaps because her poems are mildly erotic, Daisy is prompted by her grandfather, the renowned poet John Grammaticus, to recite Matthew Arnold's *Dover Beach* instead. The reading effects a profound change in Baxter, both pacifying and awing him, and the accomplice leaves in disgust. The episode concludes with Perowne and his son Theo throwing Baxter downstairs, whereupon he sustains a head injury and is rushed to hospital. Later in the evening, Perowne is called in to the hospital to operate on Baxter, an event which occasions Perowne's extended meditation on genetic determinism and personal responsibility.

Thus, a day that began in a state of inexplicable euphoria ends in a state of considerable unease. For some critics, this conclusion represents the penetration and disruption of Perowne's insular, self-satisfied worldview. James Wood, for example, writes that 'the private uncertainty and the public uncertainty – the unintended consequences of any Iraq invasion merge at the book's close' (34), and Peter Childs states that 'If there is a significant development in the novel, it is from Perowne's untroubled peace and tranquility as he wakes on Saturday morning to his feelings twenty-four hours later' (145). According to Lee Siegel, any 'possible implicit resonances' between Baxter and the 'disenfranchised, militant, impoverished Third World' ought to be apprehended as 'impressions, associations, intuitions that grow entwined with other plausible meanings as the story begins to strike the primal chords of myth,' and that 'never acquire the independent meaning of a neat allegorical subtext' (34). Richard Rorty positions the narrative involving Baxter secondary to the novel's more enduring sense of uneasy political ambivalence; the overriding feeling, he claims, is that events could just as easily have had a more damaging outcome. Others, however, have had difficulty reconciling the novel's pervasive air of ambiguity and doubt with the events involving Baxter. For Elaine Hadley, the narrative involving Perowne and Baxter displaces, and then artificially resolves, Perowne's political ambivalence. Hadley sees Perowne's diagnosis of Baxter's Huntington's as a way of abstracting from and controlling Baxter's 'embodied aggression,' (92) thereby absorbing Baxter's alterity into a private, one-to-one relation. Thus, although Hadley lauds the operation that Perowne performs on Baxter at the novel's conclusion as a 'mournful human accomplishment,' (93) she also sees Perowne's professional achievement as a profoundly shrunken domain of efficacy, as yet another example of a regrettably elevated achievement of an individual consciousness. Echoing Baxter's awed response to Dover Beach – 'You *wrote* that' – Hadley imagines Baxter's response to Perowne's composure and expertise during the operation as an equally awed 'you *did* that' (97).

Saturday, writes Hadley, is a 'sort of elegy for the individual consciousness'. Focusing on the formal, controlled tone in which Perowne's consciousness is presented, Hadley identifies 'something doggedly Victorian about the form of this in-the-moment novel and its middle-aged protagonist' (94). The text's overwhelming emphasis on Perowne's consciousness, Hadley argues, gives rise to a compelling but illusory sense of agency:

> In this novel, consciousness is the privileged site of character definition and character formation: that which makes a human and that which makes a human good. More specifically, he [McEwan] defines his protagonist as a self-reflexive agent, capable of thinking about the world beyond – about an abstract totality – but also, signally, capable of and habitually prone to thinking about his thinking of that world. These habits of thoughtfulness generate what might be called a liberal cognitive aesthetic, for, in the face of a disorienting and alien external world that fundamentally challenges individual autonomy, the liberal subject constructs through purposeful thought a feat of humane beauty. (94)

For Hadley, a novel that is so preoccupied with the singular consciousness of its protagonist cannot, by definition, engage seriously with political concerns. However, Frances Ferguson contests Hadley's claim: 'it is precisely this account of Victorian values – the celebration of culture and love as deep understanding,' she writes, 'that I think McEwan's novel challenges' (47). Whereas Hadley's argument rests on the distinction between private, individual achievement and public engagement, Ferguson argues that the salient distinction made in *Saturday* is between the *professional* and private spheres. Ferguson points out that Perowne's relations with his immediate family, although tender and amicable, are subject to frequent misunderstandings. Ferguson attributes these failures of communication to the increasing saturation of the private sphere by the media, the function of which is increasingly to 'yield[s] attention without content', to manipulate the audience's emotions rather than to transmit information (49).[1] Furthermore, the range of media to which each member of the modern family may be exposed, she observes, leads to inevitable schisms and failures of communication between family members. In contrast, brief exchanges between those individuals with a common profession – for example, between Perowne and his anaesthesiologist Jay Strauss and the two poets Daisy and Grammaticus – are immediately and effortlessly understood by the interlocutors. Professionalism, then, offers a relatively clear channel of communication, capable of 'creat[ing] both precision and greater ties of understanding than does marital or familial affection' (50), and of 'converting an impersonal relationship into something with the feel of love' (51).

Ferguson's claim that *Saturday* depicts the increasing divergence of the professional and personal spheres of life is convincing. However, it seems to me important to acknowledge that a prominent thematic component of *Saturday* is the specific capacities enabled by the profession of neurosurgery; in this context, McEwan more frequently emphasises the discomfiting *proximity* of Perowne's professional and personal worlds. As Mark Currie recognises, the representation of the consciousness of a neurosurgeon in the omniscient mode functions to juxtapose the neurosurgeon's knowledge of mind and consciousness with the novelist's, 'so that the conception of the mind as matter is also the matter of the novel's exploration of interiority'. And yet, however richly 'ironic' (127) this juxtaposition, for Currie the value of this largely 'implicit' form of epistemological reflexivity is secondary to the novel's own lack of 'explicit self-knowledge' (132) – that is, knowledge of its own fictionality. Thus, 'he [Perowne] is watched or known from above, as it were, and this omniscient knowledge of him is by far the most important thing that he doesn't know' (127).

As Currie notes, the very concept of omniscience in literature entails particular assumptions concerning the existence of 'mind ... behind the surface of fictional character' (128). Indeed, as Audrey Jaffe observes, the omniscient perspective emerged from within a culture that was intensely preoccupied with categorizing and classifying its world. In particular, Jaffe invokes the widespread belief in physiognomy and phrenology, epistemological frameworks that appeared to enable one to read individual minds through the physical qualities of the body. This relationship between mind and body, she argues, has a clear analogue in the reading practices produced by the realist novel: 'the transparency physiognomy attributes to individuals is thus a claim about the epistemological power invested in the reader's position, a power that inevitably shapes relations between individuals' (17). Furthermore, Jaffe states, in the realist novel the conventions of character and omniscience typically function co-constitutively. The well delineated boundaries of nineteenth-century character, she argues, are contingent upon the author's assumption of a disembodied, unbounded perspective:

> The inspector's or omniscient narrator's difference from those
> he observes is an effect of his position in relation to them ... At
> once refusing the boundaries of character but defining itself by
> manufacturing those boundaries, omniscient narration reflects a
> concern with character's limitations and represents an attempt to
> transcend these limitations by becoming a non-character, a presence
> but not an objectifiable participant. (12)

Jaffe is speaking in the context of the nineteenth century, a period in which the conventions of character and omniscience emerged in relatively stark contrast to former literary modes. Her argument does not, of course, bear straightforward transposition to a contemporary literary text. Nevertheless, the text depicts Perowne's knowledge as a form of omniscience, for it confers the ability to observe phenomena in excess of the constraints necessitated by human embodiment. Because the narrative is focalised solely through Perowne, the definition of character in *Saturday* is not only dependent upon the omniscient narrator's representation of the neurosurgeon's consciousness, it is also secondarily a function of the extent to which Perowne's specialised knowledge allows him to 'read' or to 'characterise' other people within the discourse of the neurosciences. The power the omniscient observer possesses is most fully, and forcefully, explored through the depiction of Perowne's volatile antagonist Baxter. Through the lens of literary character, I consider the descriptive dynamics employed when Perowne confronts Baxter for the first time, and his public acts, professional responsibilities, and private responses collide.

Character in decline

In order to consider McEwan's characterisation of Baxter more closely, let us begin by contrasting two claims concerning the matter. Elaine Hadley's statement, recall, is that 'consciousness is the privileged site of character definition and character formation' (94) in *Saturday*. Baxter, she claims, 'is primarily portrayed as a diagnosis, as a victim of Huntington's disease,' (100 n.1) necessarily peripheral to the real centre of interest (or centre of consciousness - for Hadley, they are one and the same in *Saturday*). At first glance, Hadley's claim is in direct opposition to John Banville's. For Banville, the majority of *Saturday's* characters are saccharine stereotypes, involved in improbably untroubled relationships. In contrast, Baxter presents to Banville a vibrant, resistant specificity. In short, Baxter is 'the only rounded character among a cast of pasteboard cutouts' (12). To some extent, the conflict between these statements reflects the authors' differing expectations of character. However, I believe that Hadley's and Banville's statements are also indicative of a genuine anomaly in Baxter's characterisation. As Irving Howe points out, character in literary fiction has traditionally depended upon the 'supposed correspondence between inner and outer, body and soul' (52). To understand why Baxter is depicted as he is, it is necessary to understand that McEwan has conferred upon Perowne, as a neurosurgeon, a perspective which reconfigures the relationship of the person's physical, external signs to their private, interior consciousness.

For Perowne, the practice of neurosurgery constantly underlines the 'quotidian fact' that 'the mind is what the brain, mere matter, performs' (67). As he ages, then, Perowne's sense of self becomes increasingly entropic. Perowne feels himself on the verge of both bodily and cognitive decline – after all, if brain and body are one and the same thing, then physical decline *is* cognitive decline. Thus, Perowne is someone who 'wants his prodigiously connected myelin-rich white matter intact, like an unsullied snowfield' (165). That comment occurs just after Perowne's visit with his mother, who suffers from Alzheimer's, yet the ideal it evokes extends well beyond pathological instances. In general, Perowne possesses what might be termed an ideal of neural purity, wholeness or hygiene. In relation to his children, for example, Perowne seems above all in awe of their unblemished youthfulness. In his son Theo, he admires 'the blind perfection of hair, skin, teeth, the unbent, untroubled spine – he gleams in the half-light of the kitchen. He raises his glass – mineral water...' (237). I have included even the reference to mineral water, for Perowne is uncommonly concerned with Daisy's and Theo's consumption of alcohol, drugs, or anything else that might impair their brain function, monitoring their hair, skin, teeth, nails and breath for signs of the consumption of intoxicants. As he greets Daisy, his affection once again mingles with a nearly clinical inspection:

> it is the child's body he feels as he almost lifts her clear off the floor, the smoothness of muscle under the clothes, the springiness he can feel in her joints, the sexless kisses. Even her breath is like a child's. She doesn't smoke, she rarely drinks ...What abstemious children he's fathered. (182)

As a final example, consider Perowne's oddly distant concern for Daisy in the following passage. Having just returned home from Paris, she has suddenly collapsed in tears on her father's lap. When one might expect communicative exchange, what is dramatized instead is the lack of access Perowne has to his daughter's mind. Yet McEwan does not only signal the lack of access to Daisy's thoughts, feelings, or memories, he again emphasises the physical qualities that guarantee the essential closure or privacy of Daisy's conscious mind:

> He looks down at her fondly, at what little he can see of her face. Not even the first traces of ageing or experience around the corner of her visible eye, only clean taut skin, faintly purple, like the peripheries of a bruise.... It's likely her mind is turning fast, faster than his can, perhaps around a broken mosaic of recent events – raised voices in rooms, flashes of Parisian streets, an open suitcase on an unmade bed, whatever is distressing her. You stare at a head, a lushness of hair, and can only guess. (204-5)

In Perowne's worldview, the body's youthful integrity guarantees the integrity of the conscious mind. Rather than the particularities of his daughter's face, Perowne scans for signs of 'ageing or experience.' Daisy's eyes and face are not *expressive* of her inner life; they do not provide a clear passage to her underlying feelings. Rather, Daisy's 'lushness of hair' and her 'clean taut skin' block the passage between exterior and interior, body and mind. If Daisy and Theo appear to Banville as flat 'pasteboard cutouts' it may be because, in Perowne's view of them, their clean, clinical surfaces necessarily obscure their depths. Their presentation of pure, unblemished, illegible surfaces diminishes their specificity as characters, but preserves their interiority as a private, replete and indeterminate domain. Thus it is that, in this stylistically understated, modernistic and thematically contemporary novel, Baxter emerges *as* a character - delimited, detailed, and curiously redolent of the nineteenth-century novel. Hadley's and Banville's claims, then, are oddly congruent: Perowne's close, clinical attention to Baxter's pathological signs produces a more detailed, because more invasive and inhuman, description – but it also imparts greater descriptive texture, a sense of vividness and of multi-dimenionality. In Baxter, surface and depth converge.

It is possible, now, to understand why Baxter might be at the centre of such a knotty set of significations. Consider Perowne's perception of Baxter as they face each other in the alleyway:

> Baxter is one of those smokers whose pores exude a perfume, an oily essence of his habit. … He's a fidgety, small-faced young man with thick eyebrows and dark brown hair razored close to the skull. The mouth is set bulbously, with the smoothly shaved shadow of a strong beard adding to the effect of a muzzle. The general simian air is compounded by sloping shoulders, and the built-up trapezoids suggest time in the gym, compensating for his height perhaps. The sixties-style suit – tight cut, high lapels, flat-fronted trousers worn from the hip – is taking some strain around the jacket's single fastened button. There's also tightness in the fabric round the biceps. He half-turns and dips away from Perowne, then bobs back. He gives an impression of fretful impatience, of destructive energy waiting to be released. He may be about to lash out. (87-8)

In spite of the clinical feel of the description, the depiction of Baxter as malodorous, animalistic, and primal is almost a caricature of abjectness. Here, in fact, Baxter powerfully exemplifies the 'eccentric', a specific type of minor character that, according to Alex Woloch, commonly features in the realist novel. Woloch views the realist literary text as the embodiment of a continuous interplay between the expansion and actualisation of the central protagonist, and the consequent deformation and distortion of minor characters. Thus, the description of a minor character entails that 'the free relationship between surface and depth,' which defines the novel's chief protagonist, 'is negated; the actualization of a human being is denied.' According to Woloch, the eccentric is a figure who 'grates against his or her position and is usually, as a consequence, exiled, expelled, ejected, imprisoned, or killed' (25). Furthermore, he or she is usually represented by 'the explosion of the suffocated interior being into an unrepresentably, fragmentary, symptomatic form' (24). This description clearly reflects both Baxter's functional role and his characterisation; the difference is that Baxter's 'fragmentary, symptomatic form' is literally symptomatic. Baxter is characterised by his emotional lability: 'the signature', reflects Perowne, 'of so many neurodegenerative diseases – the swift transition from one mood to another, without awareness or memory, or understanding of how it seems to others' (96). Thus, as Baxter is wrong-footed by the diagnosis and his expression changes, he suddenly appears very differently to Perowne:

> Baxter moves his head from side to side. The muscles in his cheeks are independently alive. Perowne senses an approaching shift of mood.…
> In this transitional phase of perplexity or sorrow, the vaguely ape-like features are softened, even attractive. He's an intelligent man, and gives the impression that, illness apart, he's missed his chances, made some big mistakes and ended up in the wrong company. Probably dropped out of school long ago and regrets it. No parents around. And now, what worse situation could he find himself in? There's no way out for him. No one can help. But Perowne knows himself to be incapable of pity. Clinical experience wrung that from him long ago. And a part of him never ceases

to calculate how soon he can safely end this encounter. Besides, the matter is beyond pity. There are so many ways a brain can let you down. Like an expensive car, it's intricate, but mass-produced nevertheless, with more than six billion in circulation. (97-8)

However transient, Baxter's expression of interpretable emotion and his affective attunement to his situation gives rise to a profoundly altered reading of him. Whereas Baxter had appeared strange, threatening and abject, when his motion resolves itself into a particular, recognisable emotion, Baxter too appears somehow recognisable: situated within, and responsive to, a particular history and context. However, because Perowne '*knows* himself to be incapable of pity,' (my emphasis) he chooses to use the advantage he has gained to make his escape. The abrupt shift from free indirect discourse to direct discourse here indicates that Perowne's immediate feeling, his impulse to help Baxter in some way, belies what he *knows* about himself. This moment is decisive, because it is the point at which professional detachment takes over from Perowne's immediate affective response. Baxter becomes his brain, and Baxter's brain, because it is degenerating, becomes 'mere matter.' Baxter's history, his person, dissolves into the mass of Perowne's clinical experience.

Indeed, McEwan pointedly dramatises the shift in power that occurs at the moment when Perowne diagnoses Baxter's disease. As Perowne announces his knowledge of Baxter's disease, he 'senses the power passing to him' (95). The context in which Perowne and Baxter are situated is altered profoundly: 'This fire escape recess is his [Perowne's] consulting room,' McEwan writes. 'Its mean volume reflects back to him a voice regaining the full timbre of its authority' (95). And yet, although Perowne may have been able to ward off the immediate danger that Baxter presents, his decision ultimately exposes him to a greater danger. He fails to see the further-reaching consequences of humiliating Baxter. As Perowne later confesses to his wife: 'If I'd handled things better this morning, perhaps none of this would've happened' (240). Thus, as Perowne faces Baxter, it is a (perceived) lack of affect – a lack Perowne himself attributes to his profession – that distorts Perowne's capacity to deal beneficently with the situation.

Thinking through emotion

I hope to have established that, although McEwan draws on familiar literary conventions to describe Baxter, these conventions are pointedly modulated in order to make critical comment upon both the particular limitations and capacities of the neurosurgeon's worldview. In addition, I have claimed that McEwan positions emotional expression at the border between the poles of Perowne's perspective upon other people: his clinical, diagnostic attention on the one hand, and his imputation of an inaccessible conscious mind on the other. As such, Baxter's visible movement – whether it is perceived as pathological motion or expressive emotion – becomes implicated with Perowne's perspective. The boundaries of Baxter's character, therefore, are not absolute: they expand and contract, and shift between roundness and flatness, knowability and inscrutability. In *Saturday,* the relation between interior and exterior description is adjusted rather than discarded. Emotion mediates between the bodies of individual characters, and renders the distribution of consciousness in the novel fluid. In this way, it gives rise to an effective, if momentary, narrative symmetry.

Thus, Hadley's claim that *Saturday* constitutes 'an elegy for the individual consciousness' attends inadequately to the interrelationship of Perowne's 'individual consciousness' and the affective expression of others. However, this interpretation most directly challenges Frances Ferguson's reading of *Saturday*, which views profession as an emollient to the volatility and manipulability of emotion. At one point, for example, Ferguson compares the effect of the news media to Perowne's conversations with his mother, Lily, who is in the advanced stages of Alzheimer's. By altering the tone of his voice, Perowne is able to manipulate the content of his mother's speech, so that, 'Being suggestible, she'll laugh too and her mood will shift, and the story she tells will then be happier' (165). For Ferguson, mediated and personal communicative situations are similarly 'demented', for both demonstrate 'affection without understanding' (49). Read literally, however, Perowne's power to affect his mother's mental state depicts the *convergence* of personal affection and professional understanding, and testifies to the fact that emotion remains the ineradicable substrate of interpersonal communication.

Ferguson writes that professionalism may offer a means to 'calm even when it cannot heal' (51). Yet Perowne's deployment of professional knowledge on the public city street only inflames the situation, and it is Baxter's emotional expressivity that calls forth what is ultimately a more intelligent, measured response. After all, calm is precisely the effect of Perowne's tone of voice upon his agitated mother; it is also the intention behind his uncomprehending embrace of his sobbing daughter. Even if they are uncommonly noisy, are these affective exchanges not also a channel of communication? That which is termed susceptibility or manipulability in one context might, in a different context, be more aptly termed an essential responsivity, or openness.

I am certainly not claiming that emotion always acts beneficently, nor that it constitutes some kind of panacea for political asymmetries, only that the novel's representation of emotion is more multi-valent than Ferguson allows. This view is supported by McEwan's response to an interviewer's question concerning his interest in science. 'I have always thought the defining call of literature is to do with the exploration of human nature, which is also a dominant issue within cognitive and evolutionary psychology,' he states. Observing that 'Fundamental notions like consciousness as well as the emotions – surely the novelist's domain – are studied' (127) within these disciplines, McEwan proceeds to offer an example of how one such study manifests in his fiction:

> Yesterday, I was writing a passage in the novel I'm currently doing… about my character stopping by a television shop and seeing, multiplied on several screens of different sizes, Tony Blair being interviewed. He can't hear what Blair's saying, but as he's watching, the camera is slowly zooming in on Blair's mouth. We humans are very good at looking at each other's faces, and we have many good evolutionary reasons to be so. Paul Ekman, a psychologist who I've come to admire a great deal, talks interestingly about the smile in his work. If you ask someone to fake a smile, there are muscles in the face that are not activated. What Ekman has shown is that lying smile actually has a real physiological foundation; there are muscles that do not kick in, which do when a smile is honest. As the camera zooms in, I thought, this is the question we want to pose

about a politician: is that an honest smile, or not. I could not have had
such a speculation without the work of Ekman. (127–8)

The incident McEwan describes, which appears mid-way through
Saturday, explicitly links the science of emotion to the political sphere.
Of course, the weight that should be attributed to such instances remains
an open, and highly complex, question. In closing, however, I would
like to briefly explore the link between McEwan's above reference to the
novelist's 'domain' as both that of the emotions, and 'the exploration of
human nature.' In a lecture delivered in 2002, and later published under
the title 'Literature, Science and Human Nature', McEwan recommends
that, in the face of overwhelming evidence, we once again acknowledge the
beneficent capacities of our common human nature. Focusing especially on
the expression of emotion as a human universal, McEwan remarks upon
the pronounced ideological 'reversal[s]' (17) that saw Charles Darwin
deploy his evidence for universal emotional expression against racism,
and Margaret Mead deploy her own evidence for the cultural diversity of
emotional display to the same end. Once again, Ekman's research is cited,
in this instance in support of Darwin's contention that the expression of
emotion in humans is innate, no matter how cross-culturally variable the
stimuli of specific emotions. Conceiving of the emotions as a 'vast pool of
shared humanity, of shared assumptions,' (17) McEwan concludes that it
is 'Within the emotional and expressive we remain what we are' (19). In
my view, emotional expression is the arbiter of the human in *Saturday*:
Perowne's initially fearful apprehension of his 'simian' attacker is due to a
certain shiftiness, an affective unpredictability, that Perowne will come to
identify as pathological; his altered, softened response, and more 'rounded',
human perception may be attributed to Baxter's transient expression of
emotion that is symbolic of greater depth.

******

In this essay, McEwan's broader claim is that literary expression is both fundamentally dependent upon, and an attestation to, the existence of a common human nature. In the absence of human universals, McEwan claims, literary works would be incomprehensible over time or across different cultures. In conclusion, then, McEwan writes that 'That which binds us, our common nature, is what literature has always, knowingly and helplessly, given voice to. And it is this universality which the biological sciences, now entering another exhilarating phase, are set to explore further' (19). Yet, literature is also inherently malleable. The form of the novel is particularly prone to co-vary with altered ways of understanding the workings of consciousness, with the conception of the relation of mind to brain, and the nature of the self. With a quotation from Saul Bellow's *Herzog,* McEwan suggests that 'one's biology ... predates and, by implication, is even more of the essence of being human than one's religion' (6). In addition, McEwan writes:

> Literature flourishes along the channels of this unspoken agreement between writers and readers, offering a mental map whose north and south are the specific and the general. At its best, literature is universal, illuminating human nature at precisely the point at which it is most parochial and specific. (6)

From its' opening passage, *Saturday* exhibits a heightened tension between the particular – this moment, this age, this day, this person in front of me – and the generalised operations of the 'mere matter' of the brain. Throughout the novel, Perowne's most intimate perceptions as well as his professional observations are modulated by the forms of description he has access to, as the odd, inverted practice of neurosurgery feeds back into Perowne's own subjectivity, profoundly altering his sense of what is specific and what general. On the one hand, Perowne possesses a heightened sense of the absolute inaccessibility of the specificity of another person's consciousness. On the other, Perowne has developed a sense of consciousness as a mass, stripped of particularity and individuality, and in limited supply to each individual. In *Saturday,* McEwan suggests that emotion, cutting across individual minds, across private and public space, and across biology and consciousness, may be one means of mediating between these increasingly incommensurable views of what it is to be human.

Works Cited

Banville, John. 'A Day in the Life.' Rev. of *Saturday*, by Ian McEwan. *New York Review of Books* 26 May 2005: 12–14

Childs, Peter (ed.). *The Fiction of Ian McEwan*. Houndmills, Basingstoke: Palgrave, 2006

Currie, Mark. *About Time: Narrative, Fiction and the Philosophy of Time*. Edinburgh: Edinburgh University Press, 2007

Ferguson, Frances. 'The Way We Love Now: Ian McEwan, *Saturday*, and Personal Affection in the Information Age'. *Representations* 100.3 (2007): 42–52

Hadley, Elaine. 'On a Darkling Plain: Victorian Liberalism and the Fantasy of Agency', *Victorian Studies* 48 (2005): 92–102.

Howe, Irving. *A Critic's Notebook*. Ed. Nicholas Howe. New York: Harcourt Brace, 1994

Jaffe, Audrey. *Vanishing Points: Dickens, Narrative, and the Subject of Omniscience*. Berkeley: University of California Press, 1991

McEwan, Ian. 'Journeys without Maps: An Interview with Ian McEwan.' In *Ian McEwan: Contemporary Critical Perspectives*. Edited by Sebastian Groes. London: Continuum, 2009. Pp. 123–134

———. *Saturday*. London: Vintage, 2006

———. 'Literature, Science, and Human Nature'. In *The Literary Animal: Evolution and the Nature of Narrative*. Edited by David Sloan Wilson and Jonathan Gottschall. Evanston, Ill.: Northwestern University Press, 2005. Pp. 5–19

Rorty, Richard. 'A Queasy Agnosticism.' Rev. of *Saturday*, by Ian McEwan. *Dissent* Sept. – Nov. 2005: 91–94

Siegel, Lee. ' The Imagination of Disaster'. Rev. of *Saturday*, by Ian McEwan. *Nation* 11 April 2005: 33–38

Woloch, Alex. *The One vs. the Many: Minor Characters and the Space of the Protagonist in the Novel*. Princeton: Princeton University Press, 2003.

Wood, James. 'On a Darkling Plain.' Rev. of *Saturday*, by Ian McEwan. *New Republic* 18 April 2005: 28–36

Notes

1   In a similar vein, though somewhat more cryptically, Lee Siegel states that '*Saturday* is a commentary on how politics gets invented from the stuff of emotion the way mind is created out of the brain' (35).

Chapter 9

Human Values in a Mass Society: a Reading of George Orwell's Novels

Peter Goodall
University of Southern Queensland

I

Although George Orwell's last novel, *Nineteen Eighty-Four*, is usually read as political satire, it is at heart a sustained meditation on the ethical question of what it is to be human – and the climax of such meditations in his work as a whole. There are several key passages in the novel that address this question and all are bound up in various ways with the narrative of the proles. Three examples, drawn from many in different parts of the novel, can illustrate this. The first is in a conversation between Winston Smith and Syme, his colleague in the Ministry of Truth, who is working on the Newspeak Dictionary. Syme has been enlarging on the beauty of the destruction of Oldspeak words:

> 'Has it ever occurred to you, Winston, that by the year 2050, at the very latest, not a single human being will be alive who could understand such a conversation as we are having now?'
> 'Except —' began Winston doubtfully, and he stopped.
> It had been on the tip of his tongue to say 'Except the proles,' but he checked himself, not feeling fully certain that this remark was not in some way unorthodox. Syme, however, had divined what he was about to say. 'The proles are not human beings,' he said carelessly. (55–6)

The second example is drawn from the middle of the novel, when Winston has already begun his personal revolt by conducting a love affair with Julia in the room above Mr Charrington's shop and by keeping a personal diary. As he lies in bed with Julia, he falls asleep and has a troubling dream, in which he remembers an incident from his childhood, when his family was close to starvation and he had robbed his little sister of her share of a bar of chocolate. In thinking about the event, he connects his mother's actions to the behaviour of a prole woman whom he had seen in a newsreel: "The proles are human beings,' [Winston] said aloud. 'We are not human" (173). The last example is from near the novel's end, when Winston has been tortured by O'Brien, and is desperately trying to find the hope for a better life somewhere in the system:

> 'I don't know—I don't care. Somehow you will fail. Something will defeat you. Life will defeat you.'
>
> 'We control life, Winston, at all its levels. You are imagining that there is something called human nature which will be outraged by what we do and will turn against us. But we create human nature. Men are infinitely malleable. Or perhaps you have returned to your old idea that the proletarians or the slaves will arise and overthrow us. Put it out of your mind. They are helpless, like the animals. Humanity is the Party. The others are outside—irrelevant.' (282)

II

This identification of the 'human' with the lives of the proles had, however, a long preparation in Orwell's earlier writings, and, like much else in his work, Orwell's views are often ambivalent. One of the sources of this ambivalence is that Orwell's various representations of the common people conflate two social types: the urban working class, whose lives, especially their material conditions, so preoccupied social reformers from the early Victorian period onwards; and 'mass man', identified later in the nineteenth century and the subject of considerable interest in the 1920s and 1930s.

Orwell's early work was concerned mostly with men and women of the first type, and although these figures really belong to a former historical period, Orwell was still actively writing about them in the mid 1930s. Some of the most vivid of Orwell's writing in this vein can be found in *The Road to Wigan Pier*, published in 1937. The book reveals Orwell, however, perhaps more than he would have liked, shocked and repelled by many aspects of the private lives of the working class. The first chapter, describing the lodging house run by the Brookers above their tripe shop in Wigan, paints a repulsive picture of the overcrowding, filth and laziness of working-class life. In many instances in the book, the language is almost too strong to contain the sympathy that Orwell struggles to express, an example of a kind of 'doubleness' that frequently characterises Orwell's writing about the poor. The metaphors are all of disease, filth, darkness and chaos:

> As you walk through the industrial towns you lose yourself in labyrinths of little brick houses blackened by smoke, festering in planless chaos round miry alleys and little cindered yards where there are stinking dust-bins and lines of grimy washing and half ruinous wc's. (52)

As noted above, this tradition of social commentary on the lives of the poor has its origins in the early Victorian period. There are abundant examples in the sociological work of George Godwin's *London Shadows*, for example:

> Pulling the latch of the outer door of one of the houses here, and then entering the room on the left ... we found an atmosphere so stifling that we were forced for a moment to retreat. There were two beds in the room: in one, which seemed to have heads all round it, were no fewer than nine women and children. They were stored so oddly and so thickly, that it was not an easy matter to count them even by the strong light of the police- man's lantern. In the other bed were a man and a lad, and in a small room, or closet leading from this room, three other persons were sleeping. There was little ventilation. (16)

Orwell's picture of the private life of the urban working class in the 1930s recalls many of the most repulsive features of nineteenth-century London, the sort of London that Dickens evokes in *Oliver Twist*. In *The Road to*

Wigan Pier, Orwell focuses on the factual details of the lives of the poor – the dirtiness, the overcrowding, especially in the squalid bedrooms – in a manner that recalls the practice of social investigators of the nineteenth century like Godwin. Not a single house in the working-class areas of the industrial cities had hot water laid on, for example: 'You might walk, I suppose, through literally hundreds of miles of streets inhabited by miners, every one of whom, when he is in work, gets black from head to foot every day, without ever passing a house in which one could have a bath' (52). These people, their private lives, and Orwell's ambivalent attitude towards them, recur in various forms throughout his work: the tramps in the casual wards in *Down and Out in Paris and London* (1932), the Burmese in *Burmese Days* (1934), the hop-pickers in *A Clergyman's Daughter* (1935), the Bohemian life that Gordon Comstock wants to lead in *Keep the Aspidistra Flying* (1936), and, finally, the proles in *Nineteen Eighty-Four*.

But Orwell wanted to do more than record material details like a documentary journalist, and he tried to move inside his subjects and also to confront and understand the intensity of his feelings about them. The second part of *The Road to Wigan Pier* deals at length with the cultural tradition in which middle-class people are reared from childhood to treat the 'masses' as if they were a different species:

> To me in my early boyhood, to nearly all children of families like mine, 'common' people seemed almost sub-human. (127)

What made Orwell less typical of his social class was that he was also driven in a complex way – by his political beliefs later on, but earlier by his alienating experiences as a servant of the colonial power in Burma – to try to do something about these feelings. After he returned to England from five years of service in the Indian Imperial Police force in Burma in 1927, Orwell sought out menial jobs – as a dishwasher, as a shop assistant, as a poor schoolteacher – and walked the streets as a tramp, sleeping rough in dosshouses or in casual wards.[1] In all, he was driven by an urge to *cross over*,[2] as Valentine Cunningham calls it in his study of writing of the 1930s:

I wanted to get in touch with them, I even wanted to become one of them, but I still thought of them as alien and dangerous; going into the dark doorway of that common lodging-house seemed to me like going down into some dreadful subterranean place – a sewer full of rats, for instance. (Orwell, *Wigan Pier* 152–53)

III

Although *The Road to Wigan Pier* shows how long the worst aspects of the Victorian housing of the poor persisted, the agenda and the discourse of urban planning changed in significant ways in the latter part of the nineteenth century, and the living conditions of the urban poor dramatically improved. The provision of piped water and sewage systems, the enactment of bye-laws that regulated building standards, and the improvement in the housing stock reduced fears of an imminent catastrophe caused by polluted water. That earlier anxiety, a fear of contagion by filth, both in a physical and in a transferred moral sense, was replaced, however, with fears of more gradual degeneration and morbidity – and the danger of 'contagion' of a different kind. The publication of Darwin's *Origin of Species* (1859) gave a theoretical framework to such fears; it was possible to see the English urban poor as a species that was unfit for survival. Many social commentators doubted that the current generation of city dwellers would be able to reproduce themselves, or they believed that their children would be too sickly to survive for long. Concern peaked around 1900, caused by the failure of the British army to bring a speedy end to the Boer War. Arnold White, in *Efficiency and Empire* (1901), reported that three in five men who attempted to enlist in the army at the depot in Manchester in 1899 failed to pass the medical examination.[3]

It was one thing for the urban masses to be a threat to themselves and to be faced with inevitable extinction, but fears grew at the end of the nineteenth century that they might in fact increase in numbers rather than decrease, and that their mode of life was a threat to the rest of society, to its civil and political life, its structure and institutions, but most of all to its 'culture'. Oswald Spengler's *Decline of the West*, first published in German in 1922 but available in English translation by 1928, is a key text. His fundamental theme, the twin evils of urbanisation and mechanisation leading to megalopolis and the decay of culture into a formless, inorganic mass, can be found in many of the jeremiads about culture produced in the late 1920s and 1930s: for example, Clive Bell's *Civilization* (1928), dedicated to Virginia Woolf; Karl Jaspers' *Man in the Modern Age* (1931), which sees the modern world re-enacting the fate of ancient Rome; and in F. R. Leavis' first monograph, published in 1933 by the aptly named Minority Press at Cambridge, and bearing the suggestive title *Mass Civilization and Minority Culture*. The climax of this line of thought can be found in Jose Ortega y Gasset's *Revolt of the Masses*, first published in Spanish in 1930 and translated into English in 1932.

It is important to understand that 'mass man' is not simply another name for the urban working class in the way in which it is identified by Dickens in the nineteenth century. If anything, social commentators of the early twentieth century locate mass man within the lower ranks of the bourgeoisie. His essential distinguishing feature is, paradoxically, his lack of distinction: he is 'Mr Average', totally ordinary, with a mind that is commonplace. What makes this commonplaceness threatening, however, is that mass man is not ashamed of his ordinariness but exults in it and seeks to propagate it in society. Nor can he be educated out of it. In particular, mass man cannot attain that largeness of mind that is the special product of the liberal education. The only kind of knowledge that mass man can acquire is fact, producing the curious hybrid that Ortega calls the 'learned ignoramus'. There is thus an unbridgeable gulf between the culture of the minority and the social world of mass man.

There are depictions of the private life of mass man and the suburbs – his native habitat – in several of Orwell's works, especially in the novels of the 1930s such as *A Clergyman's Daughter* and *Keep the Aspidistra Flying*, but the most complete is in *Coming up for Air*, published in 1939 on the eve of the Second World War. The novel is narrated in the first person by its anti-hero, George Bowling, whose life has followed the general history of suburban mass man in the early twentieth century. George's life and beliefs are typical. He constantly applies the word 'average' to himself: 'Five to ten quid a week,' you'd say as soon as you saw me' (13–4). Other keynotes of George's personality are the vulgarity and insensitivity that are native to the salesman. At forty-five, George has not only run to fat, but his 'life' seems to be a thing of the past: 'When I look back I realize that my active life, if I ever had one, ended when I was sixteen. Everything that really matters to me had happened before that date' (131).

IV

Orwell inherited both traditions of writing about the common people, but the distinctiveness of his treatment was to blend them and give them a subtler analysis. The word 'prole' is first used in *Coming up for Air*, but George Bowling is not himself a prole – or at least in important ways he's not. George's origins lie among the ranks of small farmers and shopkeepers in country towns, not agricultural labourers or the industrial working class. Orwell positions George very carefully: 'It wasn't so with boys of our class, the sons of shopkeepers and farmers. You went to the Grammar School and you stayed there till you were sixteen, just to show that you weren't a prole' (67). There are, in fact, plenty of examples of conventional prole lifestyle in the novel to show the contrast, recorded in the familiar language of rats, overcrowding and incest:

> [Katie Simmons's] family lived in a filthy little rat-hole of a place
> in the slummy street behind the brewery. The place swarmed with
> children like a kind of vermin [...] Poor Katie! She had her first baby
> when she was fifteen. No one knew who was the father, and probably
> Katie wasn't too certain herself. Most people believed it was one of
> her brothers. (40–41)

Orwell's aim in *Coming up for Air* is to suggest, however, that the private life of mass man is not as empty as it seems and to reveal George's distinctiveness and individuality. What makes George less typical of mass man is, paradoxically, his 'proleness'. In particular, his attitude to money is not middle class: 'I've got more the prole's attitude towards money. Life's here to be lived, and if we're going to be in the soup next week – well, next week is a long way off' (137). Another key aspect that links him to the proles is a kind of 'vitalism'.

In particular, this differentiates him from his wife's middle-class world of penny-pinching respectability: 'what Hilda lacks [...] is any kind of joy in life, any kind of interest in things for their own sake [...] It was through Hilda that I first got a notion of what these decayed middle-class families are really like. The essential fact about them is that all their vitality has been drained away by lack of money' (136).

Most important of all, buried beneath the monotony and facelessness of mass life, George does in fact have a 'culture'. What gives it value and resonance, however, is not at heart anything to do with intellectuals. It is not culture in the public, Arnoldian, sense of the term, but something personal and internalised, rooted in the private lives of families. This culture is associated, not just with George's personal past life, but with the past life of a whole generation of English men and women. As a product of this culture, George is one of nature's survivors and is unafraid of the future: 'In almost all circumstances I'd manage to make a living – always a living and never a fortune – and even in war, revolution, plague, and famine I'd back myself to stay alive longer than most people' (23). It is epitomised in the vitalism of the line from the popular song that forms the epigraph to the novel: 'He's dead, but he won't lie down'.

V

In almost all senses, life in the Oceania of *Nineteen Eighty-Four* is a perversion of human values. O'Brien ridicules Winston's faith in the agency of the individual human being and offers in response the power of collective experience: 'Can you not understand, Winston, that the individual is only a cell? The weariness of the cell is the vigour of the organism' (276). But O'Brien's notion of the collectivity is itself a mockery; almost every aspect of the *social* life of Party members is a sham. The lives they lead are, perhaps, best epitomized in the evocative title of one of the most influential books of the 1950s, David Reisman's *The Lonely Crowd* (1950). It is neither individual nor collective, neither private nor public, but one of forced and desolate solitude, albeit lived in the midst of crowded conditions. The conflicts between the Party's ideology and its reality are well caught in some of the early lines that

Winston writes in his diary: a text that is both private and public, written in solitude but reaching out to others who might read and understand it:

> From the age of uniformity, from the age of solitude, from the age of Big Brother, from the age of doublethink – greetings! (30)

Nor is friendship, since ancient times one of the explicit foundations of human social life, possible in Oceania: between Party members it is suspicious, and it is forbidden between Party members and Proles. But, even if it were not politically or criminally dangerous, there is something about life in Oceania that renders it impossible. Likewise, the particular nature of Oceanian collectivism has destroyed the family life of Party members and the personal relationship of husband and wife. Big Brother's name promises the security of the family but delivers only the oppression of a bullying sibling. Winston's first wife, Katherine, had actually been uncomfortable when alone with her husband. It is significant that Winston and his wife had had no children, but all children nowadays, Winston grumbles, are hateful creatures, members of the Junior Spies, and the principal target of their espionage is the family itself. The Party's final assault on personal relationships will be on sexuality. Winston remembers the joyless couplings with Katherine, fulfilling their duty to the Party to procreate. Even this will soon be unnecessary. In one of those moments that seem to call into question whether O'Brien is vastly prescient or simply insane, he tells Winston that eventually the Party will abolish the orgasm.

If this existence is life for one of the relatively privileged, the top fifteen per cent of Oceanian society who are Party members, it is difficult at first to see how the lives of the proles are any better, let alone how they could offer a source of hope for the preservation of humanity and its values. Our initial view of them in *Nineteen Eighty-Four* reaffirms all the modernist stereotypes of the swarming masses:

> [Winston] was walking up a cobbled street of little two-storey houses with battered doorways which gave straight on the pavement and which were somehow curiously suggestive of ratholes. There were puddles of filthy water here and there among the cobbles. In and out of the dark doorways,

and down narrow alley-ways that branched off on either side, people swarmed in astonishing numbers. (86)

The description of the course of their lives is almost identical to the view of the poor in *The Road to Wigan Pier*: 'they were born, they grew up in the gutters, they went to work at twelve, they passed through a brief blossoming-period of beauty and sexual desire, they married at twenty, they were middle-aged at thirty, they died, for the most part, at sixty' (74).

Winston's views of the humanity of the proles start to change when he begins to see them at closer quarters, less as a type – although he never penetrates their homes as Orwell the social analyst does in *The Road to Wigan Pier* or tries to present them from the inside as he does with George Bowling. For Winston, this is accompanied by a journey into the past of his own life, an awakening memory and revaluation of his childhood. His memory of where his family lived evokes comparisons with the living conditions of the poor found throughout Orwell's work:

> a dark, close-smelling room that seemed half filled by a bed with a white counterpane [...] and on the landing outside there was a brown earthenware sink, common to several rooms. (169)

It is an unsentimental picture, but the telling detail is the large (presumably double) bed that dominates the room, its whiteness set off against the dinginess of every other detail. If the lives of Party members are sexless, the sexual urge sublimated into aggression and leader-worship, prole life and revolt against the Party are always associated with sexual happiness and fulfilment. Winston is alert to the revolutionary potential of his and Julia's sexuality: 'their embrace had been a battle, the climax a victory. It was a blow struck against the Party. It was a political act' (133). We never see into the sexual lives of the proles, although we do see its consequences in the large numbers of children about.

The room in the prole quarter above Mr Charrington's shop has an especial resonance here. It is not just a place for Winston and Julia to conduct a clandestine affair; it is a quintessential private place, where the full dimensions of the 'humane' life might be manifested. Indeed, one of the things that Winston hopes is that he and Julia might create a space in which they could live in intimacy without always feeling the obligation to have sex. Although squalid, it is a place for other sensual pleasures too, such as making and drinking the real coffee that normally finds its way only into the homes of members of the Inner Party. Above all, it is a place where reading and study can take place, where Winston can absorb Goldstein's book and discuss it with Julia.

It is from the window of this room at a critical moment that Winston and Julia gaze at the monstrous prole woman as she hangs her washing on the line and sings a popular song, 'It was only an 'opeless fancy'. An ''opeless fancy' is not a bad way of describing Winston and Julia's revolt. This scene is another, perhaps the ultimate, 'crossing-over' in Orwell's work. The window through which Winston gazes on the woman performing a simple manual task emphasises the distance between them, but in every other way the scene is a supreme moment of emotional reaching-out, empathy and understanding. Winston suddenly appreciates the beauty of this woman, coarsened though she is and blown up to a monstrous size by years of child-bearing. Now, for the first time, he also sees into the historical dynamic of his society and understands the point of Goldstein's message that 'If there is hope, it lies with the proles'.

What crystallizes in his mind is the connection between human values and the values of the private world, and the way in which the lives of the proles have cherished and sustained them. He recognizes the same value system in the life of his mother:

> [His mother] had possessed a kind of nobility, a kind of purity, simply because the standards that she obeyed were private ones. Her feelings were her own, and could not be altered from outside. It would not have occurred to her that an action which is ineffectual thereby becomes meaningless. (171)

That last sentence has great importance in the novel, and might be borne in mind by those readers who find the novel so lacking in hope. Winston's mother had possessed these humane values, rooted in the security of private life, in common with most of her generation. The backward look is very Orwellian, but there is also a look into the future. These same values are now possessed and passed on in the lives of the proles.

VI

What are we then to make of the final part of the novel? Winston's last words before he is captured, echoed dramatically by the voice that suddenly erupts from the concealed telescreen, are 'We are the dead' (230). Does the novel ultimately repudiate Winston's faith in the humanity of the proles and offer instead a bleak view of the future and the final abandonment of Orwell's hope for a socialist revolution?

The reality is complex. There is no doubt that Winston himself is totally crushed, and his beliefs that the Party can neither get inside your head nor change your feelings are shown to be transparently naïve. It is not certain, on the other hand, that there will be no more Winstons in the Party who will make the same journey. Julia says that she had had sex with scores of Party members before meeting Winston; even the dutiful Parsons easily lapses into thoughtcrime when he is asleep, denouncing Big Brother. If Winston is unique in his revolt, why does the State require such an extensive and Byzantine mechanism to watch the population, why has O'Brien had to resort to writing a book in imitation of Goldstein's views (if indeed the authorship is his) in order to draw out suspected offenders? The very existence of the book, no matter who wrote it, is testament to the vigorous survival of anti-establishment ideas in Oceania. Even if O'Brien personally authored Goldstein's Book, that does not make 'Goldstein's' analysis or his solutions any the less correct.

Winston and Julia are, indeed, 'the dead', as O'Brien had warned them when he recruited them to the 'Brotherhood'. The death of the revolt by Party members is attended, however, by the birth of the revolt by the proles, but the efficacy of the proles as revolutionary agents and the related matter of the novel's pessimistic conclusion have also spawned a huge secondary literature on the novel. In one of the first books written about Orwell,

John Atkins found the picture of the future state 'almost devoid of hope' (237). Likewise, Orwell's friend Tosco Fyvel found the proles 'a picture of a completely demoralized British working class' (198). Even those writers who have stressed the continuity of Orwell's political thought – for example Stephen Ingle in *George Orwell: a Political Life* (1993) or John Newsinger, *Orwell's Politics* (1999) – have seldom seen hope in the proles as more than a delusion that is brutally crushed.

For the sake of balance, it is important to note that Orwell's view of the power of the proles, rooted in their embodiment of humane values, was not unique, but clearly in a tradition that includes similar treatments by H. G. Wells and G. K. Chesterton.[4] In Wells's *When the Sleeper Wakes*, for example, Graham cannot accept that the crowd will die: 'the Crowd, the great mass of poor men. Will that die out? That will not die out' (199). Chesterton, in *The Man who was Thursday* especially, retained a faith in the good sense of the common man. Dr Bull says 'I don't think, and I never shall think, that the mass of ordinary men are a pack of dirty modern thinkers. No, sir, I'm a democrat, and I still don't believe that Sunday could convert one average navvy or counter-jumper. No, I may be mad, but humanity isn't' (149). In a passage that seems very close to Orwell's work, Chesterton also describes the rough streets where a barrel-organ is heard, whose 'jingling music seemed full of the vivacity, the vulgarity, and the irrational valour of the poor, who in all those unclean streets were all clinging to the decencies and the charities of Christendom' (149). Much of this faith in the common people, shared by Wells and Chesterton, is based on the conviction that they, unlike the intellectuals, had never abandoned their moral code and would bring this to bear on politics eventually.

Likewise, there is a long history in Orwell's own work of similar expressions of hope and confidence. In *Keep the Aspidistra Flying*, the turning-point for Gordon Comstock, the beginning of his acceptance of society and the hope for his own future, is an appreciation that the poor have preserved their human standards: 'the money-code as they interpreted it was not merely cynical and hoggish. They had their standards, their inviolable points of honour' (255). During the war, Orwell wrote in a letter to Humphry House that 'my chief hope for the future is that the common people have never parted with their moral code' (*CEJL* 1. 532), and in a review of Noyes's *The Edge of the Abyss*, Orwell expressed the view that the common people had been less affected by totalitarian views than the intelligentsia.[5] Lastly, in 'Looking Back on the Spanish War', published in 1942, Orwell still believed the working class was the most reliable enemy of fascism (*CELJ* 2. 260).

How can the proles offer the only hope for humanity and yet, as O'Brien convincingly argues, be incapable of revolution in a thousand years? To believe both that the proles offer hope and yet are incapable of revolution is a surrender to doublethink – the simultaneous acceptance of contradictory ideas and philosophical positions, and the most basic abrogation of Aristotelian logic – as great as anything that O'Brien demands of Winston. Stephen Ingle calls the idea of hope lying with the proles 'true doublethink, embodying both mystical truth and palpable absurdity' (117). But, although this *aporia* defies logic, it doesn't necessarily defy common sense. Goldstein knows it to be true, as does Winston before torture destroys his body, mind and spirit – and I suspect that many readers believe that it is true as well. Orwell's public utterances stressed the need for clarity of ideas, truthfulness, and a prose style that was as transparent as a pane of glass. The fact is, however, that his final statement, his masterpiece, has produced one of the most controversial and conflicting sets of readings of any novel of the twentieth century: readings that have served the opposite interests of both the political left and right. But Orwell's life itself was a continual contradiction: a child of what he called the lower-upper-middle class; the Etonian who became a tramp and slept in dosshouses; the policeman who served Empire but who joined the Left; the physical wreck who fought bravely in the army of the Spanish republic; the self-confessed Tory-Anarchist. As Alok Rai puts it, Orwell's 'writing acquires the aura of unselfish fidelity to the ambivalence of reality itself' (46). It is this that gives him integrity, makes his a voice that we want to hear, and lends his views credibility even when we cannot always resolve the confusions and doubts.

Works Cited

Atkins, John. *George Orwell: A Literary Study*. London: John Calder, 1954

Chesterton, G. K. *The Man who was Thursday: A Nightmare*. 1904. Rpt. London: Arrowsmth, 1944

Cunningham, Valentine. *British Writers of the Thirties*. Oxford and New York: Oxford University Press, 1988

Davison, Peter. *George Orwell: A Literary Life*. London: Macmillan, 1996

Fyvel, Tosco. *George Orwell: A Personal Memoir*. London: Weidenfeld, 1982

Godwin, George. *London Shadows: A Glance at the 'Homes' of the Thousands*. 1854. Rpt. New York and London, 1985

Ingle, Stephen. *George Orwell: A Political Life*. Manchester and New York: Manchester University Press, 1993

Lees, Andrew. *Cities Perceived: Urban Society in European and American Thought, 1820–1940*. Manchester: Manchester University Press, 1985

Newsinger, John. *Orwell's Politics*. London: Macmillan, 1999

Orwell, George. *Collected Essays, Journalism and Letters of George Orwell*. Vol 1, 'An Age Like This.' Edited by Sonia Orwell and Ian Angus. Harmondsworth: Penguin, 1970

———. *Collected Essays, Journalism and Letters of George Orwell*. Vol 2, 'My Country Right or Left.' Edited by Sonia Orwell and Ian Angus. London: Secker and Warburg, 1968

———. *Coming Up for Air*. 1939. Rpt. Harmondsworth: Penguin, 1979

———. *Keep the Aspidistra Flying*. 1936. Rpt. Harmondsworth: Penguin, 1962

———. *Nineteen Eighty-Four*. 1949. Rpt. London: Penguin, 2000

———. *The Road to Wigan Pier*. 1937. Rpt. London: Secker and Warburg, 1973

Rai, Alok. *Orwell and the Politics of Despair*. Cambridge: Cambridge University Press, 1998

Sandison, Alan. *George Orwell: After 1984*. Dover NH: Longwood, 1986

Steinhoff, William. *The Road to 1984*. London: Weidenfeld and Nicolson, 1975

Wells, H. G. *When the Sleeper Wakes*. 1899. Rpt. Introduction by Orson Scott Card. New York: Modern Library, 2003

Notes

1 There are a number of different views of these expeditions. Sandison (56–7) sees Orwell always on the outside and self-consciously 'literary' in his descriptions of the poor: 'in the last analysis it is de Maupassant and not poverty that breathes through the elaborately laconic vignettes and the vivid, superficial drama'. Newsinger (24) takes Orwell more at face value: Orwell was virtually alone among middle-class writers in first-hand experience of 'hunger, homelessness, exhausting low-paid work and the many indignities and oppressions to which the poor were subjected'.

2 Davison (33) weighs up the different opinions of Edwin Muir, who claimed in 1952 that Orwell longed to be the 'working man' that he never could become, and Michael Meyer, who knew Orwell, and believed that Orwell never sought to identify himself with the working class.

3 See Lees (136–40) for more details and further references.

4 See Steinhoff.

5 See Sandison 45.

Chapter 10

Telling Stories at the Permeable Borders of the Human in David Malouf's *Ransom*

Yvonne Smith
University of Sydney

> *They are men from [Achilles'] home country, clear-spirited and secure in their animal nature, unacquainted with second thoughts ... They have the minds of hawks, these men, of foxes and of the wolves that come at night to the snowy folds and are tracked and hunted. They love him ... it is unconditional. But when they look at him these days, what they see confounds them ... he breaks daily every rule they have been taught to live by. Their only explanation is that he is mad. That some rough-haired god has darkened his mind and now moves like an opposing stranger in him, occupying that place where reason and rule should be, and sleep, and honour of other men and the gods. (Ransom 28–29)*

In David Malouf's novel *Ransom* (2009), based on Homer's *Iliad*, the narrator represents the human as capable of drawing upon a variety of inner capacities. It is open not only to the influence of 'reason and rule' but can also display the stealth and determination of hunting animals, as well as show the less-defined yet powerful influence of the 'gods'. Thus Achilles' men, his Myrmidons, see his wild behaviour in repeatedly desecrating the fallen body of his enemy, Hector, as due to the working of a 'rough-haired god' who has 'darkened' Achilles' mind and now inhabits it 'like an opposing stranger' (29), fighting against their culturally accepted codes of honour. What might now be called an irrational, psychologically disturbed or psychotically obsessive action – Achilles' dragging of Hector's body behind his chariot each day to assuage his grief at Patrocles' death – is represented by Malouf as a narrative of inner conflict which is explicable as a microcosm of the forces at work in the larger, mythic realm Achilles' men inhabit. In *Ransom* they belong to a world where perceptions of what is interior or exterior are only loosely bounded for the human and a cross-flow of influences constantly occurs between the natural world, humans and the gods.

As much as this worldview seems to be in keeping with the Homeric tradition, it is purposefully and imaginatively re-made by Malouf. He offers his own story-world in which the main players are very much acquainted with the subtleties of 'second thoughts', often in a distinctly unclassical vein that shows something the reader can identify as a novelist's view of complex human personalities. As I will discuss in this chapter, his choice of the final part of an epic that is foundational to the Western literary canon expresses Malouf's ongoing desire to grasp through the working of the imagination what the past can bring to bear on the present, to show how old myths and tales might become untold tales we need to hear as we make meaning in to-day's societies. In my reading, he does this particularly by means of what Adriana Cavarero has termed 'the narratability of the self … each one of us lives … as his/her own story' (34). For Malouf, '*The Iliad* reminds us that we inhabit a world of unfinished stories, and echoes, and the repetition of old horrors and miseries' ('Men and Gods' 4). I will focus on how Malouf makes a holistic view of the mind-in-the-body (thinking and feeling always interacting with bodily states) the locus of conflicted narratives of identity for Achilles and Priam and how such conflicts are at least partially redressed or re-balanced by their personal experiences at what may be termed the permeable boundaries of the human – that is, the transitional moments and places where perception seems more open, when memory brings past and present into closer relation and when 'others' including people, animals and what Malouf often calls the 'angel' or 'stranger' enter the circle of immediate experience. I will also consider briefly how such permeable borders have featured in Malouf's poetry and prose, consistent with his exploration of crossing borders of the human in works such as *An Imaginary Life* and *Remembering Babylon*. Malouf's focus in *Ransom* on the many-faceted role of the human – particularly as expressed through family ties and the male body as warrior, king, father, son, servant, labourer, farmer – gives his telling of the story a personal, even comic focus, at times, within the epic frame. He stresses subjective experience as essential in situations that would seek to deny the personal, a view also found in his novels about world wars of the twentieth century, *Fly Away Peter* and *The Great World*, as well as in his 'little book on big things' *On Experience*. As Andrew Taylor observes, the human body has become 'the site of wholeness' in Malouf's works, wholeness that occurs within social and political processes in history, yet is best felt in attentive consciousness within and between people (68–69). I will argue that Malouf's view of 'wholeness' in *Ransom* requires a consciousness that is alive through the mind-in-the-body to a present moment that is 'always with us, always open' ('Wild Lemons', *First Things Last* 1).

Malouf's blending of interior and exterior worlds is offered as a poetic reading of the human at a time when views of our species are being re-shaped in response to changes in the nature and technology of power. Donna Haraway argues that people in economically developed societies are now intimately connected with ways of living and thinking about the body that are technologically based so that the human has become a hybrid, a 'cyborg' or cybernetic organism, an 'artificial intelligence system' (206), linking organism and machine. Film and media representations of hybrid humanoid characters reflect such a trend. By contrast, the philosopher Mark Rowlands, after living with a wolf as a pet for many years, still defines what is particular to the human in terms of a basic animal nature but one shaped by belief and narratives of the self: 'human are the animals that believe the stories they tell about themselves. Humans are credulous animals' (2). Like Cavarero, Rowlands finds a strong link between the human and the need to create a story that gives expression to what Cavarero terms 'the uncontrollable narrative impulse of memory' (35). While the relation between human and animal, identity and narration has been expressed through imagination in Malouf works, he also frames the nature of the human in ethical terms, asking:

> to what extent we may be defined, each one of us, by that mixture of the
> nobly altruistic and the cowardly and mean, of a passionate dedication

to truth and a long involvement in deception and self-deception and lies, of idealism and some need we have to degrade, crush and enslave, that is the whole long, sad, occasionally uplifting story of our kind. (*On Experience*, 48–49)

As for Rowlands and Cavarero, belief in the significance of stories is a key aspect of Malouf's understanding of the human. However, his belief is not unqualified but reflects what he regards as an ethical dilemma found in the often conflicting values expressed in human behaviour. Such a view is important in *Ransom* where the lyrical voice of the storyteller is linked closely with various roles of the god Hermes, known not only as an interpreter and communicator, a bringer of messages from Olympus, but also as a trickster, liar and thief. Malouf, as omniscient narrator, weaves the engaging web of story but also invites the reader to reflect on its veracity. Is a story-teller who steals the tales of others to be trusted? Through the new characters he introduces, Somax the waggoner and his black mules, Beauty and Shock, Malouf explores not only how events might become legends over time (blending the actual and fanciful) but also how the everyday world from the margins of which they emerge provides a counter-balance to the excesses of the heroic ethic.

Ransom opens at a moment when Achilles is listening to the sounds of the sea on a beach near his camp but also trying to hear inwardly the voice of his mother, the water nymph, Thetis. His behaviour has become what the Myrmidons consider 'mad'. He longs for 'something to appear that will break the spell that is on him' (35) and seeks direction from what is both outward and inward as an answer. Thetis' voice, however, has become 'no more than a faint far-off echo to his senses, an underwater humming' (5). He has lost a gift, an inner capacity, and seeks to return to the beginning of his own bodily existence within her to find it. The dual identity which allowed him to be seamlessly a child of earth and water has waned in manhood. He is mortal, after all, like his father, Peleus. Although he waits now 'shoulders hunched, attentive' (3) for any message that his immortal water-spirit mother might have for him, he recalls that:

> Somewhere in the depths of sleep his spirit had made a crossing and not
> come back, or it had been snatched up and transformed. When he bent
> and chose a stone for his slingshot it had a new weight in his hand. (6)

Yet he is drawn still from an apparently solid to a fluid world, to 'what
accepts, in a moment of stillness, the reflection of a face, a tree in leaf, but
holds nothing, and itself cannot be held' (4). By evoking ways of perceiving
that are transitional between inwardly and outwardly focused states of
mind, Malouf works with a fluid, many-faceted sense of the subject-object
relationship, not out of keeping with Homer's multiple-perspective narrative
style, yet distinctly Malouf's own. Such a view accords with more open
concepts of self, after the work of Freud and Lacan, where the self, while
not denied as in some post-structuralist readings, is regarded as what Sarah
Spence terms 'a process, a fluidity, a tension, even between the subjective and
objective realms' (3–4). As Malouf explains regarding his own approach in a
talk at the Warana Writers' Week in Brisbane in 1983:

> I've always wanted to work and have worked (uneasily some people
> might say) between inner and outer, or at the point where objects cross
> the consciousness and become perception ... It's a point of awareness that
> engages me. I think it is where I feel I have most to discover: that is the
> point at which objects, sensations, resolve any question of object/ subject,
> and move from outside within. (Tulip 275)

The discourse of the opening paragraphs of *Ransom* is shaped by a poetic
compression of images. Time shifts seamlessly between past and present.
The sea is at once a physical force, a personality with 'many voices' and a
'membrane stretched to a fine transparency', the womb in which Achilles
once 'hung curled in a dream of pre-existence' (3). The focalisation moves
seamlessly from an exterior beach scene into the perceiving mind-in-the-
body of Achilles. Achilles is described alternatively as 'fighter' and 'farmer',
drawn to what appears solid as well as to what is 'shifting and insubstantial'.
As becomes evident when he encounters Priam as an intruder in his guarded
camp, Achilles, in Malouf's rendition, can find his 'hard, manly qualities'
suspended by a 'fluidity' that is usually obscured (172). Then his mind opens

through his bodily senses to moods and images that expand the parameters of what he experiences in the present moment.

Achilles' sense of himself is desperately conflicted by his anguish at Patrocles' death – a death he met in place of Achilles. In Malouf's earlier story, 'Ulysses, or The Scent of the Fox' (*Untold Tales* 47–58), he suggests that part of Achilles' grief is caused by another important loss. He has seen that Patrocles could imitate him in the field of battle 'so perfectly that even the gods were taken in' (57):

> Would he ever again be able to play himself without thinking of that other performance? Without, in an anxious way, trying to live up to it, if only before himself? (57)

The role of warrior and hero has been an essential element in Achilles' narrative of the self. To die nobly in battle is an ideal death, according to this code, bringing remembrance in stories and legends ever after. The prospect of such a death brings to Achilles 'a perfect order of body, heart, occasion' as he looks again, after Priam's successful appeal, at Hector's body and sees there 'the enactment ... of the true Achilles, the one he has come all this way to find' (190).

For Achilles there is 'between identity and narration ... a tenacious relation of desire' (Cavarero, 32). He longs for his story as hero to be fulfilled, even at the cost of his life, as prophecies have intimated. Yet Malouf also features Achilles' roles of son to Peleus and father to Neoptolemus who has grown to maturity without him and both are drawn upon at the crucial moment of Achilles' encounter with Priam (173-87). Family succession and affections, as well as warrior traditions, need to be acknowledged to shape a fuller life for Achilles. During his meeting with Priam, Malouf gives Achilles an experience that reveals the permeable borders of his identity and its basis in feeling:

> A figure, as yet, all hovering vagueness, has begun to take shape there
> ... The great Achilles, eyes aswarm, is weeping. With a cry he falls on
> one knee, and leans out to clasp his father's robe. ... Achilles, startled,
> looks again. The man is a stranger. Noble, yes, even in his plain robe,
> but not at all like Peleus. What tricks the heart can play! ... but for half a

hundred beats of his heart his father had been truly present to him, and
he continues now to feel tenderly vulnerable to all those emotions in him
that belong to the sacred bond. (172-74)

In book twenty-four of *The Iliad*, it is Priam who kneels first to Achilles
and reminds him of Peleus' love for him. Malouf's change here is purposeful
in having Achilles kneel to Priam because of a perceived image – half-real,
half-dream – that 'strikes him first as a startling of his blood' (172). In a
further crucial alteration by Malouf, it is of Achilles' affection for his son,
Neoptolemus, that Priam speaks first, a surprise that moves Achilles further
towards compassion when Priam appeals for the return of Hector's body.
It also brings a further vision of Achilles' own death, of Priam's murder
and Neoptolemus' revenge for his father's death after the fall of Troy. It
is Achilles' look of 'annihilating revelation' as he envisions a 'fireball' of
destruction (186) crashing on them all that makes Priam, in turn, kneel
before him in 'fellow-feeling' (187) and clasp Achilles' hand. They will
share mortality; they are not gods (184). Priam reminds Achilles that they
are creatures placed between the animal and the immortals but should
express their higher nature as 'children of the gods, not ravening beasts'
(183). The compromised, complex nature of the human is their lot, as are
their violent deaths, but in a realm where neither animal nor god reigns
human honour expressing fellow-feeling may shine.

Malouf's narrative style seek to place these moments between Achilles and
Priam out of the daily flow of the temporal, an effect largely brought about
by his extensive interweaving of flashback, flash-forward and dilation (or
digression), as found, for example, in the evocation of Achilles' perceptions
as Priam approaches (185–86). Past and present, far and near seem woven
together, crossing the borders of everyday experience and evoking their
permeability (paragraph 4, 185, for example).

Priam, too, is given a fuller interior life in Malouf's treatment. His grief
at Hector's slaughter and bodily desecration by Achilles raises memories
that show a long-felt conflict of identity in the apparently confident king.
As Malouf notes in the 'Afterword', the details of how a child named
Podarces becomes Priam ('the ransomed one' or 'the price paid') and

King of Troy is noted only in a brief passage about Hercules' labours in a work from around the first century BC called *The Library*, a history of mythology (223). Malouf offers an expanded view over thirteen pages of Priam's childhood, framed as a tale he tells to his wife, Hecuba. It is story 'at whose mid-point his own small life was suspended' (63) by warfare, reflecting Malouf's own sense as a child in Brisbane that World War II was an 'unfinished story' impacting his own emotions and future ('Afterword', 223.) Son of Laomedon, King of Troy, Podacres is hidden among lower class and slave children when his city is invaded. In imagination ever since he has lived the life of slavery that he seemed destined to follow at that moment when his sister, Hesione, saved him. However, he never really feels released. He knows what it means 'to be one of those who have no story that will ever be told' and feels that his escape was only because 'the gods had relented' (75). His life has been in the hands of a larger agency and he cannot forget it. It remains in his body as a smell 'in my armpits, on my hands' (75), a further evocation of mind-in-the-body as the locus of personal experience. He has always felt a weakness which he names 'this *lack* in me' (77). Priam's decision to go to Achilles 'stripped of all glittering distractions and disguises' (79) will allow him to act as a more vulnerable person than the role of the renowned and venerated King of Troy has permitted. It is his *chance*, a concept new to his thinking, a move in the novel from the classical towards a modern view of the human.

As Caroline Alexander observes in her study, *The War that Killed Achilles*, Zeus' directives in *The Iliad*, communicated through Thetis to Achilles and the goddess Iris to Priam, 'provide both stricken men with the means to transcend their grief according to their own almost forgotten natures' (203). Malouf, too, builds on this foundation and shows the motivation for a temporary reconciliation coming from the characters' recognition that they share a common humanity that is released when the moment is sufficiently open to the otherness each has denied. Priam needs to reconcile with the lost child that he has suppressed and Achilles to touch the maternal, fluid side of his nature. In *Ransom* the stories of these major characters gain authenticity as they each learn from experience, finding words to speak of hard lessons and acknowledge feelings. Such stories, it is implied, will survive and form a basis for a civilization's identity when they are grounded in what is personal and subjective as well as what is outward in heroic deeds, qualities Malouf admires in *The Iliad*. He discusses the importance of sustaining a subjective, interior life in *On Experience* (54-76) in terms of twentieth century writing that defies the silence imposed by totalitarian regimes.

Such an emphasis on learning from moments when personal experience opens a way to fresh perceptions is significant in Malouf's poetry and prose generally. He explains his view of how experience is acquired in terms that resonate strongly across his own works:

> How much of what we experience is direct – the impinging on our senses of actual objects, phenomena, events – and how much comes in a more oblique and subliminal way? In flashes of intuition or insight. As glimpses of a reality we had not known we had hit upon till it was there in our head, glimpses we get while we are 'looking away'. Or from what otherworld we are in when we are asleep and dreaming (*On Experience* 3–4)

The importance of both outward and inward perceptions is clear across Malouf's work, from the selection of his poems published as 'Interiors' in *Four Poets* (1962) to *Typewriter Music* (2007) where the poem 'Ombrone' notably expresses a desire 'to be at once/ in two minds and the crossing/ made without breaking borders':

> Of trees, their lucent shadow
> on water, each leaf
>
> remade, tumultuous drops
> of light coalescing.
>
> to be at once
> in two minds and the crossing
>
> made with breaking
> borders, this

the one true baptism, flames
by water

undoused, and sound by silence (43)

Water, the element symbolised by Achilles' mother, Thetis, is celebrated here, the element that 'accepts, in a moment of stillness' reflections of tree and leaf (*Ransom* 4), while producing the shiny yet dark 'lucent shadow' in the imagination of the one who perceives. The imagery of the poem offers a synaesthetic whirlpool of brightness, a tumult where flame and water, sound and silence coexist as suspended opposites. Such reconciliation occurs as the poet allows forces that oppose each other in the outer world to wrestle within the poetic imagination and find at least a momentary re-balancing through the images and rhythms of poetic language. In this regard, Malouf's concern for the present use of poetic imagination can be placed in the context of a poet who has been very influential for him, Wallace Stevens, who speaks of 'a violence within that protects us from a violence without' and of imagination 'pressing back against the pressure of reality' (36). As Seamus Heaney suggests, extending Stevens' thought in his lecture *The Redress of Poetry*:

> If our given experience is a labyrinth, then its impassability is countered
> by the poet's imagining some equivalent of the labyrinth and bringing
> himself and us through it. (3)

The open attentiveness of characters in *Ransom* to the natural world and to the spirit which 'feed[s] our bodies' is suggested in a poem such as 'Preludes':

> … a few free
> performances divert
> the air, so easily dented since it gives
> and gives more than we need
> of it to feed our bodies with its blue, or
> our spirit with what trickles
> up, invisible, as things push through out to themselves
> to the far side of the picture. (*First Things Last* 8–9)

Ways of knowing based deeply within the interaction of body, mind and nature are important aspects of awareness for many key characters in his novels such as Ovid in *An Imaginary Life* who seeks to know the language of spiders, the life of flowers and birds and to learn from a Wild Child caught among deer and wolves in the forest. Janet McIvor in *Remembering Babylon* has her body enveloped by bees to become the 'bride' of the swarm (142) and Jim Sadler in *Fly Away Peter* loves like an animal the very dirt into which, as a dying soldier, his body will fall:

> The earth smelled so good. It was a smell that belonged to the beginning of things, he could have put his nose down in it like a pig or newly weaned calf, and the thought of filling his hands with its doughy softness was irresistible. (126)

In noting Malouf's many images of the human embracing the earth and the animal, as well as the recurrence of the unexpected 'stranger' who 'taps our shoulder and we turn' ('Towards', *Typewriter Music* 77), we must now consider the new character Malouf introduces into his appropriation of the classic epic: the carter, Somax, who acts for a day as Priam's herald, who is always named Idaeus, during the king's otherwise solitary quest. Somax brings into the reader's focus the everyday world that exists in tandem with the world of kings and heroes. Somax and his black mules, Beauty and Shock, provide a balance of comic pastoral to the tragic mood of the narrative to that point. Their names, too, assert the presence in a courtly world dominated by 'psyche' (the mind and soul) of a more rustic 'soma', the Greek word for 'body', and of an aesthetic appreciation, suggested in Beauty's name, that includes the animal and traditionally 'lower' orders of life (Smith 2009b). The name Shock, too, highlights the element of surprise that has invaded the closely-guarded borders of possible ways of acting in the Trojan court, giving a counter image to the physical sense of shock felt by Priam and his family when he behaves so unexpectedly. His choice of a plain mule cart and driver brings his prophetic dream to life and when Somax and his mules enter the courtyard to prepare for the journey to the Greek camp they play the role of threshold characters, crossing an opening in a worldview as much as a physical space in a palace. They come from the margins to show that the permeable borders of the human are spaces of possibility. When, during the journey, Somax coaxes Priam to refresh himself by bathing his feet in a stream and eating a pikelet cooked by Somax's daughter-in-law, the balance of psyche and soma is enhanced. Priam seems disembodied by his kingly role and re-gains a more holistic sense of identity as he journeys to claim a body closely linked with his own: that of his son, Hector.

An alternative way of the narrating the self is made available in *Ransom* after the appearance of Somax. He values his name and is reluctant to become Idaeus. His name represents his life story so far, a narrative that he values despite his experience of poverty and the heartache of losing his wife and five children:

> It guarantees the breath that passes in and out of his mouth … is the name
> … under which he has conducted himself. (98)

Unlike Achilles for whom a prime motivation is the prospect of his heroic actions being narrated by others, or for Priam the hope of legends being told about his kingship and retrieval of Hector's body, Somax is motivated by a desire to tell and to hear his own story in the present: 'He thinks of what his cronies at the tavern will have to say of this' (96). For him, identity is not conflicted in the way it is for Priam and Achilles. His recognises the role of the animal and the gods as intrinsic to his bodily life (96, 98–99).

Cavarero argues that the disguised Ulysses weeps to hear his story told by the rhapsode in *The Odyssey* because he feels in a new way his own uniqueness. At that moment, his story 'belongs to him as an irrefutable aspect of his life, not as a guarantee of *post mortem* fame' (33). An alternative voicing of the self is offered to Ulysses linking his actions to an ongoing experience rather than the hero's death. While Achilles and Priam both focus on the deaths that await them in the epic frame of action, Somax focuses on the details of his life – his granddaughter who has been ill, for example. He becomes the companion on the hero's journey, a familiar role in quest literature through the ages, but he desires above all to return to his own life after one day and night of adventure. And he lives to tell his story, though often not believed in the tavern.

If the function of myth, as Elizabeth Baeten argues, is to 'demarcate what belongs to the truly human and what does not' (38, quoted in Bliss 726), then Malouf's appropriation and re-imagination of the myth of Troy seems motivated by a desire to highlight ethical qualities of human behaviour, especially those attributes that allow humans to redress habits that lead to repeated wars, conflicts and intolerance. He gives Priam the belief that 'the thing that is needed to cut this knot we are all tied in is something that has never before been done or thought of … something *new*' (58). Malouf's approach to myth has a double edge in this regard, as Carolyn Bliss has pointed out in her discussion of *An Imaginary Life* and *Remembering Babylon* (731–32). While recognising the power of myth to act as a conservative force that sustains an existing worldview and forbids change to what seems socially 'naturalised', Malouf also values the dynamic forces within human creativity that bring myth into being in the first instance. Such myths forge relationships between the human and the Other that are essential for our being at home in the world. By recognising the intertextuality of any myth-making, Malouf presents in *Ransom* a way to work outside the entrapment of the mythical even while celebrating its role in story-making.

Such a dualistic approach to myth is highlighted in *Ransom* by the other presence that accompanies Priam and Somax on their journey, one that influences the modulation in voice from the formal, epic tone of Priam to the novelistic chatter of Somax (a reminder of Bakhtin's distinctions, in this regard). The travellers encounter the god Hermes in a grove as they rest and both come under his influence in subtle ways. For Priam, accustomed to gods emerging in his dreams, Hermes provides safety and guidance as the cart laden with treasure crosses the threshold of the fortified camp of Achilles. His touch as a god who facilitates interpretation and communication is also felt as Priam speaks with Achilles, the sound of the lyre softening the 'madness' in Achilles and opening him to an awareness of his more compassionate nature. For Somax, Hermes seems at first a nuisance and a threat, but he softens too as his cart and mules find safe passage through a situation of extreme personal danger. For Hermes is the god of heralds, even a reluctant one like Somax/Idaeus. He is the guide in liminal places like travellers' roads and resting places, the edge of camps and the borderlands between life and death, all places featured in *Ransom*. Interestingly, he is also the god of herds and the breeding of mules, a strong reason for his prompt accord with Beauty and his naming her 'one of the true servant of the gods' (150).

The focus of the novel is certainly on Priam's quest and Achilles response, an encounter that allows each man to deal with his grief that, as Alberto Manguel observes, 'must be resolved in its confrontation with its mirror grief, a resolution more compelling that the demands of war' *(The Australian,* 1 April 2009). However, the final pages of the novel give attention to the way Somax comes to be regarded as a 'stealer of other men's tales' (124), a further link with Hermes, a trickster and thief by reputation. The stories Somax tells of his remarkable journey are engaging but must surely involve deceit, his hearers believe. How could a local cart driver have met the great Achilles or helped a king of a city that no longer exists? Ironically, only the attractiveness of his black mule, Beauty, seems credible and long-remembered. Perhaps she, too, will be the source of another story. Somax acquires a conflicted identity for his hearers as he spins his yarns. Is he Idaeus or just Somax? A connection between narrative, imagination and deceit is an intriguing theme for Malouf to highlight at this stage in the novel. As I have discussed elsewhere, such a theme is found in his poetry from the early 1960s beginning with 'Footnote for a Bestiary' and in subsequent poems such as 'The Crab Feast' and fiction such as *Johnno* and *Child's Play* (2009a, 167–81.) With his obvious belief in the power of stories, Malouf offers in the conclusion of *Ransom* a purposely discomforting scepticism that questions the double-edged 'craft' of tales and their tellers, including, by implication, his own art. It implies a need to recognise the ethical limits of story-telling which are perhaps, after all, those of the human, of the story-tellers themselves.

In this regard, Malouf is perhaps choosing to align the art of narrative with the characteristics of Hermes. His use of the omniscient narrator whose voice can move seamlessly across borders of time past, present and future gives a strong sense of trust to the reader, great confidence in the hand that guides the pen, the voice and breath that weaves the tale in the listener's ear. Such an approach to narrative relies on engendering belief. Its aim is enchantment, like the sound of the lyre in Achilles' tent. It belongs to the interpreter and translator of messages that cross the permeable borders of the human but perhaps also to one who is a master of hidden crafts, like the writer. Just as Hermes can use illusions and tricks as he guides mortals across borders of all kinds, so the narrator can engage his skills to create impressions of things that might otherwise strain belief. The extreme, the irrational and the magical find their place within a 'reality' the story-world creates and they bring, it seems, their revelations and comfort in *Ransom* as well as their dangers if relied on to excess. It is the balance that creates the human in all its complexities.

In writing in a lyrical style from the margins of epic, Malouf emphasises the intertextual nature of his own enterprise and that of story-telling across human generations. He is aware of its power and also of its boundaries. If stories are made, as Rowlands suggests, for 'credulous animals', what people are telling each other and believing and why are questions of continuing importance to the Humanities and the well-being of human societies worldwide. As the Humanities are re-shaped in these times, Malouf's works offers direction by highlighting the importance of studying writers who explore through imagination alternative paths through the labyrinths of human experience. To do so, as Malouf does very effectively, with a keen awareness of the embodied nature and potential deceptions of the imagination's own working is particularly important if the lyrical voice, in poetry and prose, is to assert its place among the competing discourses of this century.

Works Cited

Alexander, Caroline. The War That Killed Achilles: The True Story of Homer's Iliad and the Trojan War. London & New York: Viking/Penguin, 2009

Baeten, Elizabeth M. The Magic Mirror: Myth's Abiding Power. Albany: State U of New York P, 1996.

Bliss, Carolyn. 'Reimagining the Remembered: David Malouf and the Moral Implication of Myth.' World Literature Today 74.4 (Autumn 2000): 725–732

Cavarero, Adriana. Relating Narratives: Storytelling and Selfhood. 1997. London & New York: Routledge, 2000

Haraway, Donna J. Simians, Cyborgs, and Women: The Reinvention of Nature. London: Free Association Books, 1991

Heaney, Seamus. The Redress of Poetry: An Inaugural Lecture delivered before the

University of Oxford on 24 October 1989. Oxford: Clarendon Press, 1990

Malouf, David. 'Interiors'. Four Poets. Melbourne: F. W. Cheshire, 1962

———. Johnno. St Lucia: U of Queensland P, 1975

———. An Imaginary Life. New York: Braziller, 1978

———. First Things Last. St Lucia: U of Queensland P, 1980

———. Fly Away Peter. London: Chatto and Windus, 1982

———. Child's Play. London: Chatto and Windus, 1982

———. The Great World. London: Chatto and Windus, 1990

———. Remembering Babylon. Sydney: Chatto and Windus/ Random House, 1993

———. Untold Tales. Sydney: Paper Bark Press / AHRF, 1999

———. Typewriter Music. St Lucia: U of Queensland P, 2007

———. On Experience. Melbourne: Melbourne UP, 2008

———. Ransom. Sydney: Knopf/Random House, 2009

———. 'Men and Gods Behaving Badly', The Australian Literary Review 4:2 March 2009: 3–4.

Manguel, Alberto. 'Malouf the Master of Imaginary Lives', review of *Ransom. The Australian*, April 1 2009.

Rowlands, Mark. *The Philosopher and the Wolf*. London: Granata, 2008

Smith, Yvonne. 'Hunter or Hunted? David Malouf's Poetic of the Human and Inhuman', *Southerly* 69.1 (2009): 167–181. Based on a paper presented at the AULLA Conference U. of Sydney February 2009

———. 'Beauty's Clear, Round Eye', a review of the role of the animal in David Malouf's *Ransom*, Long Paddock 4, *Southerly* 69.1 (2009). <www.brandl.com.au/southerly/>

Spence, Sarah. *Texts and Self in the Twelfth Century*. Cambridge: Cambridge UP, 1996

Stevens, Wallace. 'The Noble Rider and the Sound of Words.' In his *The Necessary Angel: Essays on Reality and the Imagination*. New York: Vintage, 1951. Pp. 1–36

Taylor, Andrew. 'David Malouf, History and an Ethics of the Body.' In *Imagining Australia: Literature and Culture in the New, New World*. Edited by Judith Ryan and Chris Wallace-Crabbe. Cambridge, MA: Harvard University Committee on Australian Studies, Harvard UP, 2004. Pp. 67–81

Tulip. James. *David Malouf: Johnno, Short Stories, Poems, Essays and Interview*. St Lucia: U of Queensland Press, 1990

Chapter 11

Displacing Geographies of Memory: The Australian and New Zealand Memorials, London

Matthew Graves
University of Provence (Aix-Marseille Université)

We commonly think of monuments and memorials as objects in or of the landscape, inscribing selected memories in place and investing their sites with secular or sacred meaning. The siting of the Australian War Memorial in the federal capital is a familiar case in point: the alignment of Mount Ainslie and Capital Hill with the New and Old Parliament Houses, connected by Anzac Parade, with Lake Burley Griffin a mirror image *grandeur nature* of the Pool of Reflection between the parentheses of the Captain Cook Memorial Jet and the National Carillon, offers a spectacle linking the national war memorial to the seats of government, past and present, while making a symbolic statement about service and sacrifice in war, their relation to democratic institutions and the values of the nation. There is a performative dimension to this memorial geography. The motorist, diverted down Kings Avenue or Commonwealth Avenue, is in no position to align the distant landmarks and perceive the overall pattern. The connection can only be made from certain vantage points: the panorama on Mount Ainslie; the steps of the Australian War Memorial, or New Parliament House; or for Anzac Day marchers, in the course of the ascent of Anzac Parade.

Formative and Framing Geographies

This 'secularized sacred geography' (Johnson 7) with its aspirations towards mapping a national identity is geography as the *trompe-l'oeil* of history. The chronology of the memorial landscape's construction – its omissions, elisions and anachronisms – is invisible to the naked eye; the landscape conceals as much as it reveals. Though conceived in 1917 and approved by Cabinet in 1923, the Australian War Memorial was not opened until 1941 (McKernan 2), fourteen years after the Old Parliament, twenty-three years after the Armistice and almost a full half-century before the inauguration in 1988 of the new Federal Parliament building, which now dominates the capital's skyline. Anzac Parade, albeit central to Walter Burley Griffin's original 1912 plan for the ceremonial axis of Canberra, was not opened until 1965, twenty-four years after the Australian War Memorial.[1] While the city's memorial sites are not 'nested' chronologically in the landscape, they combine *chorologically* to create the illusion of continuity and order.[2] The conflicts and battles they commemorate were not fought here, but they have been symbolically repatriated and replanted here at the heart of the national community. Just as those which were fought here – the frontier wars – have been occluded or displaced by the supplanting geography.[3] The resultant memorial landscape is a patchwork assemblage, subject to accretion, erosion and reorientation over time. The twelve memorial stations on Anzac Parade[4] – from the Australian Hellenic Memorial (1988) to the projected Peacekeepers' Memorial (to be opened on 14 September 2012)[5] – were conceived between 1968 and 2007, by diverse agencies responding to particular political opportunities, in no pre-ordained sequence. Perhaps surprisingly, given the Keating government's record of commemorative activism, half of the memorial niches were filled at the initiative of the earlier Hawke governments.

Social scientists recognise that memory is in essence a political space: it is one of the fundamental insights of anthropology that the group comes together around a territory, that the polity is rooted in a shared home.

> In all societies, names and significant features of places are important
> means of discriminating and representing points of reference for spatial

orientation. Individuals must know where they have been and will be in order to get from one place to another. They also need to maintain a sense of self-continuity, so that past actions are connected with those in the present and future. (Haviland 333)

Notwithstanding its social construction, place is topographically grounded and is the portal to the imagined geographies of the community. In contemporary historical study, the outstanding problem is how to account for the ambivalent relationship of 'sites of memory' to the spaces which found and frame them, be they physical or figurative. Pierre Nora's *lieux de mémoire* are essentially 'a-geographical' (Sorkin xi) in their abstraction from place. Indeed, Nora allows that the three volumes of his eponymous work have since their publication (1984–1992) come to compose a place of memory of their own: as an inventory of the *hauts-lieux* of the nation and depository of the collective imaginary, they have participated in, as much as they have accounted for, 'the era of commemoration' (Nora, 2008, 34). The attendant paradox is that memory has become a dominant preoccupation among historians and in society at large just as the collective memories transmitted by traditional communities have been showing signs of decline. Significantly, Nora's dating of the 'collapse of memory' is roughly contemporaneous with Edward Relph's identification of the 'loss of place' and the progression of placelessness in modern society (Relph 117–121) – a concept extended by anthropologist Marc Augé to the 'supermodern' *non-lieux*, the ersatz spaces of consumer society (Augé 1992) – so that a loss of memory and place are seen to proceed apace as a condition of late modernity, imposing a duty of remembrance and reconstruction upon the historian, while imparting a sense of urgency to his/her mission to locate, compile and conserve pasts neglected, repressed or forgotten.[6]

In *Geographies of Remembrance*, Nuala Johnson suggests that two overlapping and complementary spatialities are at work within the memorial process: 'If memory is conceived as a recollection and representation of times past, it is equally a recollection of spaces past where the imaginative geography of previous events is in constant dialogue with the current metaphorical and literal spatial setting of the memory-makers' (Johnson 6). These we might term 'formative' and 'framing' geographies: on one hand, 'recollections of spaces past,' geographies grounded in real locations (such as battlefields and theatres of conflict) but imaginative in so far as they are finite, constructed and reproducible; on the other, landscapes of memorial reception and inscription, at varying degrees of spatial and temporal remove from their models. The two geographies are neither partitioned nor partitionable, but are coeval and operate as mirror images of each other, so that the landscapes of Anzac Cove and Ataturk Entrance at Albany (Western Australia) may be seen as exogenic and endogenic aspects of a single memorial space (Inglis, 2008, 521–2), albeit one separated by thousands of miles of continents and oceans. Accordingly, Peter Hoffenberg underlines the mimetic character of Australia's memorial landscapes; how they draw upon images of 'Australia's dream topographies,' so that Anzac Cove recalls 'the first European settlements on the south-eastern shore' and the Western Front 'the Outback's rugged, blank slate' (Hoffenberg 7).

In this way, the revival of war memorialism in the era of 'the memory boom' (Winter 1) has fashioned 'a distinct political landscape' (Mayo 62) out of the dialogue between the spaces of Australia's past and the imperatives of its present political geography. The popularity of the commemorative rituals associated with this revival – Anzac Day, Remembrance Day, Battle for Australia Day, and anniversaries in-between – might in part be ascribed to their capacity to restore meaning to the landscapes of 'the placeless society,'[7] to articulate a resurgent sense of place in a globalizing world and give it political voice, in the sense derived by Denis Cosgrove from the etymology of the term landscape: *landschaft* – a community of rights, or polity (Cosgrove 61).

In Fields now Foreign: The Australian War Memorial, London

Against the background of a burgeoning 'memorial diplomacy' begun in the Hawke era, but given a distinctly Anglo-American orientation during the Howard years, the Australian War Memorial London (AWML) is a recent overseas addition to Australia's capital monuments, in 'fields now foreign' to adapt Inglis' phraseology (Inglis, 1998, 6), at the heart of the former imperial capital. The monument is a striking interpolation in the syntax of London's memorial landscape.[8] Located on Hyde Park Corner, on the processional route connecting Wellington Arch, Buckingham Palace and the Admiralty Arch via the Mall, it is surrounded by earlier war memorials, including the Royal Artillery Monument and the Machine Gun Corps' statue of David. The parkland site, which is effectively a 1.5 hectare traffic island in the densely built environment of the city centre, was donated by Westminster City Council. The memorial was commissioned by English Heritage from the Sydney architect Peter Tonkin and artist Janet Laurence, who had previously designed the Vietnam Veterans Memorial on Anzac Parade Canberra and the Tomb of the Unknown Soldier at the Australian War Memorial. Their winning design is a landform, a curvilinear wall of stone, made from imported grey-green Australian granite; it rises like a wave, espousing the contours of Hyde Park Corner and creating an amphitheatre of contemplative space.[9] Architect Peter Tonkin chose the stone to embody the spirit of the Bush[10] and designed the form of the memorial to symbolize 'the sweep of the Australian landscape, the breadth and generosity of our people, the openness that we believe should characterise our culture' (Dedication Service booklet 15). It was formally dedicated on 11 November 2003 by John Howard in the company of Queen Elizabeth II and Prime Minister Tony Blair, symbolically bringing the 'dream topographies' of Australia 'back home' to the former imperial city, in an exercise in memorial diplomacy as much about reaffirming common cause in conflicts present (Iraq, Afghanistan) as about commemorating the wartime alliances of the past. Consequently, the ceremony turned on the elision of the site's formative and framing geographies: 'Your memory hallowed in the land you loved' (5), in the words of the dedicatory hymn to the Australian dead, which rhetorically begs the question 'which land, which love; nation or Empire'?

The originality of the AWML lies in its attempt to offer a contemporary response to the crisis of representation which faced the war memorial genre after the indiscriminate slaughter of the trenches of the First World War and the huge military and civilian loss of life of the Second World War: namely, how to reconcile the representation of human loss and suffering on an unpredented scale with a recognition of the inhumanity of war and a postmodern scepticism towards the very principle of monumentality? Working within the environmental constraints set by English Heritage – to shelter the site from traffic and to use water and stone to match the surrounding monuments and buildings; and a logistical imperative – to complete the monument within 12 months of contract, by Armistice Day November 2003 (a precipitation which betrays a political imperative), the architects sought to satisfy the functional requirements of the war monument as a ceremonial site while attempting to bridge the 'memory gap' between the surviving veterans of World War Two, represented at the inauguration, and the young Australians and Britons with no direct experience of global conflict who were expected to form the majority of the memorial's public. They set out to do so, firstly, by adopting an organic asthetic, 'a land–art earthy materiality' in the words of Paul Walker's review of the memorial for *Architecture Australia*, describing the embrace of the site's topography; the curvature of the wall suggesting gum leaves and boomerangs; the gentle rise of the wall itself and the 'redemptive qualities' of the water flowing over the stone-work; the broad sweep of the landform opposing Australian openness to the object-in-the-landscape conventionality of the neighbouring monuments (Walker). At the same time the designers strain to recall more conventional monumental forms: the planar slabs of stone which compose the wall evoke the headstones of a cemetery.

A second, complementary design strategy was to dispense with the tradition of the roll of honour, as seen in the cloisters surrounding the Court of Honour and the Pool of Reflection at the Australian War Memorial Canberra, or in innumerable local memorials throughout Australia, New Zealand and Britain, thereby circumventing the need to find room for the 101,000 names of the fallen by substituting 24,000 place names, one for each of the home towns of the enlisted. The toponyms range in scale from the 'iconically Australian' (np.), Fremantle, Perth, Toowoomba; to the local, including the suburbs and 'villages' of Sydney – Ashfield, Stanmore, Annandale; to the global in reach: Marseille, three times, with an 's,' without an 's,' even with a second 'a.' Some are voluntarily *anachoristic*: German or Japanese toponyms are presented as a corrective to the race patriotism of earlier memorial tradition and prompt recollections of immigration (John

Monash's Germanic origins, for instance) as well as of wartime internment. The effect of the emphasis on the plurality of place is to dilute and blur the attributes of nationality, just as the occurrence of place-names in indigenous Australian languages alongside more familiar toponyms from the British Isles can be seen as a call for 'tolerance' and geographical 'inclusion' (np.). This is at the initial level of perception. Viewed at a distance, the design incorporates a hologram effect whereby the inscriptions overlap and combine to reveal a bigger picture: 47 battle sites from both wars are etched out in large serif font and superimposed over the place names. The battle sites were chosen to represent the full geographical reach of Australia's theatres of conflict, from Europe to the Asia-Pacific region via the Mediterranean and North Africa, including one town on the Australian mainland, Darwin (Australian War Memorial London 9-11), whose inclusion implicitly validates the existence of a 'Battle for Australia' in 1941–42.

The late addition of the AWML to Australia's memorial landscape, 85 years after it was first proposed and 58 years after the end of the Second World War raises two issues related to the post-repatriation memorial landscape. Why now at the beginning of the new millenium, so far removed from the events commemorated; and why 'over there,' at the heart of the Old Empire and Commonwealth when British-Australia is a distant memory? It is true that with the exception of the 2nd AIF United Kingdom Force Memorial in Wiltshire, there was no major monument commemorating Australian's contribution to the Great War or Second World War on British soil.[11] Equally, there was no precedent for locating an Australian overseas war memorial in a foreign capital; the AWML is the only case to date. In his dedication speech, John Howard underlined the sense of shared home in the choice of location: 'It will join the thousands of other memorials in Australian towns and cities and settlements once called home by our soldiers, sailors, airmen and servicewomen' (Howard np.). What is surely unique about the AWML is this iteration, or duplication of the commemorative function of the Australian War Memorial Canberra overseas, which was so strenuously resisted for 85 years. After all, as Michael McKernan observes in his history of the Australian War Memorial, it was the determination to *avoid* memorial duplication and prevent Australian war records and relics from being subsumed within and subordinated to the National (and later Imperial) War Museum in London that drove forward Charles Bean's vision of an independent Australian museum-cum-memorial (McKernan 39–42).

The decision to build the memorial predates the Invasion of Iraq and the events of 9/11. It was taken at a meeting of the Australian and British Prime Ministers in London on 4 July 2000 during John Howard's visit to celebrate the centenary of Australian federation and in an indication that the project was an Australian initiative, it was announced by Howard in a door-step interview at Number 10 Downing Street. The declared objective was to provide a focus for Anzac Day commemorations in Britain. Its commemorative constituency was broadly defined to encompass Australians of all services who died 'in direct defence of Britain during World War II … and on other occasions and also generally to Australians who died fighting alongside the British in the various wars in the last century' (Howard, 2000, np.). While 'various' presumably meant all wars fought in alliance with Britain (and implicitly excludes Vietnam), Howard placed particular emphasis on the Second World War. This might be read as an attempt to challenge the near monopoly of the Labor Party over WWII memory and restore the European valency of Australia's geography of remembrance which had been given a pronounced WWII and Asia-Pacific orientation under Howard's predecessor, Paul Keating. In subsequent speeches at Australia House and at the dedication ceremony of 11 November 2003 the memorial's scope was extended to encompass 'the two great global conflicts of the twentieth century'[12] (Howard, 2003, np).

The addition of the AWML to the Anzac landscape has been discussed at length in the 2008 edition of Ken Inglis' *Sacred Places* and in James Curran's *The Power of Speech* (2004). For Inglis, the AWML demonstrates that the repatriaton of the Unknown Soldier to Canberra in 1993 had not laid to rest the ghost of the old Australian Imperial Force, nor had it quenched the government or the public's appetite for the commemoration of Australia's war history (Inglis, 2008, 535–8). The momentum of the 'memory boom' has carried over unabated into the new millenium, yet John Howard's dedicatory address offers no satisfactory answer to the question 'why now'? Inglis contextualises the memorial, setting the AWML against a background of similar iniatives launched under the Commonwealth banner in the same vicinity: the Canadian Memorial in Green Park, dedicated in 1994; the New Zealand Memorial opened in 2006, an almost mirror image of the Australian on the opposite side of Hyde Park; and the Commonwealth Memorial Gates inaugurated by the Queen in 2002 to honour the contributions of India, Africa and the Caribbean to the diversity of British Society. 'One way and another, the story of these four monuments could be read as a microcosm of imperial and post-imperial history. The Australian is the most conspicuous presence in the landscape of Westminster' (538). Alliance in war, independence in peace-time, migration and multiculturalism provide the common thematic threads in the contemporary Commonwealth extensions to London's memorial landscape.

New Symbols of Nationhood: The New Zealand Memorial, London

Yet, in many ways that 'other conspicuous presence' in Hyde Park, the New Zealand Memorial London (NZML), is anything but 'a mirror image' of its neighbour. It is the dissemblance as much as the proximity between the two which points up the tensions and paradoxes in their formative and framing geographies, between the territorial and the extra-territorial, the imperial and the post-imperial, the national and the global. Opened on 11 November 2006, three years to the day after its Australian counterpart, the New Zealand Memorial conscientiously eschews the word 'War,' although not its associations. While one of the purposes of the Memorial was 'to commemorate the shared sacrifice of New Zealanders in times of war alongside the people of Britain,' in her dedication speech Labor PM Helen Clark insists that the memorial has 'a deeper meaning,' to commemorate the depth and the durability of New Zealand's relationship with Britain and mark their 'shared heritage and values,' from Cook's voyages of discovery to the generational flows of migration between the two islands (Clark np.). The monument is not designed to be a war memorial, but an expression of New Zealand's identity as a 21st century Pacific nation in a globalised world with 'enduring bonds' to the United Kingdom. The official dedication ceremony booklet accordingly titles one chapter 'Where Britain Stands, We Stand,' wartime Prime Minister Michael Savage's declaration of empire solidarity and loyalty (The New Zealand Memorial brochure 10). It finds an echo in the text which adorns the dedication stone of the AWML opposite, taken from Robert Menzies' broadcast to the Australian people on the eve of WWII: 'Whatever burden you are to carry, we also will shoulder that burden'; a quotation chosen by the Howard goverment as a counterpoint to Curtin's 1941 declaration of freedom from the bonds of the British relationship (AWML brochure 14). Like the AWML, the purpose of the New Zealand Memorial is to provide a commemorative gathering place for expatriate New Zealanders in the UK and Europe, especially the young, on Anzac Day and Waitangi Day.

The form of the New Zealand memorial graphically demonstrates that readiness to innovate and imagine 'new symbol(s) of nationhood' (NZML brochure 18) so evident in the national Te Papa Museum in Wellington, but it is a subdued symbolism compared to its Australian neighbour which translates the reticence in Helen Clark's dedication address to acknowledge war as the sole vector of remembrance. The NZML consists of 16 bronze sculptures of varying heights spread out in a formation across Hyde Park. Baptised the 'Southern Stand,' the standards are organised into two groups. Ten are laid out in a diamond-shaped pattern, angled forward, with a 'leader' containing the dedication text; this is the wreath-laying site. The group is reminiscent of a platoon of soldiers advancing; the standards are made of intersecting plates of bronze with resemble the crosses of a military cemetery. They have also been compared to the carved posts around Maori heritage sites, or warrior-sportsmen in a Maori haka, or even to cricketers playing forward. The second group of six standards is set apart from the main group as a celestial counterpoint to the terrestrial theme, assembled in the shape of the Southern Cross constellation, a motif also found on the tomb of the Unknown Warrior in Wellington.

With its 'open-ended' symbolism, the NZML quickly became a flashpoint for political controversy and a medium for contesting interpretations of New Zealand identity. National MP Murray McCully accused the singer Dave Dobbyn, who had been asked by Clark to perform at the opening ceremony, of being 'a Lefty muso' for his choice of the song 'Welcome

Home,' which contains the verse 'the empire is fading by the day.' Allusions to the fading monarchy were deemed 'inappropriate' in the presence of the Queen (Eaton 2).

A more substantive issue was raised in the letters column of the *New Zealand Herald* where under the heading 'So Few Veterans a Poor Show,' the Clark government found itself accused of disrespect towards New Zealanders' record of war service. The government allegedly neglected the veterans' associations when composing the official New Zealand contingent for the dedication ceremony, despite inviting 32 Kiwi veterans to the ceremony, more than to the dedication of the AWML. Rick Barker, the Minister for Veterans Affairs felt obliged to point out that 'the New Zealand Memorial is not exclusively a war memorial', but 'it commemorates the broader relationship between New Zealand and the United Kingdom'; he concluded that the London service had shown 'due respect' to the veterans (Barker np.). The Anzac tradition is not lightly understated on either side of the Tasman Sea. The controversy underlines the sensitivity of departing from the Anzac myth, albeit marginally, and demonstrates the compelling authority of the century-old memorial tradition in both countries. As if in deference to the power of the Anzac myth, Helen Clark's inaugural speech attempts to strike a balance between images of wartime sacrifice and peacetime bonds, which stands in stark contrast to John Howard's war-laden rhetoric and is even at odds with the civic emphasis of the The New Zealand Memorial prospectus and her own foreword (NZML Prospectus 3).

The symbolic significance of the NZML cannot be understood in isolation from the repatriation movement, be it of the New Zealand Unknown Warrior on 11 November 2004, which followed closely in the steps of the decision to build the London monument; or of its model – the repatriation of Australia's Unknown Soldier in 1993 by the Keating government. Indeed, the New Zealand Governor-General's eulogy for the Unknown Warrior owes an undeclared debt of inspiration to Paul Keating's famous eulogy at the funeral service for the Unknown Australian Soldier (Cartwright Np.). Dame Silvia Cartwright was not alone in her admiration for speechwriter Don Watson's rhetorical skills: John Howard is said to have considered Keating's eulogy as one of the finest speeches made by any Australian Prime Minister.[13]

His secret admiration is paradoxical given that Paul Keating's version of Australia's geography of remembrance leaned so heavily towards WWII memory because of his conviction that the memory of the First World War had been hijacked by the Right, while John Howard's own emphasis on UK–Australian comradeship in war and on Australia's traditional Western allies in general can be attributed to his conviction that Keating had diminished the old alliances by his insistence on Australia's Asian identity (Curran 259). Within the all-encompassing Anzac tradition, the repatriation of the remains of the Unknown Soldiers from Westminster Abbey, followed by the symbolic expatriation of the Australian and New Zealand landscapes to London, should be seen as part of a pendular movement – an ongoing dialogue between formative and framing geographies: the body is brought home from fields now foreign; the anonymous plot of remembrance to the Unreturned Soldier is expatriated, filling the memorial hiatus at the heart of post-imperial London.[14]

From Memorial Landscape to Landscape as Monument

The framing of monuments to the war dead in a given geography is a means of draping the human and the transitory in the intemporality of landscape. Of course, that 'timelessness' itself is problematical: the urban, built environment is a palimpsest of landscapes, where memory accumulates or accretes in layers through monuments, museums, street names, memorial squares and plaques, to be displaced, replaced, erased or overlaid in time by new landmarks and memories. With increasing distance from the events, the human figure (if not the humanity) has tended to fade from the representations of war in the late modern memorial landscape. The names on the roll call of the Australian War Memorial Canberra or the Menin Gate transmute into the place names of the AWML which in turn dissolve into the toponyms of battlefields. A year on from the disappearance of the last Australian veteran of Gallipoli, the emblematic figure of the Digger is interred and merges with the landscape. True, the figure is still to be found in contemporary monuments, prominent among them Anzac Bridge in Sydney, where statues of Digger (inaugurated 2000) and Kiwi

(2008) soldiers stand guard astride the entrance to the harbour, but these are exceptions to the trend which materialise an existing feature of the urban memorial landscape – the former Glebe Island Bridge was rebaptised on Remembrance Day 1998 – by evoking associations with the formative geography of Gallipoli and the entrance to the Dardenelles Straits.

Representing the dead has been especially problematical in the Anzac memorial tradition, requiring an extraordinary projection of the geographical imagination when the remains of loved ones could neither be repatriated nor their final resting places visited. The sublimation of the figures of the fallen in the landscape which characterises the AWML and NZML, a decade after the beginning of repatriation movement, finds its corollary in memorial sculptures like Helen Pollock's powerfully evocative exhibit 'Falls the Shadow' at the Auckland War Memorial Museum which depicts the Battle of Passchendaele (Pollock 2009). The fallen are drowning in a sea of mud, their bodies submerged, their flailing outstretched arms transformed into a forest of shattered tree stumps, as war sucks the humanity from the landscape. Similarly, the bronze sculptures of the NZML tilted forward at an angle of 70° to the ground, though suggestive of a platoon of soldiers advancing, are not identifiably human – they could be Maori carved poles delimiting a sacred and communal space. Equally, the feature of the water running over stone and 'dissolving' the names on the AWML is not an isolated innovation, but part of a movement which includes the *Tears on Greenstone* memorial at the New Zealand's National Army Museum at Waiouru, where an interactive multimedia installation is substituted for the conventional stone-engraved roll of honour. These monuments aspire to anonymity in their minerality. The names of the dead are withdrawn from public display; place-name has displaced patronym in the field of memory.

There is evidence of an accompanying trend in international monumentalism to map memory and to represent war through cartographic and the topographic symbols. In the United Kingdom, we might cite the meta-maps of US theatres of operation during WWII at the American War Memorial, Cambridge; in Australia, the topographic map-sculpture of the Sandakan memorial, in Burwood Park (Sydney); in France, the Institut Géographique National's map-inventory of France's battlefields, from the 10th to the 20th centuries, or the French Goverment's *Les Chemins du souvenir* website, with its clickable map of WWI and WWII sites of memory; or the New Zealand Veterans' Affairs department's online map and database of memorial sites. The 'memory map' was one of the themes of Canada Remembers in 1995.

Conclusion

The passing of communicative memory with the death of the last of the Digger and Kiwi veterans of the First World War has arguably made new solutions possible to old representational dilemmas, but it would be premature to conclude that such solutions herald a new memorialism. The reception of the Australian and New Zealand Memorials in London and the politically-charged controversies over their shortcomings suggest a degree of inertia in the field of memory that might be attributed to secular tradition, entrenched practices, and the plurality of memorial agencies (governmental and non-governmental), or more globally to the enduring hold of the Anzac myth and its imaginative geographies on the public imagination. Initiatives like those of Keating or Clark are able to inflect or reorient the geographies of memory to a degree, but not substantially displace the landmarks of the Anzac tradition. The memorial landscape is not a straightforward product of public policy, but a given environment which has shown considerable inertia and resistance to change. The place-based components of the memorial landscape – Gallipoli, Kokoda, Tobruk and points in-between – develop the attributes of free-floating signifiers, resistant to political redefinition, imposing a degree of consensus in the memorial diplomacy of successive governments, even those as markedly different in ideological outlook as Keating and Howard's.

Nevertheless, the construction of the London memorials is evidence of a contemporary shift in commemorative focus, from the monument in the landscape, to the landscape itself as monument; from the remembrance of the fallen to growing emphasis on the study of the inter-generational effects of war on civil society. Beyond immediate political imperatives, the symbolic expatriation of national sites of memory to the former imperial capital coincides with a desire to reassess the heritage of Empire in the globalising, post-imperial world and Australia and New Zealand's places within it.

Works Cited

Augé, Marc. Non-lieux, introduction à une anthropologie de la surmodernité. Paris : Le Seuil, 1992.

Australian War Memorial London brochure, Department of Veterans' Affairs/Office of Australian War Graves, 2003

Barker, Rick. 'London Service Given Due Respect.' New Zealand Herald. 24 November 2006: Np

Clark, Helen. 'Address to the NZ Memorial Dedication Ceremony, Hyde Park Corner London.' Scoop.co.nz. 11 November 2006. Np

Cosgrove, Denis. 'Landscape and Landschaft, Lecture delivered at the 'Spatial Turn in History' Symposium, German Historical Institute, February 19 2004.' German Historical Institute Bulletin 35 (Fall 2004): 57–71

Curran, James. The Power of Speech: Australian Prime Ministers Defining the National Image. Melbourne: Melbourne University Press, 2004

Day, David. Claiming a Continent: A New History of Australia. Sydney : HarperCollins Publishers, 2005

Dedication Service Australian War Memorial London, Department of Veterans' Affairs/ Office of Australian War Graves, 2003

Eaton, Dan. '"Lefty Muso" Dobbyn Blasted by National.' The Press (Christchurch). 18 November 2006: 2

Frug, Gerald E. City Making: Building Communities Without Building Walls. Princeton University Press, 2001

Gilbert, David & Driver, Felix. 'Capital and Empire: Geographies of Imperial London.' GeoJournal 51 (2000): 23–32

Haviland, William A. Anthropology. Orlando, Flo.: Holt, Rinehart, Winston, 5th ed. 1989.

Hoffenberg, Peter H. 'Landscape, Memory and the Australia War Experience, 1915-18.' Journal of Contemporary History 36/1 (2001): 111–131

Howard, John. 'Australia in the World.' Lowy Institute for International Policy, Sydney. 31 March 2005: Np

———. 'Australia at War. Prime Minister John Howard's speech delivered at Australia House in London on November 10 2003.' The Sydney Morning Herald. 11 November 2003: Np

———. 'Transcript of the Prime Minister the Hon John Howard MP's Address at the Dedication of the Australian War Memorial, Hyde Park Corner, London.' Parliament of Australia. 11 November 2003: Np

———. 'Transcript of doorstep interview: site of the Australian War Memorial, Hyde Park Corner, London.' Parliament of Australia. 9 November 2003: Np

———. 'Transcript of the Prime Minister The Hon John Howard MP, Doorstep Interview, 10 Downing Street, London.' 4 July 2000

Inglis, Ken.'Monuments in the Modern City: The War Memorials of Melbourne and Sydney [online].' ANZAC Remembered: Selected Writings by K. S. Inglis. Lack, John (Editor); Inglis, KS (Author); Winter, Jay (Introduction by). Melbourne: University of Melbourne, University of Melbourne history monograph 23, 1998. 171–193

Inglis, KS. 'The Unknown Soldier.' Journal of Australian Studies 60 (1999): 8–17

———. Sacred Places: War Memorials in the Australian Landscape. Melbourne: Melbourne University Press, 2008

Jaisson, Marie.'Temps et espace chez Maurice Halbwachs (1925–1945).' Sciences Humaines, Revue d'histoire des sciences humaines 1 (1999): 163–178

Johnson, Nuala C. Ireland, the Great War and the Geography of Remembrance. Cambridge:

Cambridge University Press, 2003

Mayo, James M. 'War Memorials as Political Memory.' Geographical Review, American Geographical Society 78, 1 (Jan. 1988) : 62–75

McKernan, Michael. Here is their Spirit: A History of the Australian War Memorial 1917–1990. St. Lucia, Queensland: University of Queensland Press/Australian War Memorial, 1991

New Zealand Memorial ANZAC Bridge Dedication 27 April 2008. Ministry of Foreign Affairs and Trade, New Zealand Government, 2008

Nora, Pierre (ed.). Les Lieux de mémoire. Paris : Gallimard, 2001

———. 'Les lieux de mémoire, ou comment ils m'ont échappé.' L'Histoire, n° 331 mai 2008 : 32–35

Pollock, Helen. Falls the Shadow: A sculpture installation to commemorate the 90th anniversary of the Armistice. 11 November – 11 January 2009. Pictorial Gallery Auckland War Memorial Museum, 2008. Web. 31 December 2008

Relph, Edward. Place and Placelessness. London: Pion Ltd, 1976

Sorkin, Michael (ed.). Variations on a Theme Park: The New American City and the End of Public Space. New York: Hill & Wang, 1992

The New Zealand Memorial 11 November 2006 prospectus, New Zealand Ministry for Culture and Heritage, 2006

Walker, Paul. 'Australian War Memorial.' *Architecture Australia* (September-October 2008): Np.

Winter, Jay. 'The Generation of Memory: Reflections on the "Memory Boom" in Contem-porary Historical Studies.' German Historical Institute Bulletin 27 (Fall 2000) : Np

Notes

1   <URL: http://www.nationalcapital.gov.au/visiting/attractions/anzac_parade/> Accessed 04/02/09.

2   Not least through the virtual itinerary proposed by the Anzac Parade Walking Tour: <URL: http://www.nationalcapital.gov.au/index.php?option=com_content&view=ar ticle&id=213:anzac-parade&catid=57:ql-menu-visiting&Itemid=202&limitstart=1> Accessed 09/01/10.

3   For an extended discussion of the imaginative geographies of supplanting societies in the Australian context, see Day.

4   From the earliest to the latest, they range from the Desert Mounted Corps Memorial (1968) to the Peacekeepers Memorial (announced 2007, projected date of completion 14 September 2012).

5   Australian Peacekeeping Memorial Project: <URL: http://www.peacekeepingmemorial. org.au/objectives.php.> Accessed 09/01/10.

6   For Johnson, Halbwachs overlooks the geohistorical aspect of collective memory: 'While Halbwachs is right to socialise the concept of memory his analysis fails to historicise memory and to embrace the notion that the very concept of the 'social' may itself have a history and indeed a geography' (Johnson 3). However, in the last chapter of the 1997 edition of *On Collective Memory*, Halbwachs foregrounds the role of space in defining the experience of the group (Jaisson 171).

7   'Now, as Michael Sorkin argues, people live in "a wholly new kind of city, a city without a place attached to it," one that Sorkin calls the "a-geographical city". Sorkin uses the term to describe the pastiche of highways, skyscrapers, malls, housing developments,

and chain stores – the endless urban landscape of copies without an original – that constitute the place bites (…) of modern America.' (Frug 100).

8   Hereafter referred to as the AWML to distinguish it from its 'parent site,' the Australian War Memorial in Canberra.

9   See Walker's discussion of the design : <URL: >http://www.architecturemedia.com/aa/ aaissue.php?issueid=200309&article=9&typeon=2/>. Accessed 04/02/09.

10 Dedication Service, Australian War Memorial London

11 The wooden triptych in the Samaria room of Westminster Abbey dedicated to the million citizens of the British Empire who died in the Great War details the number of service personnel enlisted from Australia. United Kingdom National Inventory of War Memorials: <URL: http://www.ukniwm.org.uk/server/useSearchSession/1/viewPage/5> Accessed 04/01/09.

12 It is significant that the issue of the return of Aboriginal remains from the UK was agreed at the same discussions: the gesture might be related to the repatriation of the Unknown Soldier in 1993 as part of a broader repatriation movement.

13 I am indebted for the insights which follow to a series of conversations at the University of Sydney in 2008-09 with historian James Curran, the author of *The Power of Speech* (2004), who was serving at the European desk of the Prime Minister's Office at the time of the AWML inauguration.

14 One such model might be the anonymous Plot of Remembrance in Hinsby Park, Annandale (Sydney), which provides a common space for all to mourn, set aside from the War Memorial with its roll call of the names of the fallen. This is not a plot to the Unknown Soldier (there is no body), so much as to the ghost of the Unreturned Soldier, hence the uneasy juxtaposition of collective/public and individual/private remembrance, associating private mourning with public space and rituals.

Chapter 12

Must Humanity Perforce Prey upon Itself? *King Lear*, War, and the Humanities

R. S. White

One of many reasons why Shakespeare's plays continue to speak to modern times through productions and creative adaptations, is their incorporation of several narrative and thematic patterns brought into a unity, each of which can form the basis for a new and timely version. *King Lear* in particular is rich in such overlapping patterns, and as a result the play's significance has differed from critic to critic in country to country and from time to time. The first scene of the play raises expectations of a parable or 'winter's tale' for children, beginning something like, 'A king had three daughters and he asked each of them in turn which loved him most', and from this apparently innocuous starting point unfold consequences that draw on other narratives which in general terms are culturally familiar. One story dwells on sibling rivalries and related dynamics of patriarchal families, both Lear's and Gloucester's. There is also the psychomachia of Lear himself both as king and domestically as *paterfamilias* entering senility and dementia. One tale traces the disintegration of the state, another hinges on sexual love between Edmund and two of the Lear sisters, and yet another on Cordelia as innocent victim in her own refusal to compromise integrity, alongside her complement, the Fool. Concentrating on any one of these – and others – can generate a new interpretation or production which inevitably will differ from all predecessors.

One strand of narrative in *King Lear* which has been critically neglected concerns an issue which perennially threatens humanity, the causes and consequences of war. This theme has significance for the modern world, even, for example, in the eyes of a legal scholar who sees *Lear* 'as a drama that speaks to our current dilemmas' in law and politics (Greenhouse). I shall sketch lines of argument sharply, even starkly, not only for necessary brevity but because I aim to open up subjects for discussion rather than pursue them in any detail. A possible utility lies in suggesting how productions can be based on contemporary preoccupations, since I shall mention modern situations bearing comparison with events and ideas central also to Shakespeare's play but which may not have been perceived clearly in this light. Three issues in particular which are raised in the play as central to war are sadly as alive today as in Shakespeare's time: the divisive nature of ownership and disbursement of property; an ethic or policy of revenge; and the abiding question of where evil comes from.

The Division of the Kingdom

Most wars begin with an assertion of property rights leading to invasion, annexation, insurgent resistance and military occupation, and they end with boundaries redrawn by 'winners' rarely motivated by desire for harmonious communities. Shakespeare in *King Lear* shows that the process on a national scale magnifies the kind of conflict that all too often tears families apart – property rights precipitated by a contested will or other issues of inheritance, and leading to the kind of generational change that happens in the play: 'the younger rises when the old doth fall' (3.3.21). In such cases both Lear's and Gloucester's families provide a microcosm of the state when power is transferred. Lear's initial attempt to devolve power shows him administering his own inheritance rather than waiting for a written will to do so after his death. As the opening line of the play makes clear, he is not thinking of his daughters as monarchs or figures of power, but rather his sons in law, the Dukes of Albany, Cornwall and (he hopes) Burgundy or the king of France. However, the surprising public occasion which he orchestrates is a love test involving his daughters, perhaps to camouflage pre-empting of the more likely potential of 'future strife' between the males. Although critics berate him for inappropriately confusing issues of state and a request for expressions of love within the family - kingship with kinship - in fact there may have been no problem but for Cordelia's reluctance to voice her love in such a political arena. After her disinheritance there are only two slices of the kingdom to be apportioned along arbitrary lines to Goneril and Regan. Both later insist on the legal implications of a transaction in which Lear has willingly abdicated his regal title, powers and territory to them jointly. Their insistence that he disband his retinue of soldiers is not so much an objection to the domestic chaos they cause but due to the fact that they constitute a standing army which Lear may conceivably call upon to regain his power. They underestimate, however, the willingness of the King of France to use his army to re-assert his wife's entitlement to a part of the kingdom. In these ways an apparently domestic incident which has gone wrong turns into a civil war and later an international one concerning succession and inheritance of power in 'Albion'.

Gloucester sees clearly the process that can turn domestic conflict into national, though his astrological diagnosis ignores Lear's human culpability mirrored in the injustice he has partially perpetrated himself as a father and the reciprocal resentment created in one of his sons. Instead, he blames the 'late eclipses in the sun and moon' and fatally misjudges the virtuous one of his sons: '... there's son against father: the king falls from bias of nature; there's father against child. We have seen the best of our time: machinations, hollowness, treachery, and all ruinous disorders, follow us disquietly to our graves' (1.2.86–97). As in Lear's family, the tragic conflict in Gloucester's stems from intentions surrounding future inheritance. Lear ironically hopes that the apparent fairness of dividing his kingdom into three will avert future war, while Gloucester has already decided that despite affection for his first born and illegitimate Edmund, his title and wealth will be inherited by Edgar who, although younger, was born in wedlock. The problem, unrecognised by Gloucester, lies in the resentment sown in Edmund: 'Well then, / Legitimate Edgar, I must have your land ... Edmund the base / Shall top the legitimate' (1.2.15–22).

The actions of two old men concerning the future of their estates will literally drive blood relatives in both families (except only Edgar) violently to the grave. By the end of the play Lear's kingdom is in ruins and there is no clear monarch or route to stability, while Gloucester loses his eyes, one son, and his life, and although his fiefdom devolves as he intended to Edgar, it is at a terrible cost. In both cases, the analogy after war is the policy of 'scorched earth' where there is nothing of value left to invaders or heirs. Albany, in a gesture that ominously repeats Lear's, abdicates and nominates two unqualified, power-sharing successors, an arrangement from which Kent immediately withdraws while Edgar prevaricates. There is no obvious heir, except the one the play's Elizabethan audience would never have wanted, the King of France (White, 1988). The situation is ripe for another civil war or opportunistic war of occupation, a situation which highlights the futility of Lear's intention to pre-empt 'future strife'. The parallel process shown with a relentless logic in Shakespeare's plot and sub-plot has significance not only within warring families but also for the fragile state.

One parallel between the play and the modern world which, so far as I know, has not been noticed, is that Lear's fable-like division of his kingdom into three anticipates a moment in world history when, like the arrogant old king, national leaders – in this case not just one but three – arrogated to themselves the power to carve up the world into three spheres of influence. While not quite 'Four score and upward, not an hour more or less', none of these could claim to be in his 'perfect mind', and some would even say they were 'foolish fond old [men]': Roosevelt was gravely ill and was to die in 1945, Churchill was chronically alcoholic and depressive, while Stalin has been widely regarded as clinically insane. At the 1945 Conferences of Yalta and Potsdam in a transparent sharing out of 'war booty', Eastern Europe was handed to Stalin as the Soviet Union, Western Europe to the European allies; and 'the Far East' to the USA as its military sphere of influence. Whole new states were created, not along ethnic, traditional, historical, linguistic or cultural lines, but according to political and military priorities. Winners rewrite history along Livy's phrase *vae victis* (misery to the defeated), invariably by rewriting state boundaries. These three gentlemen, we may need to remind ourselves, were the ones who put a wall through Berlin intending 'that future strife may be prevented now' by this stratagem. Other such divisions followed. The Security Council of the United Nations in 1948 placed the boundaries of the new state of Israel along lines guaranteed to provoke Arabic hostility, partitioning Palestine and landlocking Israel between Arabic states, Lebanon, Syria, Jordan and Egypt, a situation fiercely contested down to the present despite again the apparent plan to avoid 'future strife'. Whichever 'side' one takes in that tragic situation, at the very least most people can surely agree that the borders are simply in the wrong place. Likewise, Pakistan was created, also in 1948, with imposed boundaries that caused equal offence to Hindus and Muslims, as well as horrendous bloodshed at that time and since. Bangla Desh was created by partitioning India, Bengal and Pakistan, again along ahistorical lines determined by politicians acting uncomfortably like Lear. It was widely believed in the 1930s that the Treaty of Versailles was inexorably leading to WW2, a view which history confirms. The later examples of Korea and Vietnam suggest that since the end of the Second World War 'border disputes' have been precipitated by attempts to impose divisions between north and south, by foreign politicians uncaring of ethnic, historical, and religious factors.

Lear's arbitrary division of his kingdom brings war on Celtic Britain which is not resolved at the play's end. After the violent deaths of his family there remains a power vacuum which seems to point to further bloody conflict between France and whoever is ruthless enough to emerge and assume power in Britain. It is not anachronistic to make such a reading of a Renaissance play text, since, even earlier than Shakespeare, Erasmus had said very similar things about his own world (White, 2008, 111–18) and even unworldly poets have argued since the time Chaucer wrote *Melibee* that a war solves no problems and simply leads to the next (White, 2008, 100–08). Nick de Somogyi has exhaustively traced the military threats facing Shakespeare's England and the redrawing of political maps across Europe (de Somogyi). A reading of *King Lear* which takes into account these contexts can suggest interpretations and innovative performances, just as Ian McKellan's filmed version of *Richard III* was set in Britain in the 1930s, while productions of *The Merchant of Venice* in Germany before, during and after the Holocaust were used to make comments on the situation of Jews (Jahnson). Meanwhile, Janet Suzman's multiracial *Othello* in South Africa was intended as a potent attack on *apartheid* policies (Suzman), and in the 1980s actors carried *Macbeth* from village to village in other African states as guerrilla condemnation of their own tyrannical rulers whose power, significantly, was a distant consequence of nineteenth century 'divisions of the kingdoms' by European powers.

Revenge

Apart from romance, the genre which Shakespeare most frequently revisited was revenge. Linda Anderson (Anderson) shows that even in comedies revenge can be seen as a major theme despite its negative connotations and its historical links with tragedy. Harry Keyishian argues that revenge is pervasive in all Shakespeare's plays, even in the history plays, and that revenge always concerns justice rather than remaining a simple plot device (Keyishian). Throughout even his comedies and romances Shakespeare favoured forgiveness as a more genuine answer to problems than revenge (Hunter). So he does in *Lear* when the old king and his youngest daughter movingly forgive each other, but they are not given the 'second chances' available to Leontes and Prospero. Philosophically speaking, Shakespeare's contrast between forgiveness and revenge, the one antidoting and arresting the other, seem both logical and sanctioned by the Gospels. In 'straightforward' revenge plots the logic of an eye for an eye, a tooth for a tooth – or in ethical terms a wrong for a wrong – leaves entire families dead, and the only resolution possible comes when literally nobody is left to pursue a vendetta. Shakespeare leaves us in no doubt that in all his plays he regards the agency of such self-destruction lies in human actions, no matter how often the characters call on gods above for assistance, or blame them for disaster (Elton; Maxwell). It is the logic of a destructive spiral towards universal annihilation, and René Girard, writing in the Cold War shadow of nuclear weapons, used black humour to drive home the underlying paradigm of revenge beneath the strategy officially named Mutual Assured Destruction. Speaking of those critics who condemned 'Hamlet's temporary reluctance to commit murder', he writes sarcastically, '… The only way to account for this curious body of literature is to suppose that, back in the twentieth century no more was needed than some ghost to ask for it, and the average professor of literature would massacre his entire household without batting an eyelash …' (Girard 299–300). The only way out of such a vicious circle, without causing humiliating defeat which will fuel a new revenge and defer destruction, is for one side to forgive the other for wrongs and refuse to retaliate. Politicians are not renowned for such magnanimous gestures.

King Lear shows just as clearly as *Hamlet* various actual and potential routes for revenge, located first in moments of clear injustice. Due to his incapacity to listen appropriately, Lear himself creates reasons for revenge in disinheriting his third, most loving daughter and banishing his most trustworthy courtier Kent, and alienating both Burgundy and the King of France. Others become implicated – Goneril and Regan, Albany and Cornwall. In the Gloucester family the bastard son Edmund openly seeks revenge against his father for disinheritance, and against his younger brother (or possibly half-brother) Edgar for his 'legitimacy'. Towards the end of the play Edgar kills Edmund to avenge their father and himself. In the most moving scene in the play Lear kneels to beg forgiveness from Cordelia and in her answer, 'No cause, no cause', she expresses her forgiveness, but the political events are now beyond their control. Ruth Morse has pointed out that Cordelia is legally 'in the category of prisoners executed against the disciplines of war' (Morse 67), the action most condemned in *Henry V* by Fluellen as expert in laws of war. This is certainly not the only formal illegality since the horrific blinding of Gloucester is simple torture, condemned by international law throughout history even in circumstances of war (Greenblatt 85–9), a law most recently and flagrantly violated in Abu Ghraib Prison in Iraq and Guantanamo Bay.

Albany's question is a call for God to avenge, and if a divinity will not, then humans will:

> If that the heavens do not their visible spirits
> Send quickly down to tame these vile offences,
> It will come,
> Humanity must perforce prey on itself
> Like monsters of the deep. (Quarto insert after 4.2.36)

His wife scathingly admonishes him, suggesting that 'turning the other cheek' is the cowardice of a 'Milk-liver'd man! / That bear'st a cheek for blows, a head for wrongs' (4.2.36–7), and she warns him that he should turn his attention to the military situation in Britain, calling for war in response to the hostile and apparently vengeful invasion of the French army:

> Where's thy drum?
> France spreads his banners in our noiseless land,
> With plumed helm thy flaxen biggin threats,
> Whilst thou, a moral fool, sits still, and cries
> 'Alack, why does he so?' (4.2.43–7)

Shakespeare's view arguably accords with Albany's dire predictions and condemnation of the conflict.

Is evil innate?

So far the issues which I have raised that link *Lear* with the century of conflicts from 1914 have been political ones, locating the causes of war in the existence of divisive institutions of power and property, and revenge pursued as public policy. There is, however, a more perennially offered explanation for war as for the events represented in *King Lear* – the prior existence of evil within human beings. For example, one central question that still haunts historians of the mid-twentieth century can be posed as, 'was Hitler a product of politics or of his own pathological psychology?' In favour of the second explanation are cited his racist views and the holocaust, but even so these were not in fact the reasons given in 1939 to justify the declaration of the Second World War. Rather his armed annexation of neighbouring countries in a spirit of resurgent German nationalism as an expression of collective revenge against humiliations of the Versailles Treaty were highlighted. The question had evidently occurred to Shakespeare also, given the continuing debates concerning whether Macbeth is an evil man or a potentially good man corrupted, and whether Iago is spurred by justifiable grievance or 'motiveless malignity' as a human attribute. In interpreting *Lear* critics need to address a similar set of ambiguities hanging over Goneril, Regan, Cornwall and Edmund, and perhaps even Lear himself.

It is sometimes assumed that evil – any manifestly inhumane impulse - is in some paradoxical way innately human. Such questions arise in literary discussion when we suggest that conflict is at the heart of drama and draws our interest hypnotically; or when it is suggested that evil characters are more attractive than good in works like *King Lear*, *Macbeth* and *Paradise Lost*. One of the implications is that those who hold a contrary view are unrealistic and, if they are not qualified as saints, must be severely repressed sinners. Needless to say, I am about to place myself among the latter, although I want to restrict my thoughts to the issue of war. Conflict is no doubt an inescapable part of the human condition, but murder is not even when sanctioned by the state in war, and nor is it an inevitable way to resolve conflict within families or between nations.

A range of attitudes is expressed in the play. Albany seems to believe that some are born evil: 'Wisdom and goodness to the vile seem vile: / Filths savour but themselves' (Quarto insert after 4.2.36). Edmund in his powerful speech beginning 'thou, nature, art my goddess; to thy law / My services are bound' (1.2.1-22) seems to believe that evil actions can be a consequence of injustices of 'the plague of custom' inspiring the will to revenge, and that the category of 'unnatural' is imposed by society rather than springing from a state of nature. As John Danby showed, the play presents 'nature' in different guises, from being aligned with charity to something that is red in tooth and claw (Danby). Edmund, seeing himself as begot in an act of nature, scorns the formalities of the marriage ceremony as irrelevant to nature's laws, while Kent sees 'natural' feelings and behaviour as including an impulse of familial 'kindness', humanitarian regard for the sanctity of life in animals and people alike: 'Why, madam, if I were your father's dog, / You should not use me so', he says, as does Cordelia:

> Mine enemy's dog,
> Though he had bit me, should have stood that night
> Against my fire. And wast thou fain, poor father,
> To hovel thee with swine and rogues forlorn,
> In short and musty straw? Alack, alack! (4.7.37–41)

Meanwhile, the three cruellest acts perpetrated in the play, the torture of Gloucester, the perfunctory murder of Cornwall's servant as 'whistle blower', and the hanging of Cordelia as prisoner of war, defy empathy and are justified as expediently 'convenient' (a word Regan repeats) or legalistic in the narrowest sense, as Goneril's 'Say, if I do, the laws are mine, not thine: / Who can arraign me for't' and Cornwall's

> Though well we may not pass upon his life
> Without the form of justice, yet our power
> Shall do a courtesy to our wrath, which men
> May blame, but not control.

'*Must* humanity perforce prey on itself, Like monsters of the deep?', especially when 'the dogs of war' (Neill; Penberthy) are unleashed.? The stakes today could not be higher. If the answer is 'yes' then there are enough weapons in the world to destroy the world, and many causes for revenge and national resentments dating back at least to the First and Second World Wars, the Cold War against the Russian empire, and the wars against Asian countries in the mid-twentieth century - even back to the Crusades against Islam if not the time of the Roman Empire. If the answer to the question posed by Albany's grim concern is in fact 'no', then the question we should ask ourselves today, unified as we (readers) are by a commitment to the values of academic disciplines known as the Humanities, is how best to counter the 'perforce' and halt or reverse the conditioned predatory tendencies of nations to wage war.

While the best we can say for war in relation to the Humanities is that it provides a subject for philosophical enquiry, a topic for a novel like *War and Peace*, or poems like Wilfred Owen's, yet in relation to the sciences war is more ambiguous and urgent. Many believe, for example, that science itself is 'pure' and value-free, and that pernicious applications belong in the worlds of politics, technology and commerce. But this shedding of responsibility may be misguided and the lines are surely more blurred, since scientists do at least address problems that arise from their cultural moment. Charles Darwin's theories of competition and the survival of the fittest at least provided a set of useful metaphors for British imperialism, not to mention later the Nazis and others practising eugenics and 'ethnic cleansing'. Of course Darwin did not foresee such consequences but he was uncomfortably complicit with a way of thinking, showing that science itself is not so impartial as it seems. Brecht in the 1950s tacitly represented Galileo's capitulation to church authority as an analogy for the most famous scientists of his time working together at Los Alamos under Oppenheimer to develop the atomic bomb. The rationalisation was that science is science and that the moral implications and technological applications are not part of its responsibility.

A famous correspondence between Einstein and Freud in 1931-32 encapsulates the intellectual division amongst scientists. Einstein, a pacifist appalled at the destructiveness of war, speaks with dismay of how easy a latent passion for violence existing in mankind can be raised 'to the power of a collective psychosis' in war. He is even more worried that this phenomenon is not exclusive to 'uncultured masses' but also infects 'the so-called "intelligentsia"' so even an education in humanity and the Humanities does not offer immunity. In order to find out how to eradicate this death wish from the human race, Einstein turned to Freud, 'the expert in the lore of human instincts'. Freud, far from offering hope, asserted that, 'the slaughter of a foe gratifies an instinctive craving', and advocated a kind of denial or sublimation: 'there is no likelihood of our being able to suppress humanity's aggressive tendencies... complete suppression of man's aggressive tendencies is not in issue; what we may try is to divert it into a channel other than that of warfare' (Einstein 185–204). After linking himself disingenuously with Einstein as 'We Pacifists', Freud refrains from seeing the 'unworldliness' of scientists as a reason to be reserved on the issue. To him war 'seems a natural thing enough, biologically sound and practically unavoidable'. Freud continued to believe that humans have within themselves opposite tendencies, love and hate, a desire to live and a partially repressed 'death-instinct'. If the negative feelings are directed inwards they create morbid and pathological conditions, so it is far healthier and more 'beneficial' to turn aggressive impulses outwards in the form of war. Alternatively, when the destructive impulse is suppressed in man, it will turn to sadism or masochistic eroticism as later disciples of Freud maintained. Einstein, like other pacifists before and since, disagreed and asserted that the capacity for evil at least in war lies in collective fabrications rather than individual emotions and is predominantly created by circumstances and power structures outside the human psyche itself. In Einstein's view, evil is simply not human.

However, as Brecht in *Galileo* predicted, the dropping of hydrogen bombs on Hiroshima and Nagasaki in 1945 provoked many scientists to reflect on the ethics of aiding governments to develop weapons designed to commit genocide. Some of them realised that assertions of violence as a biological necessity, is in itself a scientific issue. The result is a document sponsored in 1986 by UNESCO known as the Seville Statement. A group of scientists, mainly biologists (including an Australian) issued a 'Statement on Violence', noting that since the inception of modern science 'the theory of evolution has been used to justify not only war, but also genocide, colonialism, and suppression of the weak'. The Statement begins:

> Believing that is our responsibility to address from our particular
> disciplines the most dangerous and destructive activities of our species,
> violence and war; recognising that science is a human cultural product
> which cannot be definitive or all encompassing; ... [we] challenge a
> number of alleged biological findings that have been used, even by some
> in our disciplines, to justify violence and war. (UNESCO)

Five Propositions are listed, each opening 'IT IS SCIENTIFICALLY INCORRECT', the first being 'to say that we have inherited a tendency to make war from our animal ancestors', refuted by 'Warfare is a peculiarly human phenomenon and does not occur in other animals'. Other refutations of fallacies include '"Dominance" involves social bondings and affiliations; it is not simply a matter of possession and use of superior physical power'; 'There is nothing in our neurophysiology that compels us to react violently'; and 'The technology of modern war has exaggerated traits associated with violence both in the training of actual combatants, and in the preparation of support for war in the general population. As a result of this exaggeration, such traits are often mistaken to be the causes rather than consequences of the process' (and called 'instinct'). The signatories resoundingly conclude that 'Just as "wars begin in the minds of men", peace also begins in our minds. The same species who invented war is capable of inventing peace. The responsibility lies with each of us'. Unfortunately these wise words from manifest experts were instantly forgotten. Obviously the debate as to whether evil is natural or unnatural to human beings continues in the sciences and social sciences, as it had for thousands of years in the fields of religion and politics. There is enough evidence for an alert reader of *King Lear* to argue that Shakespeare may have agreed with the Seville Statement, and that *King Lear* is his grim warning that we ignore it at our peril..

King Lear raises the problem of evil in relation to war in a particularly intense and focused fashion often presented as juxtaposing a thesis and its antithesis. The truly evil act is the blinding of Gloucester commanded by Cornwall (who also orders Kent to be stocked) which is given no more than a metaphorical justification based on the assumption that Gloucester, as a 'traitor' and spy for the former king, should not 'see more.' The sadism is actively countered by the condemnation of Cornwall's Servant who courageously tries to prevent it happening. He fatally wounds Cornwall but is slain himself and unceremoniously thrown on a dunghill. Another dichotomy noted by textual scholars is that the Quarto text shows several comparable examples of virtue located in 'minor' characters like servants, stewards and tenants while the Folio excises or changes these, giving an irredeemably bleak view of a self-destructive society (Warren, 59–74).

To contrast groups of characters is a critical commonplace – Cordelia, Kent, Albany, the Fool, the King of France and Edgar as figures representing values of loyalty and honesty, set against the evil of Cornwall, Goneril, Regan and Edmund. Even from the actions of the second group, however, emerges a different construction of evil as lying in incremental and contingent actions reactive to circumstances, or at worst callousness rather than absolute malevolence. Machiavelli had never contemplated such actions as evil but rather as necessary to those who hold power. Given the range of options presented in the play, we can conclude that, as on many questions in all his plays, Shakespeare in *King Lear* chooses to represent rather than overtly judge, perhaps as a signature facet of his temperament, or a result of the dialecticism of his humanist education, or simply as a possibility offered by the medium of drama itself with its unmediated mouthpieces for different ideas and intellectual positions. However, the ruined state of Britain at the end of the play suggests he is aware of tragic consequences.

Conclusion

One guiding spirit behind this book, I take it, is to move us beyond opposed categories like historicism (new or old), which emphasises the 'otherness' of the past, and cultural materialism which suggests that the past is irretrievable and its remnants exist for the sake of the present. Instead, it can be argued that the past influences the present and the present illuminates the past. In terms of this chapter it is not difficult to parry accusations of anachronism, since the argument itself is that some of the patterns of significance in *King Lear* (and other plays by Shakespeare) identify issues which were topical both then and now. It should not surprise us that Edwin Muir, a pacifist, was writing just after the Second World War (Muir) and Stanley Cavell during the Vietnam War (Cavell) when they published important essays on *King Lear*. The underlying dynamics of political processes represented in the play continue to inform interpretations (Ryan; Cohen; Mack; Foakes; Kelly). Inheritance within families was just as important then as now, while political succession, whether dynastic or elected, was the most important public debate both before Elizabeth's death and afterwards. The latter is the main preoccupation in Shakespeare's history plays, and it is also still the most avidly discussed issue in all countries, whether democratic, monarchical, or tyrannical. Revenge may have been especially well known as a dramatic motif throughout Shakespeare's period because of the popularity of plays like *The Spanish Tragedy*, *Hamlet* and *The Revenger's Tragedy*, and because of the ongoing social debate about the legal status of duelling which had been deplored by the church since the thirteenth century, but Shakespeare's identification of forgiveness as the 'circuit breaker' of spiralling violence remains the logical closure to revenge. However, revenge even now underpins public policy, ranging in severity from gestures of frosty, reciprocal withdrawal of ambassadors, euphemistically named but belligerent 'off-shore military exercises', to the extreme of invasions of Afghanistan and Iraq in open retaliation after 11 September 2001. Meanwhile, enough has been said to establish that Albany's fundamentalist question has still not been answered to universal satisfaction. If one skill marks Shakespeare out from other writers, it is an uncanny judgment about his choice of issues which, while certainly topical in his own day, are based on processes which continue to delight, dismay, move, or haunt us.

Works Cited

Anderson, Linda. *A Wild Kind of Justice: Revenge in Shakespeare's Comedies*. Newark: University of Delaware Press, 1987

Cavell, Stanley. 'The avoidance of love: A reading of *King Lear*' in *Must We Mean What We Say?* Cambridge: Cambridge University Press, 1976), 278–353

Cohen, Derek. *Shakespeare's Culture of Violence*. New York: St. Martin's Press, 1993

Danby, John. *Shakespeare's Doctrine of Nature: A Study of 'King Lear'*. London: Faber and Faber, 1949

Dollimore, Jonathan. '*King Lear*: A Materialist Reading' in *Radical Tragedy*. Hemel Hempstead: The Harvester Press, 1984, 195–201

Einstein on Peace. Edited by Otto Nathan and Heinz Norden. New York: Schocken Books, 1968

De Somogyi, Nick. *Shakespeare's Theatre of War*. Aldershot: Ashgate, 1998

Elton, William. *King Lear and the Gods*. San Marino: Huntington Library, 1966

Foakes, R. A. *Shakespeare and Violence*. Cambridge University Press, 2003

Girard, René, 'Hamlet's Dull Revenge.' In *Literary Theory / Literary Texts*. Edited by Patricia Parker and David Quint. Baltimore and London: Johns Hopkins University Press, 1986

Greenblatt, Stephen. *Shakespeare's Freedom*. Chicago: University of Chicago Press, 2010

Greenhouse, Carol J. 'Lear and Law's Doubles: Identity and Meaning in a Time of Crisis', *Law, Culture and the Humanities* 2 (2006): 239–58

Hunter, R. G. *Shakespeare and the Comedy of Forgiveness*. New York: Columbia University Press, 1966

Jansohn, Christa. (ed.). *German Shakespeare Studies at the Turn of the Twenty-first Century*. Newark: Delaware Press, 2006

Kelly, Philippa. *The King and I*. London: Continuum, 2011

Keyishian, Harry. *The Shapes of Revenge: Victimization, Vengeance, and Vindictiveness in Shakespeare*. New Jersey: Humanities Press, 1995

Mack, Maynard. *King Lear in Our Time*. London: Methuen, 1966

Maxwell, J. C. 'The Technique of Invocation in *King* Lear', *Modern Language Review* 45 (1950): 142–7.

Morse, Ruth, 'Some Social Costs of War'. In *Shakespeare and War*. Edited by Ros King and Paul Franssen. London: Palgrave, 2008. Pp. 56 – 70

Muir, Edwin. *The Politics of King Lear*. Glasgow: Jackson, 1947

Neill, Michael. '"The little dogs and all": Ceremony, Nakedness, Shame, and the Deconsecration of Kingship in *King Lear*', *Shakespeare's World / World Shakespeares*. Newark: University of Delaware Press, 2008

Penberthy, Susan. 'Dogs of War and Icelandic Curs: Canine Imagery, Work and Idleness in *Henry V.*' In *'Rapt in Secret Studies': Emerging Shakespeares*. Edited by Darryl Chalk and Laurie Johnson. Newcastle-upon-Tyne: Cambridge Scholars Publishing, 2010. Pp. 317–28

Ryan, Kiernan. '*King Lear*: 'men / Are as the time is.' In *Shakespeare: Harvester New Readings*. Hemel Hempstead: Harvester Wheatsheaf, 1989. Pp. 66–73

Seville Statement. UNESCO website at http://www.unesco.org/new/en/unesco/ accessed 20/11/10

Shakespeare, William. *King Lear: The Bell Shakespeare*. Edited by Philippa Kelly. Sydney: Halstead Press, 2002

Suzman, Janet. 'South Africa in *Othello*.' In *Shakespeare and the Twentieth Century: The Selected Proceedings of the International Shakespeare Association World Congress, Los Angeles, 1996*. Edited by Jonathan Bate, Jill L. Levinson and Dieter Mehl. Newark: University of Delaware Press, 1998. Pp. 23–4

Warren, Michael. 'The Diminution of Kent.' In *The Division of the Kingdoms: Shakespeare's Two Versions of 'King Lear'*. Edited by Gary Taylor and Michael Warren. Oxford: Clarendon Press, 1983

White, R. S. '*King Lear* and Philosophical Anarchism', *English* 37 (1988): 181–200

———. *Pacifism and English Literature: Minstrels of Peace* London: Palgrave Macmillan, 2008

Chapter 13

Defining the Demonic in Ancient China

Jeffrey Riegel
University of Sydney

一女子下夜班, 一男子尾隨意圖謀不軌, 女子慎怕, 路過墳地, 靈機
一動, 對墳地說: 爸爸, 我回來了, 開門阿. 男子大懼, 哇哇大叫奔逃.
女子心安, 正要離開, 忽然從墳墓中傳來陰深神的聲音: 你又忘了帶
鑰匙啊. 女子惊駭, 也哇哇奔逃. 這時從墳墓裡鑽出個盜墓的說到:
靠, 耽誤我工作, 嚇死你們. "你趕緊挖啊, 嚇人家小姑娘幹甚麼? 我
都躺在這20年了, 憋壞了 ... 盜墓的立刻暈倒.

*A young woman who finished her night shift was on her way home when a
man with evil intentions started tailing her. The girl was frightened but, as she
passed a graveyard, had a flash of inspiration. Addressing a tomb mound she
said: 'Father I am home. Open the door!' The man following her was scared out
of his wits and ran away screaming. Now calm, the girl was about to depart
when suddenly she heard a tiny voice from deep within the tomb: 'You've
forgotten your key again!' The girl also ran screaming in fright. Just then a tomb
robber stuck his head out from the tomb and explained: 'It is because you were
interrupting my work that I scared you to death.' At which point he heard: 'Get
busy with your digging! Why waste your time scaring a young lady? I have been
lying here for twenty years and it is so stuffy I am suffocating!' The grave robber
fainted on the spot.*

I received the Chinese version of this story as a text message on my mobile
phone on 10 January 2009. The friend in China who sent it probably
downloaded the story from some mobile phone service and was circulating
it to amuse all the friends in his phone's contact list. I begin with this tale
because – simple structure and crude grammar and spelling aside – its

contents and means of circulation testify to the abiding popularity in China of supernatural tales of ghosts and demons. The tradition has deep roots in the culture.

I regard this fear of and fascination with ghosts and demons as reflections of a deep cultural anxiety about the other,' i.e., with what is not familiar or even not human. In this chapter I will present early literary artifacts of this anxiety as well as some quite self-conscious early explanations and definitions of the demonic. I do this in part because by studying Chinese attitudes toward the demonic and ghostly – things conceived of as other than the familiar and human – we can gain some understanding of how such notions as the human and the familiar were constructed and invested with value. Let me begin with two claims that will be borne out in the remainder of the chapter.

First, for the ancient Chinese, to be a human being was not to be a member of a scientifically defined species, but to be from a particular place – the homeland of their civilization, the center of 'All under Heaven.' Those distant from this center were destined to be less or other than human. Only those born and bred within it, those who had inherited and been schooled in its customs and practices – i.e., the moral, cultural, and political institutions that were the essence of humanity – were fully human. At one point in the *Analects* of Kongzi, or Confucius (traditional dates 551–479 BC), we are informed that 'The Master never spoke of prodigies, unnatural physical power, disorders, and spirits' (Hong Ye et al 7.21). This was not the case because Kongzi regarded such things as nonexistent or insignificant, but because his main project had to do with defining and teaching to others what it means to be human.

Second, the boundary between the demonic and the human was both hazy and permeable. Having the physical appearance of a human being did not make one human since non-human creatures could change into the shape of and otherwise assume the appearance of humans. Moreover, some spirits were hybrids possessed of both human and non-human characteristics. Finally, ghosts were especially problematic since they were ex-humans: some could be made, through the power of ritual, to maintain a measure of their humanity; they could be induced through offerings of food and drink to remember the bonds that linked them to their living descendants. But those who died violent or wrongful deaths became obsessed with an angry hunger for revenge that thwarted any remnants of human sentiment and twisted them into fearsome creatures.

In what follows I will present a few tales from different periods that illustrate my second claim. I will then return to a discussion of the first.

Supernatural Tales

We are probably close to the beginnings of the written tradition of tales about spirits, demons, and the like, with the *Zuozhuan*, a narrative history, mostly composed sometime during the fourth century BC, that covers the period from the 8th to the 5th centuries BC. The text is filled with references to gods and monsters that frighten people, cause illness, disrupt the state, wreak havoc, and even murder those who have offended them.

A typical story in the *Zuozhuan* tells of Bo You who, having been murdered, returned as a fierce spirit to exact revenge on the occupants of his native state of Zheng. So frequent and widespread was his mischief, the text says, that the people of Zheng would run in fear whenever someone called out, 'Bo You is here!' At one point the ghost, dressed in full armor, appeared in a dream and declared that he intended to kill two of his former enemies. When the men did in fact die, so great was the panic that swept through Zheng, it was necessary for Zi Chan, the chief official of the state, to perform rites to quell the demon and restore order and calm. Though possessed of fearful powers, Bo You nonetheless looked human to those who saw him. Other early sources make clear that, though former humans, ghosts were identifiably different. Humans, having been born and raised in the heartland of civilization, wore clothes and tied their hair up. Ghosts ran about naked with their hair down and flat against their backs. Only powerful rites of exorcism would drive them out from the lands inhabited by humans.[2]

Mozi, a fifth century BC teacher who offered policies for ensuring political order and social stability starkly different to those of Kongzi was, unlike Kongzi, quite happy to teach his followers about ghosts and spirits. The text gathers several stories under the title *Minggui*, or 'Explaining Demons,' not only for the purpose of proving that ghosts and spirits exist but also to show that they are agents of divine surveillance and reciprocity. Here is a brief tale, now embedded in the *Mozi* chapter, that was probably once part of a cycle of stories about spirits of the four directions:

> In the past, Duke Mu of Qin was in his ancestral temple at the crack of dawn when a spirit entered the gate and alighted on his left. It had the body of a bird and the face of a man, wore a plain white robe with three layers of down feathers, and had a grave and somber expression on its face. When Duke Mu saw it, he quaked with fear, and started to flee. The spirit said: 'Fear not! God on High savors your bright virtue and has sent me down to bestow on you an additional nineteen years of life, to make your country flourish, and your descendants thrive and never lose Qin.' Duke Mu, bowing twice and knocking his head against the ground, said, 'May I be so bold as to ask the spirit's name?' 'I am Goumang,' the spirit replied.[1]

It was perhaps necessary that Goumang have a human head so that he could speak Chinese with the humans to whom he delivered the messages of God-on-High.

The *Zuozhuan* and *Mozi* are famous, well-studied sources that survive from the early period having been preserved in imperial libraries and transmitted across the centuries by scholars who faithfully copied and handed them on to their students. In the last several decades archaeologists working in China have unearthed numerous manuscripts written on wooden tablets, bamboo strips, and lengths of silk that were not transmitted and so were lost before their recent discovery.

Among these are eight bamboo strips discovered in a 3rd century BC tomb at the Gansu site of Fangmatan in northwest China inscribed with a bizarre story of resurrection that can be paraphrased as follows.[2] It was reported to a local official that a man named Dan had committed suicide after he had murdered someone else. After Dan's body was exposed in the marketplace for three days and then buried, he was he was brought before underground judges who were persuaded that it was not yet his time to die. Thus they ordered that he should return to life above ground. A white dog—the ancient Chinese Cerberus?—dug an opening for him and Dan emerged. Though he had regained consciousness, he was still like a zombie having lost the use of his four limbs and otherwise been scarred by his death and burial. The story concludes that, though bruised and incapacitated, this man, having been resurrected from the dead, would nevertheless give lectures on what the dead desire. For the humans to whom he lectured the knowledge he had gained was essential because he had traveled from the human realm to the netherworld, a realm as alien and distant as any foreign kingdom.

I regard the Fangmatan tale of resurrection as the distant ancestor of the ghost-story text-message I received on my mobile phone: it was written on bamboo strips the ancient means for recording and broadly distributing stories in antiquity and it, too, tells of a dead man who did not wish to remain in his tomb.

The preoccupation with demons and the supernatural continued into the era of the imperial Qin and Han dynasties. There survives from that period a handful of texts that chronicle the clash between the human world and demonic forces.[3] Rather than quote these surviving sources, I will simply list a few of the titles of demonological works that were once part of the Han dynasty imperial library:

Portentous and Propitious Mutant Prodigies, in twenty-one scrolls;
Declarations of Odium for Mutant Prodigies, in thirteen scrolls;
Seizing the Unpropitious and Subjugating Spectral Entities, in eight scrolls.[4]

With the collapse of the Han dynasty in 220 AD, China entered an unsettled era that witnessed invasions by nomadic tribes from the north, the displacement of the traditional culture of the valleys of the Yellow and Wei rivers to the more southerly basin of the Yangzi, the introduction from India of Buddhism, and the emergence of Daoism as China's great native religion. Parallel to these developments and no doubt influenced by them was the appearance of collections of ghost stories and tales of the supernatural. In time the contents of these collections came to be recognized as constituting a genre of literature that in (much later) Ming dynasty times (1368–1643) was given the name *zhiguai* or 'records of prodigies.'

One of the earlist of the so-called *zhiguai* collections is the *Soushenji,* a text attributed to Gan Bao, a mid-level official in the E. Jin (217–419).[5] Typical of the style and humor of the stories in the collection is one that recounts the fate of an elderly lady who took such long baths that she transformed into a giant soft-shell-turtle, nevertheless recognizable as her former self because, when glimpsed, the turtle still had silver hairpins stuck in its head. The story concludes with the observation that henceforth her relatives did not dare to eat turtle meat. Just as creatures might assume the shape of humans, so might a human being transform herself into something else.

The *Yuanhunzhi* by Yan Zhitui (531–c.591) dates to a few centuries later. That Yan Zhitui – one of the great literary figures and scholars in the years of division between the imperial Han and Tang dynasties – compiled such a collection testifies to the high regard in which ghost stories were held during this period. A story in the collection that reflects Buddhist influences tells of how some marauding soldiers stole a valuable piece of rock crystal from a temple and then sold it to buy food. All subsequently died, except the one soldier who did not get a share of the ill-gotten food.[6]

Even as superficial a recounting of the *zhuiguai* literature as the present one would not be complete without reference to the sub-genre of 'fox-spirit' tales. These are the stories of foxes (*hu*) that were both feared and found fascinating for their power to metamorphose into handsome men or beautiful women to pursue sexual relationships with humans. There was a certain self-satisfaction implicit in the tales: humans and their existence are so desirable that they are pursued by demonic forces. However, the stories did give voice as well to an anxiety over how criminal behavior could occur in the heartland of the civilization, how wickedness could exist in this idyllic land of Oz, how there could be evil in 'All under Heaven.' This was especially so in the late Tang dynasty examples of short stories known in Chinese literary history as *chuanqi* or 'tales that transmit the odd and unexpected.' *Chuanqi* were composed by some of the most famous literary figures of the Tang. Features that immediately distinguish them from earlier tales include not only their much greater length and the fact that we know the names of their authors, but also that the stories provide vivid glimpses into Tang dynasty daily life, especially the romantic lives of the inhabitants of the great Tang capital,

Chang'an. The *chuanqi* are, however, too involved to attempt to capture one here in a simple paraphrase. Instead I will quote a poem by the famous Tang poet Bai Juyi (772–846) that wonderfully summarizes what late Tang society found most troubling about fox-spirits:

> When a fox specter of an old grave is growing old,
> It changes into a woman of lovely features;
> Its head changes into a female coiffure, its face into a painted countenance.
> The big tail it trails behind becomes a long red petticoat.
> Slowly she strides along the paths between the rustic hamlets,
> And where at sunset no human sounds are heard.
> She sings, she dances, and alternately laments and wails.
> Without raising her eyebrows velvety as the kingfisher, but bowing her pretty face,
> She bursts into a fit of laughter, a thousand, a myriad of joys.
> Eight or nine out of ten who behold her are beguiled;
> If false beauties may fascinate men in such a manner,
> The attraction exercised by genuine beauties surely will surpass it.
> Such false and such genuine beauties both can bewilder a man,
> But the human mind dislikes what is false and prefers what is real.
> Hence a fox disguised as a female demon can do but little harm.
> Nor can a man's eyes for longer than a day or night;
> But a woman acting like a fox-enchantress is the cause of absolute ruin,
> For the harm she does to a man's mind grows with each passing day.[7]

After the collapse of the Tang in the early tenth century, the tales of the supernatural continued to flourish as a popular literary tradition. Indeed, the fourteenth century ushered in a long period when story-telling more generally reached unprecedented levels of artfulness and sophistication. With respect to popular literature, the period is perhaps best known as that when the great Chinese dramas and novels were written. But it also produced perhaps the best examples of ghost-stories and related genres.

The recognized master of the ghost story during this time is Pu Songling (1640-1715). Pu's collection of stories – the *Liaozhai zhiyi* – 'is not just the culmination of the classical tale [i.e., the *zhiguai* and the *chuanqi*] in style, complexity, and range; it is no exaggeration to say that this collection has come to define our very notion of the genre.'[8] What most characterizes all of Pu's stories – and there are hundreds of them – is the 'deliberate blurring of the boundaries between the real and the illusionary.' And the protagonists – probably like Pu Songling himself – are often unrestrained romantics who long for any opportunity to move from one realm to the other.

A marvelous example is the story of a rather overweight – Pu calls him 'fleshy' – scholar who had read another of Pu's stories about a stunningly beautiful fox-spirit called 'Blue Phoenix' and could think of nothing or no one else. So intense were the longings inspired by Pu's literary creation, the 'Blue Phoenix' visited the fat scholar and awarded his ardor by granting him her fifteen year old daughter – also, of course, a fox-spirit – in marriage. After their marriage was consummated, the young girl took the scholar to meet her sisters, foxes all. After a night of drinking with them the scholar awoke the next morning convinced the whole night had been a dream. The girl explained, 'My sisters appeared to you in a dream because they feared you were a wild carouser. Actually, it was no dream.' Eventually the two parted because the fox-spirit girl had been called by the gods to perform higher spiritual duties. When they parted, the scholar promised to fulfill the girl's wish that Pu Songling write her biography so that she would be as famous in literature as her mother 'Blue Phoenix.'[9] I am doing my part by including the story in this chapter. I do so as well because the story illustrates how fox spirits were capable not only of assuming human shape but also of performing all the social rituals and niceties of the human world.

Another noteworthy author of classical tales – though not the equal of Pu Songling – is Yuan Mei (1716–1798) who is best-known as a poet and scholarly provocateur.[10] Yuan Mei entitled his very large collection of tales of the supernatural *Zibuyu – What the Master Never Spoke Of* – a reference of course to the passage from the *Analects* with which I began my presentation. Yuan Mei's point was that his interests were not related to Confucius's concerns with morality but rather had to do with the 'prodigies, unnatural physical power, disorders, and spirits' that filled and punctuated the lives of his contemporaries.

Yuan Mei's collection of supernatural tales ranges from pointed social criticism – focusing on the plight of women and others victimized by 18th century Chinese society – to humorous tales that poke fun at monks and priests and at the pompous stuffed shirts who occupied high office in the government. All the stories, in one way or another, shed valuable light on the central roles played by religious belief and superstition in everyday life. An example is seen in this excerpt from one of the *Zibuyu* tales:

> In Guizhou there was a wicked rascal whose offenses were as numerous as a mountain is large. The local magistrate had him killed and tossed his body into a river. After three days, his soul came back and, thus restored to life, he wreaked havoc over a five-day period. This happened several times, leaving the local magistrate no choice but to report the matter to the provincial governor who became enraged and, with the permission of the emperor, had the rascal beheaded and then buried his body and his head in two different places. But after three days, he was once again restored to life and his body and head were joined together, though at the side of his neck one could see the faint trace of the strand of red thread used to sew him back together. He proceeded to commit crimes as he had done before. Later, when he beat his own mother, she came to the magistrate to file a complaint, and had a jar in her hand. 'This is the jar in which the soul of my rebellious son is hidden. Realizing that his offenses were great and his crimes extreme, when he was at home he removed his own soul and, after refining it by means of the Daoist arts of immortality, he was able to store his soul in this jar. Thus when the officials punished him, it was his body they were destroying, not his soul. A soul that has been refined for a long time can restore health and renew life to a battered body. After but three days one can be completely renewed. But now his wickedness has gone too far, even to the point where he beats his old lady, but this old lady cannot tolerate such treatment. I beg that the officials first destroy the jar, use a rotating fan to scatter his soul, and only after that should you inflict corporal punishment on his body. Then this evil son of mine should be truly dead.' The official did as the woman advised and had the rascal clubbed to death. When his corpse was later examined it was found that, in less than ten days time, it had fully rotted.[11]

One of the things I find fascinating about this story is that archaeologists have unearthed what they identify as *hunping* or 'soul jars' from tombs in the Yangzi river basin that date mostly to the 3rd and 4th centuries. These jars were perhaps placed in tombs as receptacles for the soul, incorruptible surrogates for the corpse. Their iconography is complex: some show what is perhaps a maternal figure cradling a child that may represent the deceased; others appear to have been influenced by Buddhist reliquaries and hence display representations of the Buddha; still other jars are reminiscent of granaries on which birds perch, symbolism perhaps meant to attract the soul of the deceased and encourage it to alight and stay put. What Yuan Mei's story seems to suggest is that in doing their evil ghosts find their human bodies to be impediments and so require containers made of more durable stuff, porcelain rather than flesh.

Theories of the Supernatural

In Yuan Mei's story we find a reference to 'Daoist arts' for refining the soul as part of an explanation for how the evil protagonist of the tale could continue to survive though his physical body had been destroyed. Implicit in most classical tales is an explanation of how ghosts and other supernatural beings come to exist. When asked if it is really possible for a ghost like Bo You, the *Zuozhuan* trouble-maker, to exist, Zi Chan, the Zheng minister who succeeded in quelling the demon, provides more than an implicit answer. Setting out what could be read as instructions for would-be ghosts, he says, in effect, that prominent men like Bo You, by virtue of their wealth and high station, are able to consume refined foods the properties of which effectively ensure that their spirits will survive them. In other words, some humans can, through being human, master the means to transcend their own humanity. This interesting notion – that wealth and power not only serve you when alive but ensure privilege after death – is reflected in countless ancient burials that have been excavated in China in the last several decades.[13]

Such explanations, implicit or otherwise, and the ghost stories and supernatural tales they were meant to rationalize were so popular and widespread that some early thinkers found them detrimental to a well-ordered society and challenged them as just so much unattested lore and empty speculation. In my view the most compelling, and certainly the most interesting, of these challenges was formulated by Wang Chong (27–c.97), a Han dynasty scholar who – in a set of eighty-five essays given the overall title of *Lunheng* or *Balance for Judging Theories* – otherwise tried to formulate rather elaborate views of the material workings of the universe. Typical of his approach is his attempt to demonstrate that thunder does not occur because Heaven is angry – as was popularly believed – but because of excessive heat in the atmosphere. Wang Chong devoted four *Lunheng* essays to criticizing popular views of death, ghosts, and supernatural beings. In the first three of these he argued that death is a terminus that no part of life transcends or survives. When people claim to see ghosts or demons they are, he explains, dreaming or their faculties have been impaired by illness or the onset of their own imminent deaths.

But in his fourth essay on the subject – one entitled *Dinggui* or 'Defining the Demonic' – while still repeating some of these ideas, Wang Chong allows that in some instances those who see ghosts when ill are in fact witnessing demonic beings. These beings, he elaborates, are not however deceased humans, i.e., ghosts of the dead. They are, he suggests, not at all related to the category of human being! Wang Chong then describes just what categories of demonic being they are.[14]

The first of Wang Chong's categories of demonic beings mistaken for ghosts consists of the animals – presumably both the domesticated as well as the wild animals – of ancient China's agrarian society and its rural setting. Some animals by their nature, Wang Chong claims, are capable of metamorphosis. He perhaps had fox-spirits in mind. Or maybe he had observed that pets sometimes come to resemble their masters. Wang Chong explains this phenomenon by noting that animals and people live in close quarters and that in their breathing and other activities they therefore share the material essences of their surroundings. Wang Chong offers as proof of such metamorphosis the examples of bestiality he evidently observed. He does allow that such human and animal intimacies are most likely to occur when the human is physically ill. Wang Chong concludes that, in any case, when someone ill claims to see a ghost coming towards him – like a dead man beckoning him from the grave – it is likely to be nothing other than one of the six domesticated beasts (the ox, horse, sheep, chicken, dog, and pig) commonly found in his neighbor's villa.

Another of Wang Chong's categories is made up, he says, of those who are 'originally born of humans' but do not mature. Instead, as infants, they flee into the wilds where they become the source of deadly plagues that infect human society. These disease-ridden demons prey on the old and feeble by disguising themselves as ordinary humans. Wang Chong's characterization of children as less or other than human is part – albeit a negative one – of the underpinnings of the traditional emphasis on the critical need for education and attentive parental nurturing. Wang Chong observes that even the most moral of men can father such creatures and that, being the offspring of moral men, they have the appearance of moral individuals when in fact they are the bearers of the most harmful diseases. What events and individuals inspired these observations in Wang Chong are unknown to us. But they do remind us that being born in the heartland of the civilization was not sufficient to make one human; it was necessary that one be raised to adulthood there.

A third category of the demonic consists of many who are reading this chapter. Wang Chong says:

> Demons are creatures that are no different from humans. Inhabiting the world between Heaven and Earth these demonic creatures usually remain outside of our four borders. But on occasion they come to the Middle Kingdom where they wantonly comingle with humans. They are the most unfortunate and loathsome species of beings. That is why those who are sick and about to die see them.

When Wang Chong wrote this, he and his contemporaries were becoming deeply aware of how large the world is and what a small part of it the Han Empire occupied. Diplomatic missions had been sent deep into Central Asia; Buddhism was knocking at the door. Soldiers in Han armies had served on campaigns in what is now Vietnam and in what were for them other far-flung places in Southeast, Central, and Northeast Asia. The geographical knowledge that resulted from all this was often quite fanciful as in Wang Chong's account. In the same passage, Wang Chong quotes from an ancient text entitled *The Classic of Mountains and Seas*, a compilation of myths and stories about odd creatures arranged according to their supposed locations on the empire's periphery. Like other early bestiaries, its 'anomalies were collected for purposes of instruction, curiosity, and delight.'[15]

> *The Classic of Mountains and Seas* says, 'In the northern direction is the Land of Demons.' . . . The text also says, 'In the midst of the Deep Blue Sea is Dushuo Mountain, on which there grows a giant peach tree three thousand *li* around. The northeast part of its branches is called 'Demon Gate,' the place through which the myriad demons enter and exit. Atop the gate are two spirits: one is called Shendu; and the other Yulei. They are the masters of the myriad demons. The loathsome and harmful demons they bind with rope and feed to the tigers. That is why the Yellow Sovereign created the seasonal rites by which the demons are driven away. They consist of erecting a giant peach-wood man, painting the entrance to the home with images of Shendu and Yulei and suspending from the top of the gate a rope with which to harness the demons.'[16]

The Classic of Mountains and Seas was probably illustrated when it was first composed sometime between the 4th and 1st centuries BC. The earliest surviving illustrations are woodblock prints that date to the Wanli era (1573–1620) of the Ming dynasty. A relevant example is an illustration (dating to the period 1628–1644) of the passage that describes the Land of Demons to which Wang Chong refers. In this illustration we see:

> The Land of the Demon People lies north of the Corpse of Erfu. The people have human faces with one eye.
> According to another version, the god Erfu dwells east of the Land of the Demon People, He has a human face and a snake's body.
> The Tao-Dog resembles a dog that is green. It is a man-eater and devours its prey head first.
> Thoroughly-Odd resembles a tiger with wings. He devours people head first, and those he devours wear their hair long. He dwells north of the Tao-Dog. According to another version, he devours people feet first.
> Tafei has a human body and a beast's body that is green.[17]

Fantastic ideas such as those found in Wang Chong and *The Classic of Mountains and Seas* would persist for centuries even when contradicted by the experiences of the many medieval travelers who ventured to distant lands. Let me close with two modern examples of the persistence of these traditions.

The Chinese-Australian artist Guan Wei migrated to Australia in 1989. Years later, when reflecting on his cross-cultural journey, he imaginatively recast it as an exploration of the South Seas by the famous admiral Zheng He (1371–1432). As part of an exhibition – entitled 'Other Histories' – that was on display at the Powerhouse Museum in Sydney in late 2006 and early 2007, Guan Wei created historical 'artifacts' that would have been produced by Zheng He's exploration (and of course relate to his own journey from China to Australia). Among these artifacts are illustrated pages of creatures that are reminiscent of but not quite humans. Though artworks created by Guan Wei, the illustrations are copied from *The Classic of Mountains and Seas* and thus reflect the abiding power of that text to capture for all times and circumstances the look of the demonic threats that await a human being who dares to exit the confines of China's borders.

When I was a student studying Chinese language in Taiwan in the early 1970s – a time when the island was a stronghold of Chinese tradition well prior to its becoming the cosmopolitan center it is today – it was not unusual for children, at the sight of a foreigner, to shout with gleeful mischief, *yangguizi laile* 'a demon from across the sea is here.' Though shouted partly in jest, the words were meant, as the ancient warning that 'Bo You is here!' had been, to alarm and alert their friends and neighbors. At the time I was a bit offended by the suggestion that I was demonic and not human. I might have felt otherwise had I known that this epithet applied to someone from abroad had a distinguished pedigree that might be traced back through China's rich literary history to the ghost stories of the *Zuozhuan* and *Mozi* and to the speculations of Wang Chong and the fanciful accounts of *The Classic of Mountains and Seas.*

Works Cited

Crump, James, and Kenneth DeWoskin. *In Search of the Supernatural: The Written Record*. Stanford: Stanford University Press, 1996

De Groot, J. J. M. *The Religious System of China*. Leiden, 1907

Dien, Albert E. 'The *Yüan-hun Chih* (Accounts of Ghosts with Grievances): A Sixth-Century Collection of Stories.' In *Wen-lin: Studies in the Chinese Humanities*. Edited by Chow Tse-tsung. Madison: University of Wisconsin Press, 1968

Gansu sheng wenwu kaogu yanjiusuo, and Tianshuishi Beidaoqu wenhuaguan. 'Gansu Fangmatan Zhanguo Qin Han muqun de fajue.' *Wenwu* (1989.2): 1–11, 31

Harper, Donald . 'Wang Yen-shou's Nightmare Poem.' *Harvard Journal of Asiatic Studies* 47 (1987): 239–283

———. 'A Chinese Demonography of the Third Century B.C..' *Harvard Journal of Asiatic Studies* 45 (1985): 459–98

———. 'Resurrection in Warring States Popular Religion.' *Taoist Resources* 5.2 (1994): 13–28

Hong Ye, et. al. (eds.). *Lunyu yinde*. Harvard-Yenching Institute Sinological Index series supplement, no. 16. Originally published: Beijing: Yanjing University, 1940

Kang, Xiaofei. *The Cult of the Fox*. New York: Columbia University Press, 2006.

Li Xueqin. 'Fangmatan jian zhong de zhiguai gushi.' *Wenwu* (1990.4): 43–47

Liao, W. K. (trans.). *Han Fei Tzu: Works from the Chinese*. London: Probsthain, 1959

Ma, Y. W., and Joseph S. M. Lau (eds). *Traditional Chinese Stories: Themes and Variations*. New York: Columbia University Press, 1978

Mathieu, Rémi. *Étude sur la mythologie et l'ethnographie de la Chine ancienne*. Paris, 1983

Riegel, Jeffrey. 'Kou-mang and Ju-shou.' *Cahiers d'Extrême-Asie* 5 (1989-90): 55-83.

Schmidt, J. D. *Harmony Garden: The Life, Literary Criticism, and Poetry of Yuan Mei*. London, 2003

Strassberg, Richard E. *A Chinese Bestiary: Strange Creatures from the Guideways through Mountains and Seas*. Berkeley and Los Angeles: University of California Press, 2002

Waley, Arthur. *Yuan Mei: Eighteenth Century Chinese Poet*. London, 1956

Wang Chong. *Lunheng*. Shanghai: Renmin chubanshe, 1974

Wang Yingzhi. *Yuan Mei Pingchuan*. Nanjing, 2002

Yuan Mei. *Yuan Mei quanji*. Jiangsu: Guji chubanshe, 1993

Zeitlin, Judith. *Historian of the Strange*. Stanford: Stanford University Press, 1993

Notes

1 A story that illustrates these various features of a ghost's appearance and the steps required to exorcise a ghost is found in the third century BC *Hanfeizi*. See Liao II.7–8

2 For a more detailed discussion of this passage, see Riegel 55–83

3 For the excavation report of the tombs at Fangmatan, see Gansu sheng 1–11, 31. For the resurrection story see Li 43–47, and Harper, 1994, 22

4 See Harper, 1987

5 Adopted from Harper, 1985, 460

6 See Crump and DeWoskin

7 For a study of the text and this particular anecdote see Dien 211–228

8 For translations of the Tang *chuanqi* that involve fox-spirits, see Ma and Lau. For a study of the cult of the fox and literature, see Kang. This translation is adapted from De Groot 589

9   Zeitlin 4
10 This paraphrase is based on the translation found in Zeitlin 211–216
11 There are three comprehensive treatments of Yuan Mei's life: Waley; Wang Yingzhi; and Schmidt.
12 Yuan IV. 98–99
13 Though the chapter on supernatural beings in the *Mozi* is entitled, 'Explaining Ghosts,' it does not explain their existence but rather presents an argument for why belief in them is essential for political order and social stability
14 What follows is a paraphrase of Wang Chong 342–345
15 Strassberg xiii. For a complete translation of the text, see Mathieu
16 This passage is not part of the transmitted *Shanhai jing*
17 Adopted from Strassberg 197–99

Chapter 14

Hamlet and the Crisis in the Humanities

Bob Hodge
University of Western Sydney

This chapter addresses, from a particular angle, the core set of problems raised by *What is the Human?* Is there a problem facing humanity today that can be located via the Humanities, that set of intellectual disciplines concerned with the condition of being human? If so, what is it, and how might we address it?

Shakespeare and his Hamlet provide a point of departure for these broad reflections on these questions. Can literary works and their study become part of the solution as well as the problem of the 'crisis of the Humanities'? Can they contribute today to the perennial task of better understanding the world and humans in it?

The crisis of Humanities

The word 'crisis' is sometimes over-used, to exaggerate difficulties and (usually) to sell the One Solution, harsh, expensive but necessary. Yet this language is sometimes required to draw attention to a problem that is large and serious, but seen as too hard. In what follows I will not invent a 'crisis,' but examine claims that there is one, or several. My reference point is a recent work by Martha Nussbaum (2010). Nussbaum is a distinguished Humanities academic, an influential philosopher and classicist, and a public intellectual. She begins her most recent book with this call to arms:

> We are in the midst of a crisis of massive proportions and grave global significance. No, I do not mean the global economic crisis that began

in 2008. At least then everyone knew that a crisis was at hand, and many world leaders worked quickly and desperately to find solutions … (2010:1)

After invoking and dismissing the fashionable economic 'crisis' as not so serious after all, she moves to what she calls a 'silent crisis':

> Thirsty for national profit, nations and their systems of education are heedlessly discarding skills that are needed to keep democracies alive: … complete citizens who can think for themselves, criticize traditions, and understand the significance of another person's sufferings and achievements (2010:2)

Nussbaum yokes together two crises, establishing a powerful, important, potentially interdisciplinary field which should encompass the discipline of the Humanities in all its forms, and also economics and business studies. Yet her ambivalent tone keeps the two apart, staging a dichotomy. This is often the case in her polemic on behalf of the Humanities, even though she herself has intervened in economics arguably more successfully than any other Humanities academic today, through her collaboration with Nobel-Prize winning economist Amartya Sen (Nussbaum and Sen). From her practice rather than her polemic we can draw the idea of a more inclusive form of Humanities, in a challenging new interdisciplinary form, capable of transforming both economics and Humanities into a new form of Humanities.

There is another invisible division in her concept of Humanities, around the role of 'tradition.' One key quality in the Humanities for Nussbaum is a 'critical' attitude to tradition. Yet she laments the loss of a set of skills and capacities which were previously strong, in Humanities understood as a discipline. This corresponds to a tendency in her work to look backwards to a past before the 'crisis,' when things were clearer and less perceptually idiosyncratic. Her own background as a classicist reinforces this tendency. This was manifest in her earlier defence of the Humanities (1997) where she attacked 'post-modernism,' accusing Derrida for instance of being 'simply not worth studying,' and Foucault of 'historical incompleteness and lack of conceptual clarity.' She perceives a fault line in the Humanities in terms of which its true (traditional) form needs to be defended from false accretions.

For Nussbaum it is especially the true (traditional) Humanities which faces this double crisis: a crisis from neglect by the world in crisis, and another crisis from contamination with its new forms. This means that the double crisis falls on a fault-line in Humanities itself. Unless this pair of crises can be managed, then Humanities is weakened as a player just when it is most needed, according to Nussbaum's own analysis.

Yet the connections Nussbaum wants are also demanded from the other side of the divide she sees between Humanities and Business Education. Even before the GFC, business educators were expressing concerns at the lack of the Humanities concerns raised by Nussbaum. For instance, in 2008 Philip Delves Broughton reflected on his experience only 4 years before while studying his MBA at Harvard Business School. He says that he sensed even then a seismic shift. It pivoted around issues of ethics in business:

> In 2003, Harvard introduced a class called 'Leadership and Corporate Accountability' to allow students to discuss the perils of chasing dollars down ethical sewers. (2008:4)

In one class he reports a flash-point in a discussion of an argument that once would have encapsulated the ethical position of classic capitalism of the 1960s:

> Many successful business people lived by one set of ethical issues in their private lives and a quite different set in their professional lives ... Knowing that you could win the game of business playing all manner of tricks which you would never inflict on your spouse, children or friends made for a calmer, less complicated life. (2008:4)

This strategy, solving ethical dilemmas through a total split between ethical values and professional strategy, now seemed problematic to the class. In the 1960s this was seen as a way of removing complexity. If difficult questions were not asked, it was as though the problems themselves were resolved. Now, in an environment perceived as already highly complex, such simplicity is no longer tenable.

Heavy criticisms also come from Management mainstream. Already in 1994 Henry Mintzberg, a distinguished Canadian management theorist, had denounced the dominant style of MBA as exemplified by the Harvard model. Instead he argued that 'much of (its) success is delusory, that our approach to educating leaders is undermining our leadership, with dire economic and social consequences' (Mintzberg 5). Two other management heavy weights, Warren Bennis and James O'Toole, published an influential critique in the *Harvard Business Review* entitled: 'How Business Schools lost their way.' These writers begin bluntly: 'Business Schools are on the wrong track' (96). They are graduating students 'ill-equipped to wrangle with complex, unquantifiable issues.' This is the 'stuff of management,' they say, out there in the real world. Yet back in Schools of Business, even the best, there is an obsessive but irrelevant focus on 'scientific' models. 'When applied to business - where judgements are made with messy and incomplete data - statistics and methodological wizardry can blind rather than illuminate' (99). The problem, they say, 'is not that business schools have embraced scientific rigour, but that they have forsaken other forms of knowledge' (102).

These other forms of knowledge clearly include the Humanities. Solutions to the general malaise affecting the world of business are being looked for where Nussbaum locates them. Her two crises converge, one the solution to the other. Yet for this to happen, we need to bring the two domains still more closely together, economic life as a source of inspiration as well as impediment for Humanities knowledge? Humanities, I suggest, cannot just be the mixture as before, backed up by a better PR machine.

How might the particular case of Shakespeare and his Hamlet play a part in a new kind of business education, and how might issues from the world of business offer rich, new insights into and from a work that might seem already interpreted to death? I have in mind a range of possible pedagogic outcomes. Business students can incorporate these texts and issues into their courses. There are already some authors from Business who try to do this, even using *Hamlet* as a text: for example, successful CEO Norman Augustine shares his infectious enthusiasm for Shakespeare, which some

Humanities academics might find naive, along with insights into tricks of power in action which he understands better than most of them (Augustine and Adams). He analyses Claudius' situation as a case study in crisis management, which it also is. Humanities students can stretch their imagination to incorporate these areas of life into their own studies. Or more integrated options can come onto the agenda, with students from Business and Humanities sitting in the same class, their teachers engaging in the interdisciplinary research required to give a scholarly context to this new area of study, discovering together their common problems and the different forms of their common humanity.

Layered time

Shakespeare lived mostly or entirely in England between 1564 and 1616. His play *Hamlet* can be dated 1600. But this may have incorporated earlier versions, and the copy we have today incorporates some later editorial decisions. But even if the date were more precise we can still ask: should this be seen as recent? Or long ago?

A great deal hangs on this doubt. Different attitudes to time create different fissures in the body of the Humanities. Nussbaum, for instance, includes the ancient classics of Greece and Rome firmly within it. From this perspective, Shakespeare and *Hamlet* are part of this continuum in time. Her conception of the Humanities is equally generous in terms of space, including literature and culture of India and China as part of the multicultural education of her idea of the 'world citizen' who will be formed and nurtured by the Humanities. Yet as we have seen, this generosity does not fully extend to the recent 'postmodernists,' or business barbarians from the present.

There is an analogous line in literary studies, between what is called 'Presentism' and 'Historicism.' In polemics, these two approaches are often presented as incompatible. Presentism is seen as locked into a solipsistic present which can only see its own preoccupations, against an Historicism claiming to eschew subjective judgements and record only 'the facts' (Holbo). 'Historicism' here must be sharply distinguished from 'New Historicism' (see, for example, Greenblatt), which offered itelf as mediator between historical and current contexts and interpretations, but seemed, to Historicists, marred by the assumptions of Presentism.

Neither Presentism nor Historicism in a pure form could serve the animating function Nussbaum wants for the Humanities. Her form of Humanities is needed to save Democracy in the present, not in a hermetically sealed past. Terence Hawkes, influential in putting this term into circulation, described 'presentism' as 'taking one's present situation fully into account' (Hawkes 2). That is what Nussbaum does with the Humanities, so she is a 'presentist,' in these terms. So is Hamlet, when he says 'The play's the thing / Wherein I'll catch the conscience of the king' (II.ii.616–7).

Foucault made some historiographical observations which (despite Nussbaum's skepticism about his value) are helpful here. He identified one tendency in history which moves towards ever larger units of time, which aims to 'distinguish various sedimentary strata; linear successions, which for so long had been the object of research, have given way to discoveries in depth,' and he asks 'in what large-scale chronological table may distinct series of events be determined?' At the same time he notes that the history of ideas, including the history of literature, tends in the opposite direction: 'away from vast unities like "periods" or "centuries" to the phenomena of rupture, of discontinuity' (2, 3).

In these terms, the contrast between 'presentism' and 'historicism' comes from two different lenses, each a legitimate form of History. Neither perspective is simple or automatic. 'Long history,' to give it a label, has different strata. It is not a single, undifferentiated sweep of time, but tries to identify a small number of significant interruptions, creating smaller units of history which are nonetheless larger than the units in the history of ideas.

The historical imagination Nussbaum wants to foster covers a vast terrain, until she comes to the present, when she drastically alters her focal length to react to a local subjective change in the present. Yet it would be possible to move in the other direction, beyond the boundary formed by the High Civilizations of Europe, Asia and America to reach what is often called 'pre-history,' which continues back through time to the dawn of the human species, and beyond. Nussbaum insists on recognising the animal origins of humanity. This kind of long history allows it to be included. From this perspective, *Hamlet* is not at or beyond the limits of our (21ˢᵗ century, English-speaking) capacity to understand and connect. On the contrary, it is almost too close to the centre of an extended field.

The 'post-human,' a category put on the agenda by this book, extends in the other direction, towards an imagined future which is only just beginning, unless we can stop it. But in terms of this Foucaldian temporal framework, the 'post-human' is produced by ever more minute subdivisions of time. Paradoxically these make both the 'human' and the 'post-human' only briefly thinkable before they melt away, before the 'human' is cut up into countless temporally-bound strata, and the 'post-human' waits anxiously for almost immediate obsolescence.

Hamlet can, I suggest, help business and literature students alike grapple with these important issues of time, assisted by the most nit-picking forms of traditional scholarship. This text is a palimpsest. There are different versions written or over-written by Shakespeare, and earlier versions he may have incorporated. One is probably a now-lost play by a minor dramatist, Thomas Kyd. Kyd and Shakespeare got the story, via a circuitous route, from Saxo Grammaticus, recording legends around 1185 about Danish Prince Amleth. Saxo was a compiler himself, working with even earlier oral versions, some of which survived in his near contemporary, Snorri Sturluson, including an enigmatic reference to 'Amlódi's churn' as a mythological reference to the sea. These in turn come from the same mythological matrix as the stories of the Nibelung, later the basis for Wagner's famous 19ᵗʰ-century opera, and less directly Tolkien's *Lord of the Rings*.

Palimpsestic analysis like this could be a valuable exercise for business students, applied to concepts that are important to them. For instance, one widely-used text book in Management Studies says this about 'globalization,' a keyword for defining the modern conditions of business:

> Globalization was initially conceptualised as the worldwide process of economic and industrial restructuring. Industrial countries invested in factories in developing nations with lower wage structures, and reduced their costs at home through restructuring and technology change. Today,

> globalization is also seen to include the process of continual change to
> gain competitive advantage. (Davidson and Griffin 146)

This description unhelpfully reduces the vast, complex object referred
to by 'globalization' to a two-stage history of a particular economic
strategy, with an unstated starting date ('initially') and a more recent
break ('today'). The brief content given indicates that 'globalization' began
with the post-war strategy of building factories in developing countries,
the second change coming around the 1970s. Such 'globalisation' has a
shallow history. Its history is outside history, concerned only with ways
of organising industry and investment, not with the development of the
'world citizen' Nussbaum records from the time of the Stoics of classical
Greece and Rome 2000 years ago.

With the idea of a palimpsest we can track earlier layers of this single but
discontinuous process further back, till at a certain point it mirrors the layers
in the text of *Hamlet*. 16th-century Elizabethan sailors were at the leading
edge of an early stage of European global expansion. In the 11th-century
Scandinavian sailors ranged across Northern Europe, including Britain and
Ireland, on to Iceland, Greenland, and the Americas. Movements of peoples
in 'Dark Age' Europe are barely known today, yet they constituted forms of
'globalization,' forming strata which still underly Europe today. In tracing
this process, there is no conflict between good literary scholarship and the
deeper understanding of processes of globalization which business students
need. This inclusive 'Humanities' approach brings out connections to look
at. It does not have to generate specious or unsound analyses of them.

Shakespeare the Elizabethan

In these terms there is no incompatibility between 'presentist' and 'historicist'
perspectives, or between Humanities and Business perspectives. Each will
calibrate history in its own way, but none will comprehend the whole.
Bounded in a nutshell, the mind can comprehend infinite space: and yet in
reaching toward infinite space the mind is yet encased within its nutshell in
a *particular* space and time.

How, then, might the GFC connect with Shakespeare? What mutual light might be generated by putting these two worlds and times together, across a complex, interrelated but stratified temporal field, drawing on as many disciplines and traditions in the Humanities as are needed?

In fact, Shakespeare's England knew about Great (or Global) Financial Crises. An extended period of inflation for over a century between 1500 and 1620 had massive, destabilizing effects on all countries, including England. Between 1542 and 1554 England suffered an exacerbation of the crisis, as a result, it is now agreed, of a policy of debasement of the coinage (Clay). The author of the diagnosis and cure was Sir Thomas Gresham, extremely successful speculator and financial advisor to Protestant King Edward VI, Catholic Mary and Protestant Elizabeth. His so-called Law, known as Gresham's Law, states that 'Bad money drives out good'. In his analysis, bad money, coins with impurities which are therefore cheaper to produce, circulate alongside 'good money' made of purer metal. Because all money looks the same and is equally authorized by the government to have the same value, the government makes a loss on all the 'good money', so they cease to make it. 'Bad' money has driven out the good.

A prophet of Neo-Liberal economics, Milton Friedman, specifically cited Gresham and his law as a forerunner of his Monetarist theory (Friedman 296). The monetary system has not changed greatly over 500 years. It is a sufficiently stable series, in Foucault's terms, to unite then and now as aspects of a single system. Reflections on it are not 'presentist', but incorporate different experiences of a sufficiently common object.

Shakespeare did not directly address the monetary system, but his works have many incidental reflections. Marx quoted *Timon of Athens* IV.3 on money with approval: 'The equation of the incompatible, as Shakespeare nicely defined money' (Marx 163). Timon's virtuoso harangue against gold and money in that scene would be a good text for a whole class of Humanities and Business students on the effects of money on all aspects of life. In this chapter I limit myself to *Hamlet*, where the theme is present but not foregrounded. In this play as in others Shakespeare suggests connections between value in monetary and other systems which provide a rich basis for general reflections.

For instance, Hamlet confronts his mother, Queen Gertrude, with two portraits, one of his father, the other of Claudius his uncle:

> Look here upon this picture, and on this,
> The counterfeit presentment of two brothers (III.iv.54–5)

The two represent a form of Gresham's Law, whereby bad money (Claudius) has driven out good (Old Hamlet). For Hamlet this fact is inexplicable, as devaluation of the currency was for Gresham's contemporaries until he explained it. We can ask: does this question come from outside Shakespeare, from our present knowledge, even though Shakespeare lived after Gresham, and hence was capable of it?

But there is a jarring word in this speech, 'counterfeit'. Should this just refer to the fact that the images are painted, not real? Hamlet certainly acts as though the truth of the painting is irrelevant. He compares image to image as if he were comparing realities directly. But Elizabethans knew well that paintings of monarchs could flatter, and normally did. So Hamlet is comparing what is the equivalent of two coins, neither of which may contain pure metal. In fact the Gresham principle can be applied to every aspect of life, in Elizabethan times as in contemporary business. Words and images are out of synch with what they refer to. Aberrations from Gresham's Law create Global Financial Crises in one sphere of life, and corruption, pain and madness in another.

The question of Hamlet

Hamlet is full of much-quoted phrases, but the most famous of all is the first line of Hamlet's soliloquy: 'To be, or not to be: that is the question' (III.i.56). A Business student might ask, of this, just why is it so famous? And many Humanities students might find it hard to give a good answer. The explication of this enigma and the line that provokes it illustrates many things I have to say about what form of the Humanities may be able to best respond to Nussbaum's interlocking set of crises.

Looking at this line through Linguistics, one discipline that makes up the Humanities, we may note that this is not itself a question. It is a statement that there is a question about these alternatives, which Hamlet is not asking at this point. Moreover, the two alternatives are unclear. Hamlet is supposedly contemplating suicide, so 'to be' can be glossed as 'to live', but this is not a natural interpretation, in Elizabethan or modern English. 'Not to be' likewise can be glossed as 'not to live', but that is equally strained. From these two alternatives we can get to what is taken as the real question: 'shall I live or shall I kill myself?' However, it is a long route.

Business students in my imagined class might well ask: Is this the best a so-called master of the English language can do? Asking a question which is not a question, about alternatives phrased so obscurely that it is not clear what the question would be if it were asked? These questions raise others: how could such poor English be treated as the pinnacle of English poetry, as it is? And how can the analysis of such a phrase contribute to a Humanities response to its many crises?

A first response to make is to recognise that Shakespeare here is not trying to write the first premise in a philosophical treatise, but to dramatise the movements of a human mind facing huge, intractable problems. In these terms we can see that Hamlet is posing a question he cannot face, evading it by obscuring the reality of the choices he does not want to choose between, and by making it not even a question. He takes 13 more lines of musing before he can even formulate a question.

When he does, this is a different question, now displaced from himself ('Who would bear …?' III.i.70) followed by another 6 lines of musings. The question-form with the conditional 'would' implies that this is an answer to his first question: No-one would bear this life. But this form of question allows the positive answer to come that actually comes: most people do, including me. By exploiting the ambiguity of this form of question he comes up with a positive, which we see growing out of his negative by a psychological chain of reasoning. He then finishing by casting the action of suicide, which would have prevented him from carrying out any other actions, as a form of cowardice, in which 'the pale cast of thought' affects 'enterprises of great pitch and moment' so that they 'lose the name of action'. That is, the only action that counts as action is the one that prevents all other actions.

Questions have been recognised as a distinctive quality of this play by traditional Humanities scholars. For instance Maynard Mack wrote:

> Hamlet's world is pre-eminently in the interrogative mood. It reverberates with questions, anguished, meditative, alarmed. There are questions that in this play, to an extent I think unparalleled in any other, mark the the phases and even the nuances of the action, helping to establish its peculiar baffled tone. (Mack 505)

For Mack, this quality characterises the play, and contributes to its 'tone', which he calls 'baffled'. He identifies the problem with the form of the questions in the play, and connects this problem with the play's themes. This leads into further questions, with more urgent connections with interests from the present from Business and Humanities students alike.

Questions are important for everyone who uses language, and they take a variety of forms. The topic is covered in management handbooks as part of a manager's basic toolkit. It is made to seem simple in principle, needing only some advice as to when and how to use this mode. For instance, one popular handbook has this discussion:

> Good listening techniques are vital, especially in intimate, informal settings. Encourage the speaker by appearing to listen intently, and not interrupting too often ... Ask open questions ('What do you think we should do about X's career development?' which will generate discussion and let you deploy the key listening techniques of empathy, analysis, and synthesis. Avoid closed questions ('Should we promote X?') that can be answered with just 'Yes' or 'No.' (Heller 154)

There are many differences between this treatment of questions and the theme in *Hamlet*. Most obviously, this writer and the Business people he addresses are not wracked with doubt and indecision, as Hamlet famously is. In this respect *Hamlet's* main function might seem to be to provide a model of what a manager should *not* be or do.

Yet the contrast helps bring out some curious aspects of this advice. First there is the odd use of 'appearing', implying a contrast with 'being'. A crucial problem in Hamlet's world is presented as unproblematic here. Yet in economics, Gresham's Law applies to the 16th and 20th centuries alike. Only 'appearing' to listen is likely to function like bad money, driving out good, making it harder to be believed.

Where Hamlet is troubled by too much introspection, too many doubts to be able to be effective, there is no sense that these ideal business persons have any inner life or any doubts. Everything is 'impression management', calculated and guaranteed to work as advertised. *Hamlet* refers to a kind of 'impression management'. Polonius advises his son Laertes that 'the apparel oft proclaims the man' (I.iii.72). But Polonius is presented as a buffoon in the play, not a source of wisdom.

In business practice, the situation is more complex. Studies of how business discourse occurs in practice show that the use and form of questions depends on the shifting dynamics of the communication (Pilegaard), with differences in different cultures and at different times. These differences are highly functional and reflect decisions made by participants in the exchanges. This makes them sensitive indicators of the situations and cultures concerned. Anderson for instance showed differences between English and Danish speakers. English speakers use repetitions, for instance, 'to evade disclosing a firm stand when faced with a direct question'. Danish speakers, in contrast, show 'an undertone of "definiteness" and consequently a streak of "uncooperativeness" in the negotiation process' (Anderson 240).

These practically-orientated business micro-studies show that the act of asking and answering questions is shrouded in complexity. People do not ask questions just because they want to know something. Questions are social acts, depending on social factors and forces which inhibit who can ask what of whom. Hamlet's inability to ask questions is typical of situations of power and danger, because questions and answers alike may expose dangerous knowledge.

The Neo-Liberal myth that everyone is free to ask questions clashes with a common dysfunctional reality. The Enron bubble grew out of control until it burst because no-one, inside or outside the organisation, was able or willing to ask the right questions (McLean and Elkind). The inability of major corporations to allow real questions to come onto the agenda has proven a major factor in the persistence of the systematic unethical behaviours that concern business educators like Bennis and O'Toole (2005) just as much as crises like the GFC.

As well as being sensitive to local conditions of discourse, question are basic to human communication, part of a Long History. English *wh-* and Latin *qu-* both derive from an Indo-European root **kwi-*. Questions turn discourse into an interactive process where knowledge flows or is blocked from one or both sides by willingness or refusal to exchange.

Hamlet grows out of a body of myths, and its nucleus contains story elements from pre-capitalist societies. The anthropologist Claude Levi-Strauss (1967) argues for a deep pattern he finds in many myths from this strata of Long History in which questions play a crucial role, linking with other fundamental social processes. Celtic myths like *Parzival,* the Greek Oedipus cycle, and Amerindian myths all have a significant relation between incest and the solving of riddles, through parallels between sexual and discursive processes and the well-being of society. Oedipus answers the riddle, the question without an answer, and marries his mother, like an answer without a question. Parzival is an anti-Oedipus, who does not ask the question he should, of the Fisher King, and does not have the sacred marriage that the Kingdom needs.

Hamlet is like Parzival, and the Amleth-myth comes from the same body of myths. He is unable to ask or answer the right question, unable to form a couple with Ophelia, paralysed by the incestuous feelings provoking his disgust at the incest of another. Myth-criticism is often seen as a distraction from real history and real politics. As part of Long history it can point to connections that are no less real because they are also old.

According to Lévi-Strauss, Parzival and Oedipus are the two forbidden extremes. Each leads in the myth to disaster for the country, plague in the case of Oedipus, famine in the case of the Parzival cycle. For Lévi-Strauss these myths are found across many different 'primitive' societies because they arise from intractable human dilemmas, related to contradictions and paradoxes of speech and sexuality.

In *Hamlet*'s case, this structure raises questions as relevant to modern capitalism as Shakespeare's society. What happens when the barrier Broughton refers to between public and private values collapses (Broughton 8)? Is Hamlet's acute misogyny towards Ophelia (III.i.101ff.) just Elizabethan normalcy, to be accepted as such by 'historical' criticism? Or is it part of what is 'rotten' in the state of Denmark, in 16th-century England, in 21st-century corporate culture, as it was in Amleth's warrior society, or Oedipus's very ancient Greece?

Conclusion

My purpose is to use Shakespeare and *Hamlet* to show how they can stimulate thought and discussion between Business and Humanities about the multiple crises we face, and what kind of knowledge the many disciplines of the Humanities (including Business Studies) might try to provide, to each other and themselves. Such a dialogue would benefit from the richer sense of what questions can be and what they can show, triggered by Shakespeare's text and going beyond it. It would weave around fundamental issues about the relations between the present and the past, about what is unique about our own time and others, what we can and cannot know, and how we can get by with real but imperfect knowledge. It might see how economic laws like Gresham's may also reflect more basic social truths about ethics and integrity, without which the current crises will be mere harbingers of an increasingly ugly, dysfunctional world.

Works Cited

Anderson, F. 'English and Danish communicative behaviour in negotiating simulations of the use of intratextual and intertextual repetition.' In *The languages of business: an international perspective*. Edited by F. Bargiela-Chiappini and S. Harris. Edinburgh: Edinburgh University Press. 1996

Augustine, N. and K. Adams. *Shakespeare In Charge: The Bard's Guide to Leading and Succeeding on the Business Stage*. New York: Hyperion. 1999

Bennis, W., and J. O'Toole. 'How business schools lost their way.' *Harvard Business Review* (May 2005): 96–105

Broughton, P. Delves. 'Harvard loses its Lustre.' *Australian Financial Review* (19 Sept. 2008): 3

Clay, C. *Economic Expansion and Social Change: England 1500–1700*. Cambridge: Cambridge University Press. 1984

Davidson, P., and R. Griffin. *Management: Australia in a global context* (2nd edition). Brisbane: John Wiley & Sons. 2003

Foucault, M. *The Archaeology of Knowledge.* London: Routledge. 1972

Friedman, M. and R. *Freedom to Choose.* Harmondsworth: Penguin. 1980

Greenblatt, S. *Renaissance Self-fashioning: From More to Shakespeare.* Chicago: Chicago University Press. 1980

Hawkes, T. *Shakespeare in the Present.* London: Routledge. 2002

Heller, R. (ed.). *Manager's Handbook.* London: Dorling Kindersley. 200

Holbo, J. 'The function of Presentism at the Critical Time.' *Literature Compass* 5.6 (2008): 1097–1110

Lévi-Strauss, C. *The scope of anthropology* London: Jonathon Cape. 1967

Mack, M. 'The World of *Hamlet.*' *The Yale Review* 45 (1952): 502–23

McLean, B, and P. Elkind. *The Smartest Guys in the Room.* Harmondsworth: Viking. 2003.

Marx, K. *Grundrisse.* Harmondsworth: Penguin. 1939

Mintzberg, H. *Managers not MBAs: A Hard Look at Soft Practices of Managing and Management Development.* San Francisco: Berrett–Kohler. 1994

Nussbaum, M. *Cultivating Humanity.* Cambridge, Mass.: Harvard University Press, 1997

———. *Not for Profit: Why Democracy needs the Humanities.* Princeton: Princeton University Press. 2010

———, and A. Sen. *The Quality of Life.* Oxford: Clarendon Press. 1993

Pilegaard, M. 'Politeness in written business discourse.' *Journal of Pragmatics* 28.2 (1997): 223–44

Chapter 15

Reel Life: Representing the Human in Michael Almereyda's *Hamlet*

Marina Gerzic
University of Western Australia

In the last decade there has been a particular explosion of Shakespeare on film, with over forty filmed Shakespeare adaptations released to varying degrees of box office achievement and popularity. These 'new generation' Shakespearian films, termed 'Post-Shakespeares' by Michael Anderegg (Anderegg 177–202), are modernised renditions of Shakespeare's plays, which have reconfigured Shakespeare for a modern audience, and re-popularised Shakespearian works into popular culture. One such 'Post Shakespeare' film is Michael Almereyda's recent adaptation of *Hamlet* (2000), starring actor Ethan Hawke. Almereyda's *Hamlet* was made at a time of political and economic upheaval in the United States of America. The film was released shortly after the first large-scale anti-globalisation protests broke out at the World Trade Organisation Conference in Seattle, Washington in late November 1999. Following the film's release in 2000, American energy company, Enron, announced bankruptcy in late 2001. The collapse of the company was revealed to be a result of institutionalised and well organised accounting fraud by many high ranking executives. All was not well in the state of US economics and business, and this sense of shady practices, manipulation and corruption is reflected in Almereyda's *Hamlet*.

Elsie Walker goes so far as to refer to Almereyda's film as an 'anti-capitalist *Hamlet*' (Walker 17). Robert Shaughnessy points out that unlike previous filmed versions of *Hamlet* 'the domain of the film's actions is neither military nor political but economic' (Shaughnessy 54). I agree with Shaughnessy that the focus of the film is largely on the economic, and how it affects the personal relationships and humanity of each of the characters in the film. Most obviously this is seen in the film's setting, the business world of New York City. The connection to the economic is strengthened through references to foreign film versions of *Hamlet* such as Akira Kurosawa's *Warui yatsu hodo yoku nemuru* (English title: *The Bad Sleep Well*) (1960) and Aki Kaurismäki's *Hamlet liikemaailmassa* (English title: *Hamlet Goes Business*) (1987). Both films are set in business worlds, and as with Almereyda's film, they offer a critique of global corporate power. However, the political context of the time is also influential and shouldn't be discounted when analysing Almereyda's film. What I refer to here is specifically the election of George W. Bush to the US presidency and the subsequent conspiracy surrounding the halting of the recount of votes in the state of Florida (at the time John Ellis 'Jeb' Bush, the brother of George W. Bush, was serving as Governor of Florida). Hamlet's uncle Claudius (Kyle MacLachlan) is equally handed control of the kingdom of Denmark under suspicious circumstances, and this can be argued is a comment by Almereyda on the state of US politics at the time.

Almereyda's *Hamlet* is characterised by a bombardment of visual information throughout the film. Shakespeare's 'original' play-text has been significantly edited and visually displaced and rearranged. What is left is a film dominated by image over Shakespeare's words. Almereyda himself clarifies the abundance of images in the preface to the film's screenplay:

> The film admits that images currently keep pace with words, or outstrip them, creating a kind of overwhelming alternate reality. So nearly every scene in the script features a photograph, a TV monitor, an electronic recording device of some kind. (Almereyda, 2000, iii)

Almereyda thus explains that his Hamlet is trapped not in a mental world of 'words, words, words' (II, ii, 194) but in one of 'images, images, images.' Many trademarks and logos, mistaken by viewers for product placements, when in fact Almereyda paid for the privilege of using all the brand names, bombard the screen space, leading to a sense of claustrophobia. Hamlet's ability and desire to reproduce those images is therefore both a way to organise his thoughts and represent his reality, but also his curse. Hamlet declares to Rosencrantz and Guildenstern that 'Denmark is a prison' (II, ii, 242), and this prison is 'defined by the advertising, by all the hectic distractions, brand names, announcements and ads that crowd our waking hours' (Almereyda, 2000, xi).

There are two main types of imagery present in Almereyda's film; what I term 'the corporate' – as mentioned above, the product placement purchased by the director Almereyda, as well as 'the artistic,' Hamlet's 'Pixelvision' video diaries and short film *The Mousetrap*, where words are dispensed with altogether. This analysis will focus on the video diaries and short film, and how they are used to characterise Hamlet as a man obsessed with images, who is only able to find himself on screen. An examination of what happens to the character of Fortinbras (Casey Affleck) within the film, reveals that in Michael Almereyda's *Hamlet* the human is displaced with images.

Almereyda's Manhattan

In his cinematic adaptation of *Hamlet* director Michael Almereyda transplants Shakespeare's story into modern New York City. Here Denmark is a corporation, a powerful media conglomerate that is under a hostile takeover bid by outside interest Fortinbras. Elsinore is now a hotel where Ophelia (Julia Stiles) suicides in the lobby fountain. Shakespeare's speeches are delivered by phone and fax machines, or, as is the case with Rosencrantz (Steve Zahn) and Guildenstern's (Dechen Thurman) communiqué to the King of England, via floppy disk. Almereyda's Manhattan is a place of corporate intrigue and conspiracy, where each person is constantly visible, constantly watched and contained. Hamlet and Ophelia are at odds with this urban world of claustrophobia and global corporate power that surrounds them. Unlike the corporate elite of Denmark who use images to monitor and control, Hamlet and Ophelia are artists, one a photographer the other a film maker. Their visual means of recording are used as a form of introspective art in which they can express themselves. The choice to present Hamlet and

Ophelia as artists may have its foundations in that both characters were popular subject matter for artists (notably painters) from the late eighteenth to early nineteenth century. British portrait artist Thomas Lawrence, impressionist Édouard Manet, French romanticist Eugène Delacroix, and pre-Raphaelites Edwin Austin Abbey, John Everett Millais, Dante Gabriel Rossetti and John William Waterhouse all painted portraits and scenes from Shakespeare's *Hamlet* during the period.

Hamlet, played by actor Ethan Hawke, is a man obsessed with filming on his portable Pixelvision camera, and constantly replaces human interactions with virtual ones. His exchanges with real people come across as awkward and forced, and are often interrupted, such as when he shows up in Ophelia's loft on her birthday only to be intruded upon by her father Polonius (Bill Murray). Hawke's Hamlet is instead most comfortable in front of his television screen, reviewing images and working on his short films. Hamlet plays out his life and his inner thoughts via the medium of film. He obsessively replays, reconfigures and manipulates images in an unsuccessful attempt to make the virtual 'real.' The two examples in the film are Hamlet's video diary and his short-film *The Mousetrap*.

Hamlet's video diary

Hamlet's video diary is filmed on his personal Pixelvision camera. The term Pixelvision refers to recordings made on a Fisher–Price PXL 2000 toy black and white portable video camera produced in the 1980s. Its images are recorded not on videocassettes but on audiotape. A characteristic of recordings produced by the camcorder is a reduced frame rate output and a picture that is both monochrome and low in resolution. Pixelvision has seen a revival in popularity since the early-to-mid 1990s among alternative and experimental filmmakers, such as Richard Linklater, Sadie Benning and Michael Almereyda. The use of Pixelvision technology has been a characteristic of Almereyda's work for some time. His earlier feature length films, such as *Another Girl Another Planet* (1992), and vampire film *Nadja* (1994) both use Pixelvision extensively. Almereyda has also made several short films exclusively using a Pixelvision camera, and has written an article about the technology (see Almereyda, 1994). The resurgence in popularity of the camera can be attributed to its grainy image, unique rendition of contrast, and accompanying 'bipod' stand, a simple cradle to hold the camera still on a table. This allows filmmakers to immediately set up the equipment, and experiment with the camera.

Visual artist Sadie Benning's work with Pixelvision is of particular interest, as Almereyda credits Benning with his introduction to, and immediate love of the medium of Pixelvision (Almereyda, 1994, 101–03). Furthermore her work with Pixelvision parallels Ethan Hawke's use of the technology in *Hamlet*. Benning's early work took the form of video diaries, autobiographical mediations narrated in the first person. Almereyda describes the intimate nature of Benning's video diaries as, 'You have the sense that you're watching something intensely fragile and secret, on the threshold of visibility' (1994, 103). This same sense of intimacy and private introspection also characterises Hamlet's video diaries. In his analysis of Pixelvision, Peter S. Donaldson suggests that the technology lends itself to such video diaries due to its 'unusual degree of privacy because of its incompatibility with other media' (Donaldson 218). Unless an adaptor is used, playback is limited to the camera as no other equipment is able to render a video image from audiotape.

In Almereyda's *Hamlet* one of the primary functions of Hamlet's video diary is to reflect the 'fractured and tormented state of Hamlet's soul and imagination' (Crowl 195). In the film's published screenplay actor Ethan Hawke reveals that making the video diary was a great way for him to get inside the character (Almereyda, 2000, xv). The video diary is a device used to record and reflect the bits and pieces of Hamlet's soliloquies that are retained by Almereyda in his film adaptation of *Hamlet*. The video diary is an instrumental way in which Hamlet expresses himself and his internal thoughts and feelings about the state of the world and his relationships with others. Its importance is underscored by its presence at the very beginning of the film. In a divergence from the film's published screenplay, which like Shakespeare's play-text opens with Bernardo's exclamation of 'Who's there?' (Almereyda, 2000, 5), the film instead opens with an entry in Hamlet's video diary. Almereyda reveals in the screenplay (135) that this change came about after a botched attempt to film the scene as it exists in the screenplay (55) contributed to an unsuccessful test screening organised by the film company Miramax (who holds the distributor rights for the film). As a result both Almereyda and Ethan Hawke admitted that the film needed a more immediate and urgent start, and so Hamlet's speech to Rosencrantz and Guildenstern (II, ii) was shifted to the beginning of the film. The scene with Bernardo (Rome Neal), Horatio (Karl Geary) and Marcella (Paula Malcomson) was instead moved to a flashback sequence during their report of the first ghost sighting later in the film (Almereyda, 2000, 135–36). Speaking directly to the camera, in a grainy distorted black and white image, Ethan Hawke delivers an out of sequence and truncated version of Hamlet's speech to Rosencrantz and Guildenstern:

I have of late, but wherefore I know not, lost all my mirth.

What a piece of work is a man?
How noble in reason, how infinite in faculties, in form and moving how express and admirable, in action how like angel, in apprehension how like a god! The beauty of the world, the paragon of animals –
And yet to me, what is this quintessence of dust? (Almereyda, 2000, 55–56)

In Shakespeare's text Hamlet's utterance can be interpreted as a performance put on for Rosencrantz and Guildenstern, who he knows have been sent for and are spies for the King. Rosencrantz and Guildenstern are absent from the scene at the beginning of Almereyda's film; Hamlet is alone and the video is his direct address to the camera. The scene has less of a performative quality and seems more like a private introspection on the nature of humanity, as will be the case with his video diary throughout the film. This is a stark contrast to his short film *The Mousetrap*, discussed below. Unlike the short film, Hamlet's video diary is extremely personal and intended for his eyes only. For example, Hamlet hides his camera away when he notices Polonius surreptitiously looking over his shoulder at some replayed footage from the video diary. In constructing *The Mousetrap* Hamlet only uses previously recorded images to capture his own ideas. The clips from various sources stand in for The Players of Shakespeare's text, and thus the entire composition has an intended performative quality. Through opening his film with Hamlet's diatribe, Almereyda frames his adaptation as Hamlet's personal struggle with his thoughts and feelings rather than as a simple tale of revenge.

In Almereyda's *Hamlet* one of the most remarkable and significant moments of Hamlet's video diary is when James Dean is cast, by proxy, as Player King. As I will later show is the case with Fortinbras, in this scene we have an example of a significant character, one who here inspires Hamlet with his performance, being made up of images. As Hamlet watches images of James Dean on screen in clips from both *East of Eden* (1955) and *Rebel Without a Cause* (1955), a connection is established between Dean's conflict in both films with 'repressive parental institutions' (Burnett 59) and Hamlet's own disconnection from his feelings and inability to deal with repressive and dysfunctional parental figures. As images of James Dean appear on screen they are also captured by Hamlet and amalgamated into his video diary. Dean's appearance on screen coincides with Hamlet's 'O what a rogue and peasant slave' soliloquy (II, ii) where Hamlet questions the passion of the Player King (James Dean) in his performance:

> O what a rogue and peasant slave am I!
> Is it not monstrous that this player here,
> But in fiction, in a dream of passion,
> Could force his soul so to his own conceit
> That from her working all his visage wanned
> His whole function suiting
> With forms to his conceit? And all for nothing!
>
> What would he do,
> Had he the motive and the cue for passion
> That I have? (Almereyda, 2000, 58)

Hamlet wonders how James Dean is able to be so convincing and poignant in his acting when he himself is so apathetic about his own problematic real life situation. Dean's presence as Player King functions as a projection of Hamlet's wish fulfilment and is a figure of inspiration for Hamlet (Burnett 59). James Dean's famous 'haunted and alienated melancholy becomes a rich cultural icon for Hawke's Hamlet' (Crowl 195). Hamlet wants to be able to deal with things as James Dean does in these movies, and during this soliloquy Hamlet is finally moved to action. Samuel Crowl suggests that there is a morose self-absorption to Ethan Hawke's conception of Hamlet, and argues that he 'seems only to be able to find himself on the screen' (Crowl 195). Richard Burt summarises Hawke's portrayal in his observation that 'Hamlet sees himself everywhere' (Burt 296). Ethan Hawke himself elaborates on the intertextual tone of his depiction of Hamlet, suggesting in his introduction to the film's screenplay that: 'Hamlet was always more like Kurt Cobain or Holden Caulfield' (Almereyda, 2000, xiv). Furthermore, Hawke's introduction in the screenplay is prefaced with a quote from J.D. Salinger's novel *Catcher in the Rye* (1951), where Holden Caulfield talks about Hamlet, describing him as a '*sad screwed-up type guy*' (Almereyda, 2000, xiii; Hawke's italics). Like James Dean, both are figures of teen angst, isolation and introspection and have become idols in popular culture. Hawke's Hamlet is therefore a sum of all the references around him especially those he watches on his television screen. These images he sees all around become influential in how he expresses himself in his short film *The Mousetrap*.

The importance and influence of Hamlet's video diary, particularly to Hamlet himself is further punctuated by its 'presence' at the very end of the film, thus bookending Hamlet's story. As Hamlet lies dying his memories of events that actually happened to him are visualised in the same grainy low resolution as those captured on his video diary. He sees images of his mother, his father the Ghost (Sam Shepard), his brawl with Laertes (Liev Schreiber) at the graveyard, himself as he is beaten in the Laundromat by Claudius' bodyguards, and finally Ophelia. Her appearance at the very end of this sequence highlights how important she is to Hamlet and how Almereyda has shifted the focus of his film to Hamlet and Ophelia's tragic love story. The ending of Almereyda's film reveals that Hamlet's obsession with video images has totally consumed him and he now sees everything as if looking through the lens of his camera. Hamlet has become a 'reel' man, only able to communicate and 'be' via the medium of film.

The Mousetrap

As well as his video diary, Hamlet's short film *The Mousetrap* is another example of how he expresses himself via film. *The Mousetrap* is Almereyda's filmic equivalent of the player's performance of *The Murder of Gonzago* in Shakespeare's play-text. The 'play-within-a-play' becomes a 'film-within-a-film.' In order to try to prove Claudius' guilt Hamlet decides to put on *The Mousetrap*, and invites family and friends, including his uncle to a screening of the short-film. Hamlet instructs Horatio to watch his uncle during the screening:

> I prithee, when thou seest that act afoot,
> Observe my uncle. If his occulted guilt
> Do not itself unkennel in one speech,
> It is a damned ghost that we have seen.
> Give him heedful note,
> For I mine eyes will rivet to his face,
> And after we will both our judgements join
> In censure of his seeming. (Almereyda, 2000, 65)

Hamlet reasons that if Claudius is guilty of his father's murder then he will react to what he sees in the short film; however, if Claudius does not respond to what he sees on screen, the Ghost's previous utterances to Hamlet are not to be trusted.

The Mousetrap created by Hamlet is an experimental short film assembled from footage from a variety of different films and television shows. These source clips range from silent film, animation reminiscent of that by Terry Gilliam in the television series *Monty Python's Flying Circus* (1969), to explicit pornography. Each clip is only present on screen for a moment before it quickly cuts to another image; the result is that the audience is forced to 'piece the story of *The Mousetrap* together by assimilating the cinematic montage' (Walker 27). Tying together all the various clips is Pyotr Ilyich Tchaikovsky's 'Hamlet,' op. 67, an aural allusion to both the history of and continued inspiration of Shakespeare (and *Hamlet*) to the world of music. The film begins with a red title card featuring stark bold white lettering, on which appears the writing: THE MOUSETRAP/A TRAGEDY BY/HAMLET/ PRINCE OF DENMARK. The title card is identical in appearance to that shown at the very beginning of Almereyda's film. This deliberate similarity connects Hamlet not only with the act of filming, but with the director Almereyda himself, and illustrates how film and filming is embedded within Hamlet's identity. Hamlet is thus positioned as both director and auteur who exerts total control over the entire filmic text.

Hamlet's short film *The Mousetrap* paints an 'ideal' family of the 1950s and its eventual corruption. The screenplay describes the film's opening as: 'rose blooming; an idyllic happy family: man, wife and a little boy. The earth spins calmly on its axis. All is well in the world' (Almereyda, 2000, 68). These pleasant almost 'schmaltzy' images of 'perfect' family life are then juxtaposed with grotesque and pornographic images of decay, death and sex. Hamlet's short film goads Claudius into reacting to what he sees in the film, and is furthermore a critique on the state of Hamlet's new family dynamics. Mark Thornton Burnett argues that the film implies that there is 'no equivalent example of a functional familial unit in the Elsinore of the millennium' (Burnett 59). The short film highlights the dysfunction in Hamlet's current family situation and the unrealistic expectations and projections he has for his former one. Hamlet's short film is also a commentary on his situation and how he views the difference between his parents' relationship and the one his mother and uncle Claudius now engage in. Like the references to James Dean in the video diary, the childhood family depicted in Hamlet's short film is also a figure of his wish fulfilment and nostalgia. Hamlet positions himself as the innocent boy whose world is unwittingly destroyed as he sleeps. Sleeping becomes an analogy for Hamlet's absence. He is away at school in Wittenberg when his father is murdered. Waking symbolises his return to Elsinore and the discovery of his uncle's involvement in his father's death. The family who appear on screen is symbolic of Hamlet's view of his own family before his father's death. This 'picture perfect' 1950s' family symbolises the perfect familial relationship he believes was destroyed by sinister and perverse figures, represented on screen by images of sex and death, and one whose impossible return he longs for. However, Hamlet's strained encounter with his father's ghost throughout Almereyda's film suggests the relationship between them to have been less than ideal when he was still alive.

Fortinbras, the 'reel' man

What happens to humans in this *Hamlet* is conveyed most strongly by the character of Fortinbras – he is completely disembodied. The virtual absence of Fortinbras in productions of *Hamlet* is not a new characteristic of stage and screen adaptations of the play. From the seventeenth century through to the end of the nineteenth century the play's political aspects, the core being Fortinbras' threatened invasion of Denmark, was removed from staged versions of the play. This cut has still sometimes been made in twentieth and twenty-first century productions. In his now iconic film adaptation of *Hamlet* (1948) Laurence Olivier excises the political elements of the play, and eliminates the characters of Fortinbras, Rosencrantz and Guildenstern from the film. Famed director Peter Brook's millennial stage production starring British actor Adrian Lester (later filmed for television in 2002) takes a similar course. Brook eliminates the conflict with Norway and subsequently the character of Fortinbras is excluded from his production, although unlike Olivier's adaptation the characters Rosencrantz and Guildenstern still appear. Franco Zeffirelli in his film adaptation of *Hamlet* (1990) starring Mel Gibson also removes the character of Fortinbras in order to shift the film's focus onto the personal relationships within the play, and more specifically like Olivier before him, accommodate a Freudian reading of the Hamlet's relationship with his mother Gertrude.

Not all recent productions have chosen to eliminate the character of Fortinbras. Kenneth Branagh's visually stunning *Hamlet* (1996), a full text film of the play, not only includes all political aspects including Fortinbras (played by actor Rufus Sewell) but makes him a fully realised character from the moment he appears on screen. This is achieved through the use of cinematic flashbacks. The audience is not only told about Fortinbras' military campaigns, they are shown them. Fortinbras is overtly presented to the audience as a man of action, and what Hamlet might have become. Furthermore, Fortinbras is intended to be an obvious visual opposite to

Branagh's Hamlet. Whereas Hamlet is blond haired and blue eyed, Fortinbras has dark hair and brown eyes, and appears more rugged and brutish than Branagh's more refined Hamlet. Another more recent stage production which decides to include Fortinbras is the Royal Shakespeare Company's 2008/2009 production of *Hamlet* starring Scottish actor David Tennant, best known for his role as The Doctor in the re-imagined *Doctor Who* (2005) science fiction television serial. As with Almereyda's film, in this production Fortinbras (played by actor Robert Curtis) is virtually eliminated. Max Cooter in his review of the West End run of the production observes that Fortinbras only briefly shows up at the end of the play and says nothing (Cooter web) his appearance we can infer would be all the more menacing in its apparent silence. As Cooter rightly suggests, by ending this performance with Horatio's heartfelt farewell to Hamlet, this production 'emphasises the personal above the political' (Cooter), which is also a prominent aspect of Almereyda's *Hamlet.*

In Almeredya's adaptation Casey Affleck's Fortinbras is not Hamlet's direct physical opposite, but acts as a symbol of what Hamlet could potentially achieve and become if he had a desire to join the 'family business'. Like Branagh before him, Almereyda had originally intended Fortinbras to act as Hamlet's opposite, describing him in the screenplay for the film as a

> proud fatherless prince like Hamlet, but deprived of Hamlet's melancholy, his self-loathing, his talent for introspection. Fortinbras is decisive and active; a warrior, a winner. (Almereyda, 2000, 141–42)

Just as Hamlet is preoccupied with images, Fortinbras is just as concerned with images, and the way they can be manipulated. At the film's beginning he is the mogul of a multimedia empire attempting a takeover of Denmark Corp. Like Claudius he is savvy with the press, appearing on the cover of the technology focussed magazine *Wired*. Hamlet on the other hand is critical of the press; he shuns them on the red carpet as they interview Gertrude (Diane Venora) and Claudius, and casts a critical eye (and lens) as he films the assembled press at the conference announcing Claudius' new role as CEO of Denmark Corp. The image of Fortinbras and article title on the cover of *Wired* magazine is also particularly fortuitous regarding Claudius' death and Fortinbras' eventual conquest of Denmark. In the cover photo Fortinbras covers his eye with his left hand (a skull shaped ring adorns his finger - an image which connects him further with Hamlet), just as Claudius will do after being shot by Hamlet. The title proclaims 'The Wired interview with Fortinbras: Moving into the new millennium', announcing to the viewer that Fortinbras (and not Claudius nor Hamlet) will take Denmark Corp. into a new era.

The screenplay to the film indicates that Fortinbras initially had much more of a physical presence within the film. In particular Fortinbras closes the film. When Fortinbras arrives by helicopter on Elsinore's rooftop he takes out his digital video camera and films the scene before him. Documenting the final carnage that he has come upon, the screenplay notes that 'Fortinbras steps past Claudius, tracking bloody prints as he stands on the King's chair for a better view' (Almereyda, 2000, 129). For Almereyda, Fortinbras is the embodiment of history. He describes Fortinbras' actions as

> History's bloody bootprint, stamping remorselessly among the corpses
> of all overcomplicated young men, the ones who hesitate, who stun
> themselves looking into mirrors, the poets, the losers. (Almereyda, 2000,
> 142)

Unlike Hamlet's videoing, which is a mean of artistic introspection and observation, Fortinbras' filming of the dead bodies seems a cold, macabre way of documenting that which he has conquered, an act fitting a man who is now the face of a global media empire. Differing from what is presented in the screenplay, the final film diminishes Fortinbras' presence, with certain characters appropriating his characteristics. For example, Fortinbras is described in the screenplay as a 'scruffy young man wearing a sharp suit, a hat with earflaps, a bag slung on one shoulder' (Almereyda, 2000, 128); these physical features and costuming are transferred in the film to Hawke's Hamlet and define him throughout the film.

In the film Fortinbras is reduced to being a man made of images, seen only on the covers of newspapers and magazines. For example in the newspaper that Claudius rips up at the press conference, as mentioned earlier on the cover of *Wired* magazine that Guildenstern reads on the fateful plane trip to London, and on screen on the television news program which Hamlet watches on the plane. Almereyda states that Fortinbras' presence in the film became 'fragmentary, nearly anonymous, as befits a prince in the age of faceless corporate power' (Almereyda, 2000, 142). The reduction of Fortinbras to image is a comment on the power of image. In the end image, the reproduction of reality, symbolised by Fortinbras, is what completely takes control of Denmark and displaces the human. The film aptly ends, not with Fortinbras showing up in human form to claim 'victory,' but with news of his takeover conveyed via a television report. In an obvious allusion to Baz Luhrmann's *William Shakespeare's Romeo + Juliet* (1996) where an anchorwoman acts as both prologue and epilogue, Robert MacNeil, formerly of the *MacNeil/Lehrer News Hour* (1975) delivers lines taken from a speech given by the Player King, as a conclusion to the film:

> Our wills and fates do so contrary run
> That our devices still are overthrown;
> Our thoughts are ours, their ends none of our own. (III, ii, 192–194)

As MacNeil reads the lines aloud the camera reveals he is reading from a teleprompter – MacNeil's thoughts are not his own, but words that he is reading from a screen. Ironically the final image we are left with in Hamlet, a film saturated with images, is of words.

Almereyda's *Hamlet* can be read as providing meditations – particularly timely ones – on both the corruption that is endemic in the business world (the Global Financial Crisis, non-executive chairman of the NASDAQ stock exchange Bernie Maddoff defrauding investors of billions of dollars, and the collapse of mortgage corporations Fannie Mae and Freddie Mac are three recent examples), and on the obsession and reliance on images, particularly in the way we can create and display our lives in the cyber world. The rise of the internet in the 1990s has lead to an increase in user-generated content online. One of the prime examples is the recent craze for 'broadcast yourself' websites such as YouTube, where users edit, perform and display their thoughts, feelings and lives for others to view and comment on. Like Hamlet and Fortinbras, users are being stripped of their humanity and reduced to images on a screen, 'reel' people communicating into the abyss.

Works Cited

Anderegg, Michael. *Cinematic Shakespeare.* Rowman & Littlefield, 2004

Almereyda, Michael. 'My Stunning Future: The Luxuries of Pixelvision.' In *Projections 3: film-makers on film-making.* **Edited by John Boorman and Walter Donohue.** London: Faber and Faber, 1994. Pp. 101–107

———. *William Shakespeare's Hamlet.* London: Faber & Faber, 2000

Burnett, Mark Thornton. "To Hear and See the Matter': Communicating Technology in Michael Almereyda's *Hamlet* (2000).' *Cinema Journal* 42.3 Spring (2003): 48–69

Burt, Richard. 'Shakespeare and Asia in postdiasporic cinemas: spin-offs and citations of the plays from Bollywood to Hollywood.' In *Shakespeare the Movie II: Popularising the Plays on Film, TV, and Video and DVD.* Edited by Lynda E. Boose and Richard Burt. London; New York: Routledge, 2003. Pp. 265–303

Cooter, Maxwell. 'Hamlet (RSC).' *Whatsonstage.com.* Bandwidth Communications Ltd. 10 Dec. 2008. Web. 29 Sep. 2009. <URL: http://www.whatsonstage.com/reviews/theatre/london/E8821218018187/Hamlet+(RSC).html>

Crowl, Samuel. *Shakespeare at the Cineplex: The Kenneth Branagh Era.* Ohio: Ohio University Press, 2003

Donaldson, Peter S. 'Hamlet among the Pixelvisionaries: Video Art, Authenticity and Wisdom in Michael Almereyda's *Hamlet.*' In *A Concise Companion to Shakespeare on Screen.* Edited by Diana Henderson. Oxford: Blackwell's, 2006. Pp. 216–237

Shakespeare, William. *Hamlet, Prince of Denmark.* Edited by Phillip Edwards. Cambridge; New York: Cambridge University Press, 1985

Shaughnessy, Robert. 'Stage, Screen and Nation: Hamlet and the Space of History.' In *A Concise Companion to Shakespeare on Screen.* Edited by Diana Henderson. Oxford: Blackwell's, 2006. Pp. 54–76

Walker, Elsie. 'Getting Back to Shakespeare: Whose Film Is It Anyway?' In *A Concise Companion to Shakespeare on Screen.* Edited by Diana Henderson. Oxford: Blackwell's, 2006. Pp. 8–30

Media Cited

In chronological order by original theatrical or television release date (in brackets).

Hamlet (1948). Dir. Laurence Olivier. Perf. Laurence Olivier. The Criterion Collection/ Carlton International Media Limited, 2000. DVD

East of Eden (1955). Dir. Elia Kazan. Perf. James Dean, Raymond Massey. Warner Brothers/ Warner Home Video, 2005. DVD

Rebel Without A Cause (1955). Dir. Nicholas Ray. Perf. James Dean, Sal Mineo, Natalie Wood. Warner Brothers/Warner Home Video, 2000. DVD

Warui yatsu hodo yoku nemuru (English title: *The Bad Sleep Well*) (1960). Dir. Akira Kurosawa. Perf. Kurosawa Production Co. Ltd/Home Vision Cinema, 2001. VHS

Monty Python's Flying Circus (1969–1974). Perf. Graham Chapman, John Cleese, Terry Gilliam, Eric Idle, Terry Jones, Michael Palin. BBC/Python (Monty) Pictures/A&E Home Video, 2005. DVD

Hamlet liikemaailmassa (English title: *Hamlet Goes Business*) (1987). Dir. Aki Kaurismäki. Perf. Pirkka-Pekka Petelius. Villealfa Filmproduction Oy, 1987. VHS

Hamlet (1990). Dir. Franco Zeffirelli. Perf. Glen Close, Mel Gibson. Icon Entertainment International/Warner Brothers, 1995. VHS

Another Girl Another Planet (1992). Dir. Michael Almereyda. Perf. Elina Löwensohn. Screen Edge, 2005. VHS

Nadja (1994). Dir. Michael Almereyda. Perf. Perf. Martin Donovan, Peter Fonda, Elina Löwensohn. Kino Link Company/Siren Visual Entertainment, 2002. DVD

William Shakespeare's Hamlet (1996). (Four-hour director's cut version). Dir. Kenneth Branagh. Perf. Kenneth Branagh, Julie Christie, Derek Jacobi. Castle Rock Entertainment, 1998. VHS

William Shakespeare's Romeo + Juliet (1996). Dir. Baz Luhrmann. Perf. Claire Danes, Leonardo DiCaprio. 20th Century Fox/20th Century Fox Home Entertainment, 1996. DVD

Hamlet (2000). Dir. Michael Almereyda. Perf. Ethan Hawke, Julia Stiles. Double A Films/Miramax Films/Buena Vista Home Entertainment, 2000. DVD

Hamlet by Brook/Brook by Brook (2002). Dir. Peter Brook/Simon Brook. Perf. Adrian Lester. BBC Worldwide/Facets Video, 2002. DVD

Doctor Who (2005–2010). Perf. David Tennant. BBC. Television

Chapter 16

Milton and the Fit Reader

Ronald Bedford
University of New England

A primary marker of the human is the possession, both oral and written, of language. Indeed, it is language in all its directness or equivocation that defines us as a species. But warnings about the deceptive potential of this notoriously slippery medium have been frequently rehearsed, from Plato to Shakespeare to Orwell to Derrida, and by present day arbiters of our language practices in popular works such as Don Watson's *Death Sentence: The Decay of Public Language* (2003) or his most recent *Bendable Learnings* (2009). John Milton's way of sharpening our discursive engagements was to define and create a *fit* reader, able to respond competently to Milton's own persuasive and educative rhetorical feats. Yet in his own time, through the eighteenth and nineteenth centuries, and right up to the present, these interactions were (and are) fraught with paradox and misunderstanding, exposing fascinating gaps between intention and reception, between speaker and hearer, between writer and reader, and between reader and reader. Human language, it seems, can be understood but just as readily misunderstood.

It began early in the mass marketing of books. In an essay in the collection *Milton's Legacy* (2005), Stephen B. Dobranski demonstrates how Milton shared with his contemporaries the disturbing perception that readers could not be counted on to read in ways desired by authors. He studies several hundred seventeenth-century prefaces by authors and publishers to readers to argue that Milton's effort to shape his readers into a 'fit audience' constituted an unusually sophisticated version of a common anxiety about the act of reading itself – and hence also about the nature of authorship and authorial intention. It is not difficult to discern ways in which such communicative uncertainties anticipate modern debates about the assembling of 'interpretive communities,' the formation of 'the competent reader', and the primacy or irrelevance of 'the author'.

We may then wonder whether, in Book 7 and his reference to a 'fit audience ... though few', Milton is merely looking for an appropriately sympathetic audience, 'fit' in the sense of holding proper values regarding civil and political life and of being classically and biblically literate enough to understand the allusions and intertextualities that shape his certain meanings. Or is he assembling an audience of subversive initiates trained in cryptography, eager to look sceptically under every verbal stone, and prepared for conclusions in which nothing is concluded? For in recent times in Milton scholarship the distinction between fit and unfit readers or hearers seems to have morphed into – in the words of Stephen Fallon – those who hold that 'Milton is a poet of unqualified certainty, that his works cohere', and those for whom 'Milton is enmeshed in uncertainty', and for whom coherence is an illusion. In this way the fitness or unfitness of readers is complicated by their view of the fitness or unfitness of the writer. It is a complication which characterizes the current critical stand-off regarding Milton's intentions and methods as an author and the nature of his 'legacy'. For example, Tobias Gregory's recent commentary on Joseph Wittreich's *Why Milton Matters: A New Preface to his Writings* (Palgrave, 2007) in the *London Review of Books* (6 March 2008), describes how, for Wittreich, Milton is the great, striving neo-Romantic individualist whose authorial 'trademarks' are 'discontinuities, inconsistencies, eccentric theories; discrepancies and contradictions', and whose poetry is marked by 'a spirit of contradiction' and full of 'deconstructionist propositions' – a position summed up in Wittreich's (unsupported) claim that '*Paradise Lost* was the text the Hell's Angels packed away in their hip pockets'. Gregory counters with the claim that 'if Milton could not justify the ways of God to men, could not explain away the difficulties ... it wasn't for lack of trying.' It is argued that Milton, despite his heterodoxy on many issues, is struggling with intractable ethical, political and theological questions that exercised many others of his generation. 'The uncertainties, tensions, contradictions, injustices, ambiguities, subversions, evasions, horrors' in Milton's poetry, writes Gregory, 'do indeed exist; the mistake ... is to suppose Milton put them there on purpose. They are there despite his best efforts'. And thus our competence as interpreters of Milton's intentions is put to the test. But whether the fittest readers are reading a Milton who always means what he says, a Milton who doesn't always mean what he says, or a Milton who doesn't know what he means, is still an open question.

Milton's famous reaching out to an audience in the invocation to Book 7 has its particular context in *Paradise Lost* that is simultaneously autobiographical ('though fall'n on evil dayes,/ On evil dayes though fall'n' of the Restoration), and mythologically allegorical: Urania is invoked to drive off 'the barbarous dissonance/ Of *Bacchus* and his Revellers' – an allusion to the celebrations of Charles's new reign – and Orpheus is invoked to symbolize the inspired but spurned poet as likely to suffer dismemberment as the heroes of the revolution like Vane or Cook or Harrison.[1] But Milton's gesture is also about writing and reading strategies. I want therefore to dwell for a moment on the notion of 'fitness' as Milton uses it.

The phrase 'fit audience' is a resonant one, at once congratulatory – for those who suppose themselves among the fit – and, of course intimidating for those who may not be so sure. It suggests a line between the initiated and uninitiated, sheep and goats (a cliché of course, but a seriously biblical one), and everyone wants to be *inter oves* In *Eikonoklastes* Milton imagines 'readers; few perhaps, but those few, such of value and substantial worth, as truth and wisdom, not respecting numbers and bigg names, have bin ever wont in all ages to be contented with' (*CPW* 3.339f.).

There is, then, an immediate paradox about the 'fit audience ... though few': on the one hand it suggests the expectation that any writer, other than an unscrupulous crowd-pleaser, must hold that his audience will be limited to those who love truth and wisdom – a naturally selected elite beyond the vagaries of 'licentious and unbridl'd democritie' and above 'the noise and shouting of the rude multitude', as Milton described the English readership in 1660 in *The Readie and Easie Way* (*CPW* 7.438–9; 442). The competence of such readers, their 'value and substantial worth', resides in their alignment with the values espoused by the writer. On the other hand, the 'fit audience' may be few because the writing itself is encoded in such a way as to select, target and train its own audience, to *create* an audience whose competency will be tested through the reading experience. Some such notion of a reader informs Stanley Fish's influential *Surprised by Sin: the Reader in Paradise Lost* and also those many studies which pursue a similar investment in the homiletic or reader-response dimensions of the poem. In the one formulation, Milton is preaching, writing (and can only write) to the converted; in the other he is evangelizing and educating his readership. In the one, then, his readership is cumulative and self-selecting; and in the other his readership is prospective and selected and shaped by himself – or rather, by his writing strategies.

But what are those writing strategies? 'Fit' is part of a binary, 'fit' and 'unfit', creating the kind of double audience so characteristic of *ironic* discourse, and competition between percipient and impercipient readers or hearers. And irony is a narrative method that modern scholars – along with Renaissance and Puritan scholars – identify as a key feature of biblical narrative, particularly of the Gospels, and which, arguably, Milton seeks to reproduce in his biblical epics where the issues at stake are eternal salvation or damnation, and the presumption is that both author and the initiated reader know what the right answers are, and what the wrong ones are.[2]

That Milton often means by 'fit' something close to what is meant by the term 'literary competence' or 'the competent reader' can be demonstrated by reviewing some of the ways in which he deploys the word. Frequently it is synonymous with 'competence' in the sense of qualified or properly informed, but the term 'competence' in this primary modern sense was less readily available to Milton than it is, say, to Jonathan Culler or Stanley Fish. According to the concordances, Milton uses 'competent' only twice in his prose writings and never in his poetry, and the *OED* suggests that the word's sense of 'sufficiency of qualifications' or of 'capacity to deal adequately with a subject' is an eighteenth-century usage and its earliest citation from Edmund Burke, 1790. Milton had to make do with the various nuances and contexts of the word 'fit', which the *OED* takes back, in the sense of competence, to the sixteenth century. 'Fit' can be both competent, qualified, or socially or ceremoniously correct or apt, and such lexical shading is frequent: Milton speaks of men 'fit to be our Justices of the peace' (*Of Reformation, CPW*

1.661), of 'fit professors' (*Animadversions, CPW* 1.719), of 'a fit person to do the noblest and godliest deeds' (*Reason of Church Government, CPW* 1.842), or of 'that which makes a fit minister' (*Considerations, CPW* 7.315). In all of these, aptness or suitability may compete with a notion of competence for primacy of meaning, but his programme of a 'generous Education which fits a man to perform justly, skilfully and magnanimously all the offices both private and public of peace and war' (*Of Education, CPW* 2.378), or his ambition 'to make the people fittest to chuse, the chosen fittest to govern' (*Ready and Easie Way, CPW* 7.443), are unequivocally about knowledge, qualifications and competence.

But why is it so important for readers of Milton to be so super-fit – more, that is, than being merely politically informed? Anyone who ventures into this astonishingly complex, complexly organized and deeply allusive text soon feels their readerly competence put severely to the test. But there are also plenty of interpretative difficulties that do not depend on prior knowledge, but only on alert ears – as in Raphael's description of the angels in the War in Heaven as 'Fit to decide the Empire of great Heav'n' (6.303), a fitness or competence modified by 'seemd' (301). Seemed to whom? The fitness of not only angels is at issue here: Raphael's fitness as narrator, that of the reader in perceiving or failing to perceive the inauthenticity, even, it might be argued, Milton's authorial fitness in allowing it to pass. We as readers are invited to decide not the empire of great heaven but the nature of the levels of narrative competence or incompetence, the levels of possible irony, and the question of at whose expense such irony – if any – is being deployed.

Currents of ironic verbal inflection frequently eddy about the word 'fit' as Milton uses it as in the way in which the fallen and self-excusing Adam in Book 10 tries out irony or 'dry mocke' on 'the sovran Presence' to whom he seeks to justify himself:

> This Woman whom thou mad'st to be my help,
> And gav'st me as thy perfet gift, so good,
> So fit, so acceptable, so Divine,
> That from her hand I could suspect no ill ...
> Shee gave me of the Tree ...   (10.137–43)

Adam's disreputable catalogue of the supposed virtues of Eve takes the form of a satirical jibe at the creator's incompetence: 'some perfect gift', Adam implies, as Milton expands on the laconic and equally pointed 'The woman whom thou gavest to be with me, she gave me of the tree, and I did eat' of Genesis. In significant contrast, Eve, 'not before her Judge/ Bold or loquacious' – that is, practising neither *dissimulatio* nor *antiphrasis* nor *sarcasmos* – responds with a poignant brevity and simplicity: 'The Serpent me beguil'd and I did eate' (160–2). The subtlety of the inversion 'me beguil'd' for 'beguil'd me' is not an archaism, or a bending to iambic metrics, but shows Eve putting herself forward as the one who failed – in sharp contrast with Adam's bluster. Adam's own words to Christ recall not only his earlier enthusiastic encomium of Eve to Raphael (8.548–50) – a recycling of his own words that provides an ironic contrast for the reader - but also recall for the divine listener (and the attentive reader) God's promise in Adam's dream in response to the lonely Adam's request for a companion 'fit to participate/ All rational delight' (8.390–1): 'What next I bring', says God, 'shall please thee, be assur'd,/ Thy likeness, thy fit help, thy other self' (8.449–50). For the fallen Adam, in this desperate moment of self-excuse, even God can become, if not an incompetent reader, an unfit author.

Around this phrase, 'thy fit help', Milton had, in the 1640s, energetically and passionately negotiated with the intractabilities of canon law and of custom in arguing - partly as an allegory for the fitness of rulers and the rights of subjects – for a new doctrine and discipline of divorce, for an ideal of marriage based on the 'conjugall fellowship of a fit conversing soul' (*Doctrine and Discipline of Divorce, CPW* 2.251) conforming to God's purpose of the 'fit help' of a true mate: 'Let it be made also a fit society, as God intended it' (2.310). Christ's injunctions against divorce, Milton argues, are intended not literally but *ironically*, in order to separate 'the Religious from the irreligious, the fit from the unfit' (2.653). Such fitness is specifically related to an ability to distinguish between good argument and specious argument, between irony and literalism, between the truly religious and the irreligious. In his attack on the 'glib & easie' and 'counterfeit knowledge and literature' of custom and error Milton sees the Saviour prevailing against both 'the crabbed texturists of his time' and flat-footed modern literalists who offer 'a misinterpretation of Christ' (2.222–33) because they cannot read irony. In canon law Christ's words were 'congealed into a stony rigor' (2.236) yet Christ 'meant not to be taken word for word' but rather 'as when we bow things the contrary way, to make them come to their natural straitnes' (2.282–3). In *Tetrachordon* the Pharisees, tempting Christ, may expect 'that their answer will bee such as is fittest for them, not so much a teaching, as an intangling' and designed 'to perplex and stumble them purposely with contriv'd obscurities' (2.642–3). For Milton, Christ is an ironist inviting readings of 'literal rigidity' but speaking with the 'mouth of charity' (2.668–9), and his object is to address one community of readers by satirizing another. And the *Doctrine and Discipline of Divorce* concludes with a fine example of Milton's own invective directed against those who cannot see metaphor or irony when it is under their noses:

> And if none of these considerations with all their wait and gravity, can
> avail to the dispossessing him of his pretious literalism, let some one or
> other entreat him but to read on in the same 19 of *Math* till he come
> to the place that sayes *Some make themselves Eunuchs for the kingdom of
> heavens sake.* and if then he please to make use of *Origens* knife, he may
> doe well to be his own carver. (2.334)

Above all, Milton idealizes and privileges the reader. Awareness of an audience was an essential part of the rhetorical tradition in which Milton was educated, both in English and in Latin, and his prose writings exhibit an acute awareness of 'the reader' and, indeed, of the multiplicity of kinds of reader, from his earliest jocular or teasing *Prolusions* at Cambridge to the jeremiad of *The Ready and Easie Way*. For example, the *Apology for Smectymnuus* is rhetorically constructed throughout as an address to a reader or readers – 'heare me out now Readers ... I beseech ye friends' – and is full of appeals to 'the jury of Readers': 'Take him at his word Readers, but let him bring good sureties' (*CPW* 1.876; 886).

Throughout the prose writings a multifarious array of readers, competent and incompetent, are constructed and invoked: there is 'the ingenious Reader' (*Animadversions, CPW* 1.639), 'the elegant Learned reader' or the 'knowing reader' (*Reason of Church Government, CPW* 1.807; 820), 'the judicious Reader', 'the common reader' and the 'acute reader' (*Areopagitica, CPW* 2.512; 517; 533), the 'intelligent Reader' (*Colasterion, CPW* 2.750), less diligent and 'more diligent readers' (*Eikonoklastes CPW* 3.406). Readers may be 'credulous' (*Of Prelatical Episcopacy, CPW* 1.627) or 'charitable' (*Reason of Church Government, CPW* 1.806), they may be 'outlandish' (*D.& D of Divorce, CPW* 2.233) or, as the added Preface to *Paradise Lost* notes, they may be 'vulgar readers' who cannot do without jingling rhymes. The wiliness and disingenuities of writers constantly put pressure on readers' alertness, and most especially when those writers are prelates and 'dancing Divines' who come 'with Scripture in thir mouthes, gloss'd and fitted for thir turnes with a double contradictory sense' (*Tetrachordon, CPW* 3.195). Milton constantly warns, 'But marke Readers, the crafty scope of these Prelates' (*Animadversions, CPW* 1.727), and at moments of victory in debate the solidarity of reader and author may be celebrated, in a manner very like Fielding, by an ironic and conspiratorial 'what think ye Readers, do you not understand him?' (*Reason of Church Government, CPW* 1.771).

Among the strategies used by those who would deceive the lazy or credulous reader is the linguistic feat of 'doubling'. *Tetrachordon* castigates 'our doubling Divines': 'At thir turnes and doublings no men readier' (*CPW* 3.198; 255). *An Apology* diagnoses 'deceitful and double dealing propositions' offered to Parliament (*CPW* 1.918), and the notion of doubleness and contradictoriness is intimately associated with the *fitness* of audience or reader to interpret it, or to see through it: 'For Liberty hath a sharp and double edge, fit only to be handled by Just and Vertuous Men' (*Character of the Long Parliament, CPW* 5.448), and the 'dancing Divines' quoted above have their mendacities and 'double contradictory' senses 'gloss'd and fitted for thir turnes' for the judicious reader to deconstruct and unfit.

However,, the characteristic of doubleness – saying one thing and meaning another - is also one of the primary defining features of allegory and irony and such doublings, elaborately glossed and fitted, seem to be a fundamental verbal characteristic of Milton's own poetic discourse, constantly confusing simple-minded literalists. Such explicative, rather than deceiving, doubling may be justified not only by modern theories of difference and opposition as elementary structures of language but also by the ancient philosophical principle of contraries as expressed, for instance, in Chaucer's *Troylus and Criseyde*, 'by his contrary is everything declared', or in Milton himself by the assertion that 'That which purifies us is triall, and triall is by what is contrary' (*Areopagitica, CPW* 2.515). And in *Paradise Lost* that 'trial of man' is specifically a trial by language, the attempt to resist the 'falsities and lyes' of Satanic corruption by which 'the greatest part/ Of Mankind' have been misled (1. 366–69).

Several problems now arise. Considering the gleefulness with which Milton exposes the deviant doublings of others and the confidence with which he throws open 'the Temple of *Janus* with his two *controversial* faces' (of Truth and Falsehood) (*Areopagitica, CPW* 2.561), the adoption of similar methods of concealing and revealing – 'Where more is meant than meets the ear', in the powerfully proleptical line from 'Il Penseroso' – would seem to require some justification of its cunning and duplicity, some baptism into that kind of song which is governed by Urania. Milton had already in the divorce tracts characterized Christ as an ironist, and in that he was following a long tradition deriving from St Mark's identification of a fit and an unfit audience: 'He that hath ears to hear, let him hear' (Mark 4.9). Many commentators on the Scriptures, both patristic and Renaissance, had noted the divine author's penchant for irony, mockery and sarcasm as well as for allegory and parable. At the same time, a counter-tradition of an Augustinian and Puritan suspicion of eloquence, rhetoric and figuration enjoins readers to individually study and meditate on the tropes and figures of Scripture in order to discover its devices and categories of rhetoric – the 'science of the saints' – and the importance of this activity is emphasized in the epistle preceding Milton's *Christian Doctrine*. In one of his only two uses of the word irony, Milton discusses falsehood and its relation to various rhetorical strategies:

FALSEHOOD must arise from EVIL INTENT and entails EITHER THE DELIBERATE MISREPRESENTATION OF THE TRUTH OR THE TELLING OF AN ACTUAL LIE TO SOMEONE, WHOEVER HE MAY BE, TO WHOM IT IS THE SPEAKER'S DUTY TO BE

TRUTHFUL. [...] It is evident from this definition [...] that parables, hyperboles, fables and the various uses of irony are not falsehoods since they are calculated not to deceive but to instruct [*parabolas, hyperbolas, apologos, ironias mendacia non esse*]. (*CPW* 6.760–1)[3]

The instructive possibilities of *Aenigma, Metaphore, Allegorie, Ironia, Hyperbole* or *Parable* (as George Puttenham lists them) are not exactly endorsed, however, in the fullest critique of the practice of reading to be found in Milton's poetry, the rebuke of Satan – the arch-doubler and father of lies – by the Son in *Paradise Regained*. Satan has offered the Son all that classical learning might lend to his 'empire', pointing out that learning includes not just Jewish law and prophecy, for 'The Gentiles also know, and write, and teach/ To admiration' (4. 227–28). To which the Son replies:

However many books
Wise men have said are wearisom; who reads
Incessantly, and to his reading brings not
A spirit and judgment equal or superior,
(And what he brings, what needs he elsewhere seek)
Uncertain and unsettl'd still remains,
Deep verst in books and shallow in himself. (4. 321–27)

The unfit or less 'equal' readers the Son describes as 'collecting toys,/And trifles' or as 'Childern gathering pibles on the shore'. The Son's minimalist gesture of rejection points up the enduring paradox for Protestant readers of the sufficiency of Scripture and the inner workings of divine grace, and also indicates perhaps Milton's final suspicion of the very educational tradition in which he had been brought up and in which he had become so deeply implicated. But up till this *terminus ad quem* - and indeed in the framing of it - Milton had vigorously proclaimed the joys and responsibilities of reading, writing, publishing, disputing and reasoning within the community of readers, satirical in *Areopagitica* of those who live under a perpetual childhood of prescription, and yet himself always sceptically conscious of the limits of being 'alwaies learning and never knowing, alwaies infants' (*CPW* 7.320). The returns from such huge literary investment in the form of social change, action and reform may have become for Milton visibly fewer and fewer, but the sanctification and justification of the rhetorical arsenal of writing practices for defending truth and liberty, including irony, doubleness and deception, and the reader competence (or one might say connoisseurship) implied by their deployment, are ruthlessly scrutinized by the Son. The Son's analysis of Satan's rhetorical techniques and their motives represents Milton's most direct comment on the problem of doubleness, prophecy, and the uses of ambiguity and deceit-by-irony:

> The other service was thy chosen task,
> To be a lyer in four hunderd mouths;
> For lying is thy sustenance, thy food.
> Yet thou pretend'st to truth; all Oracles
> By thee are giv'n, and what confest more true
> Among the Nations? that hath been thy craft,
> By mixing somewhat true to vent more lyes.
> But what have been thy answers, what but dark
> Ambiguous and with double sense deluding,
> Which they who ask have seldom understood,
> And not well understood as good not known? (1. 427–37)

While this appears to fix Satanic rhetoric in its ethical place, it also suggests the waveringly thin line that separates bad from good rhetorical practices. This critique of subversive speech, deceiving language and allegory ('Oracles') is curiously similar in tone to George Puttenham's view that although 'figures be the instruments of ornament in every language, so be they also in a sorte abuses or rather trespasses in speach', drawing the ear and mind 'from plainnesse and simplicitie to a certain doublenesse, whereby our talke is the more guilefull and abusing'. Milton here allows the Son's words to echo Puttenham's, poignantly, and even embarrassingly, focusing on those constant paradoxes of Renaissance and especially Protestant rhetorical theory, of plainness versus eloquence, of openness versus dissembling, or of wit versus devotion – as in Donne's 'when wee are mov'd to seeme religious/ Only to vent wit, Lord deliver us' (*A Litanie*, XXI), a metaphor repeated in the Son's scornful 'vent more lyes', as in the venting of literal hot air. The question may be a crude one, but we might ask whether Milton believes in the power of rhetoric, figuration and irony to move us to the good, or whether they are only and always part of Satan's 'dark materials'? And if they are not, how and when can their deployment be justified?

'The Western ethical and aesthetic scrutiny of irony,' writes C. Jan Swearingen, 'and of related notions of linguistic deceit and lying, is as old as rhetoric and literacy.'[4]

For Plato rhetoric and irony were morally wrong because they were deliberate, knowing lies, and following in that tradition Augustine was persistent in his critiques of mendacity: 'the Scripture does not say "the multitude of the eloquent" but "the multitude of the wise" is the welfare of the whole world' (Augustine). Aristotle's or Cicero's successful rhetorician, like Milton's Satan, is able to persuade an audience that things are the way he says they are, and the way he says they are may not be so. Satan's famous opening address to Beelzebub – from a prone position – claiming the near-success of the rebellion, rewrites history and defiantly lies about 'the Glorious Enterprize' (1. 84–124). It is a lie, not an error or a *pseudos*, but designed knowingly and deliberately to mislead others. But if the ironist too is misleading a section of his audience – even for reasons of polemic or of instruction – what is the ethical difference between such irony and lying? The proximity of irony and lying as speech acts could find *ironia* as a proper form of discourse for characters like Satan or Herod. Genesis 3, 4–5,

> And the serpent said unto the woman, Ye shall not surely die. For God doth know that in the day ye eat thereof, then your eyes shall be opened, and ye shall be as gods, knowing good and evil,

which combines both a lie and a truth, was cited in Otto Casmann's *Rhetoricae tropologiae* of 1600 as *ironia*, as was Herod's devious communication to the wise men, 'Go and search diligently for the young child; and when ye have found him, bring me word again, that I may come and worship him also' (Matthew 2, 8).[5] Herod's words, like the serpent's, are more lies than ironies, and the relation of lying to irony would seem to reside in a difference of intention: a lie is essentially self-serving and designed to be believed; irony, though it may be believed by some, is designed to be understood.[6]

Lies are not usually intended to be interpreted *as lies*, and only become ironical when decoded – often at the prompting of an ironist recording the lie – by a reader or listener who knows better than the liar. Defenders of such figurations would argue that exposure to irony or mockingly educative dissimulation trains the reader or listener in detecting the black arts of others and such training is, as commentators both ancient and modern have asserted, a major strategy of biblical rhetoric – and thus endorsed by the very highest authority.

There is too a further complication for the literalists which resides in the nature of dramatic narrative itself. In the example of Jesus' rebuke of Satan's lying in *Paradise Regained*, the Son is there represented not by scriptural paraphrase but as a dramatic character in a text, a voice contesting another voice. In other words, both his figurative dramatization and the poem itself are an endorsement of the rhetorics of fiction. The rapidly expanding canons of literary character and voice in the Renaissance encouraged the creation of speaking personae not only in drama but in poetry and, later, the novel. The speaking voice *understood as fictitious* could be mediated not only by a competing voice, as in the dialogic form of *Paradise Regained*, but could be authorially and structurally controlled in dramatic monologue, as in many of Donne's or Herbert's poems, or in an epic poem like *Paradise Lost* so as, for instance, to show inferentially that voice's deviations, its status as victim of dramatic irony, its self-deceptions, or its lies. Milton's Satan is not merely an inveterate liar deploying a deceitful, nonteleological, irreligious and illicit use of language; he is also himself a counter-ironist, as a character placed within a larger story, a victim of a better, or at least differently, informed perspective which – as the history of responses to the Satan of *Paradise Lost* amply evidences – competes for the reader's attention and assent. In a manner designed to create a special kind of ironic *dissimulatio*, the epic narrator interjects facets or implications of the story to which the characters are blind ('nor ever thence/ Had ris'n or heav'd his head, but that the will/ And high permission of all-ruling Heaven' (1. 210–12)), and a subtle tension is set up between the two perspectives, a tension reflected in an internal dissonance within the consciousness of the audience itself. It is this narrative characteristic of ironic competition that has been identified as a key feature especially of Gospel narrative, and it is clearly recognizable as a key feature in both the narrative mode and the reader experience of *Paradise Lost*. The epic ends with the famously falling cadence that Dr Richard Bentley found too pessimistic and proposed to change,

> They hand in hand with wandring steps and slow,
> Through *Eden* took their solitary way (12. 648–49),

while *Paradise Regained* too ends with what may appear to be an anonymous withdrawal or even rejection:

> hee unobserv'd
> Home to his Mothers house privat returnd. (*PR*, 4. 638–39)

Both of these narrative strategies of withheld closure, in their under-statements or mis-statements which both deny and affirm, mirror exactly the challenges to the interpretative powers of the reader which form the epilogue to Mark's gospel – whose narrative abruptly ends with Jesus hanging from the machine of his death – and are embodied in the reactions of the women in the garden: as Donald Juel asks, 'What sort of good news closes with "And they said nothing to anyone, for they were afraid"?' (Juel 169–70). In all three examples here what might be pointed to is the paradox of the certainty of uncertainty, or – and it is a version of the same thing – the uncertainty of certainty, in the relation of humans to divine purpose, whatever that may be.

It is a paradox – in a different sense, relating not to divine but to authorial purpose – that seems to be currently exercising Milton's readers and critics. As has been argued, they are paradoxes of long standing inherent in the human project of speech and discourse, and which Milton's writings manifestly continue to expose and anatomize.

Works cited

Augustine, St.. *De Doctrina Christiana*, IV. Trans. by D.W. Robertson. New York: Bobbs–Merrill, 1983.

Casmann, Otto. *Rhetoricae tropologiae*. E. Collegio Musarum Paltheniano, Frankfurt, 1660

CPW - Complete Prose Works of John Milton. 8 vols. New Haven: Yale University Press, 1953–1982

Dawsey, James. *The Lucan Voice: Confusion and Irony in the Gospel of Luke.* Macon GA: Mercer University Press, 1986

Dobranski, Stephen B. 'Milton's Ideal Readers.' In *Milton's Legacy.* Edited by Kristin A. Pruitt and Charles W. Durham. Selinsgrove, PA: Susquehanna University Press, 2005. Pp. 191–207

Duke, Paul. *Irony in the Fourth Gospel.* Atlanta: John Knox Press, 1983

Fallon, Stephen. 'Inspired with Contradiction: Milton's Conflicting Certainties', paper given at the 'Milton in Intellectual and Cultural History' symposium. University of Queensland, August 2008

Fish, Stanley. *Surprised by Sin: The Reader in* Paradise Lost. 1967; rpt. London: Macmillan, 1997.

Good, Edwin. *Irony in the Old Testament.* London: SPCK, 1965

Gregory, Tobias. *London Review of Books* (6 March, 2008

Jankélévitch,V.. *L'Ironie.* 1936; rpt. Paris: Flammarion, 1964

Jónsson, Jakob. *Humour and Irony in the New Testament: Illuminated by Parallels in Talmud and Midrash.* Reykjavík: Bókzútgáfa Menningarsjóds, 1965

Juel, Donald, *Introduction to New Testament Literature,* Nashville: Abingdon, 1978

Knoppers, Laura L.. *Historicizing Milton: Spectacle, Power, and Poetry in Restoration England.* Athens and London: University of Georgia Press, 1994

Knox, Dilwyn. *Ironia: Medieval and Renaissance Ideas of Irony.* Leiden: E.J. Brill, 1989

Milton, John. *The Poetical Works of John Milton.* Edited by Helen Darbishire. London: Oxford University Press, 1958

Pruitt, Kristin A., and Charles W. Durham (eds.). *Milton's Legacy.* Selinsgrove: Susquehanna University Press, 2005

Puttenham, George. *The Arte of English Poesie.* 1598. Edited by G. D. Willcock and A. Walker. Cambridge: Cambridge University Press, 1936

Swearingen, C. Jan. *Rhetoric and Irony: Western Literacy and Western Lies.* Oxford: Oxford University Press, 1991

Watson, Don. *Death Sentence: the Decay of Public Language.* Vintage Australia, 2003.
———. *Bendable Learnings.* Sydney: Knopf, 2009

Wittreich, Joseph. *Why Milton Matters: A New Preface to his Writings.* London: Palgrave, 2007

Notes

1   For a fine discussion of this passage and its context see Knoppers 88-90. Quotations from Milton's poems are from the Darbishire edition (Milton).

2   See for example, Good; Jónsson; Juel; Duke and Dawsey.

3   *Christian Doctrine,* trans. by John Carey, *CPW* 6. For hyperbole as a frequent figure in the gospels and one often used by Christ, Carey refers to *Doctrine and Discipline of Divorce, CPW* 2.281, and *Colasterion, CPW* 2.745.

4   Swearingen ix. For a detailed history, see Knox 39–57.

5   Casmann 118, cited by Knox 52.

6   Jankélévitch, for instance, makes a distinction between what he calls 'La bonne conscience' of irony and 'la mauvaise conscience menteuse' (59–60).

Chapter 17

Paradise Lost Aloud:
Then and Now

Beverley Sherry
University of Sydney

What sets human beings apart from other living things? Seventeenth-century writers had firm beliefs about this: 'Speech is the only benefit man hath to express his excellency of mind above other creatures' (Jonson 570); it is 'the only companion, and witnesse of reason' (Goodman 295). Milton explores this idea in *Paradise Lost*: in his desire for a mate, Adam complains that he cannot speak with animals: 'I by conversing cannot these erect / From prone, nor in thir ways complacence find' (8.432–33), and so God gives him Eve.[1] The subject or 'great Argument' (1.24) of Milton's epic is how we as fallible human beings got to be the way we are, and this subject finds expression in a wide range of speaking characters, pre-eminently Adam and Eve, and through the ever-present voice of the narrating poet. The poem calls attention to itself as oral, and it has been kept alive for more than three hundred years by people reading it aloud or listening to others read it aloud.

So how was *Paradise Lost* heard in the past, how is it heard today, and how does this enquiry aid our understanding of the poem? Beginning with the scant records from Milton's own time, this essay moves to evidence from the eighteenth and nineteenth centuries, and then to the late twentieth and early twenty-first centuries, where oral performances and ear-witness accounts are abundant.

Milton placed a high priority on poetry as vocal. In composing *Elegy V*, for example, he felt 'sacred sound' filling his brain: 'what song is my spirit singing so loudly with wide-open mouth?' (*The Poems* 86); and in an autobiographical passage of *The Reason of Church Government*, he describes the poetry he wants to write as inspired 'utterance,' alluding to the prophet Isaiah's anxiety about his unclean lips (Isa. 6:1–8) and hoping that, like Isaiah, his lips might be touched with sacred fire.[2] Consequently he insists that his poetry needs to be heard. Invoking his muse in *Paradise Lost*, he draws on the Latin *audire* ('to hear'): 'still govern thou my Song, / *Urania*, and fit audience find, though few.' Such 'fit' listeners are contrasted with the barbarous rabble who would not hear Orpheus's song but killed him (7.30–36).

Paradise Lost (1667) is unrhymed, which mystified Milton's first readers, so he provided a prefatory note on 'The Verse' for the 1668 issue, in which he distinguishes between readers with 'judicious ears' and 'vulgar' readers. Milton rejects rhyme, defining 'true musical delight' as consisting only in 'apt Numbers, fit quantity of Syllables, and the sense variously drawn out from one Verse into another, not in the jingling sound of like endings.' Three intended characteristics of *Paradise Lost* are signalled here: the pleasure of its sound, the aptness or fitness of its sound, and the prevailing enjambment of the verse.

Because of Milton's method of composing, *Paradise Lost* was inescapably oral, issuing from his lips. The blind poet had to dictate every word, which has prompted one critic to remark, 'in an important sense, *Paradise Lost* is an oral artefact' (Steggle 15), another to imagine it as 'excitedly breaking forth from the poet's imagination and passing, even now, through the poet's lips to our ears' (Teskey 19). We would certainly not have the poem but for Milton's voice, and half way through the epic he reassures the reader that, amazingly, his voice has not become 'hoarse or mute' (7.25).

One characteristic of that voice has been recorded. The biographer John Aubrey observed that Milton 'pronounced the letter R very hard' (Darbishire 6). While there is no fundamental difference between the spoken English of Milton's time and today's educated speech of southern England ('Received Pronunciation'), the 'r' before consonants or before a pause was sounded in Milton's time but disappeared by the middle of the eighteenth century (Barber 210–12, 243).[3] So Milton possibly sounded the 'r' before a consonant, for example, in the opening lines of *Paradise Lost*, 'First,' 'mortal,' 'World' (1.1–3), and the 'r' before a pause, as in 'that be from thee farr' (3. 153), 'infinite despaire' (4.74), and 'happier farr' (12.587). In view of Aubrey's comment,

Milton might well have dictated the lines about the grating sound of hell's gate (2.879–83) with rasping 'r's and this line about Eve's primal sin with harsh relish, 'Greedily she ingorg'd without restraint' (9.791).

Those who actually heard Milton dictate *Paradise Lost* noted particularly the flow of the verse. Far from the 'jingling sound of like endings,' the lines came out in expansive verse paragraphs. Cyriack Skinner observed that, on waking in the morning, if an amanuensis was late, Milton 'would complain, Saying *hee wanted to bee milkd*' (Darbishire 33).[4] Milton's nephew Edward Phillips recalled that he would dictate 'a Parcel of Ten, Twenty, or Thirty Verses at a Time' to any available scribe (Darbishire 291, 73). Jonathan Richardson reported that he would deliver 'perhaps 40 Lines as it were in a Breath, and then reduce them to half the Number,' and that, once the lines came to him, they flowed abundantly, 'with a certain *Impetus* and *AEstro* ['inspiration'], as he himself seem'd to Believe' (Darbishire 291). Richardson alludes here to Milton's claim that his muse 'deignes / Her nightly visitation unimplor'd, / And dictates to me slumbring, or inspires / Easie my unpremeditated Verse' (9.21–24).

The finished product, however, did not come out in an ungoverned rush, for, despite his blindness, Milton took care to check punctuation with his amanuenses (Darbishire 73). In the seventeenth century, punctuation was often rhetorical, and pauses – indicated by commas, semi-colons, colons, or full stops – suggest how Milton delivered the lines and are a guide to oral performance. In addition, apostrophes indicate elisions which preserve the metre, as in, 'Him the Almighty Power / Hurld headlong flaming from th'Ethereal Skie' (1.44–45). Despite the pauses, Milton's characteristic punctuation in *Paradise Lost* is light, so that it 'builds up and maintains an energetic, pulsating tempo' through the verse paragraphs (Lewalski ed. xxxiii).

In the seventeenth century the most eloquent tribute to Milton's flowing lines came from the poet Andrew Marvell in his dedicatory poem, printed with the second edition in 1674:

> Thou singst with so much gravity and ease;
> And above humane flight dost soar aloft
> With Plume so strong, so equal, and so soft.

Sherry Paradise Lost *Aloud: Then and Now*

> The bird nam'd from that Paradise you sing
> So never flaggs, but always keeps on Wing. (36–40)

Marvell 'sees' *Paradise Lost* moving in an unflagging body of sound, always on the wing, like the legendary footless bird of paradise.

In the eighteenth century the majestic, sustained lines of *Paradise Lost* were considered central to its sublimity, and Milton was regarded as 'the British Homer' (Shawcross 68). Joseph Addison concludes that, 'Milton has copied after Homer, rather than Virgil, in the length of his periods, the copiousness of his phrases, and the running of his verses into one another' (Thorpe 43). The reference to Homer links *Paradise Lost* with oral epic; Homer was indeed Milton's favourite poet and John Toland reported that Milton could almost recite Homer's epics 'without book' (Darbishire 179). The auditory effects of Milton's verse were analysed in a mass of prosodic criticism that appeared in the eighteenth century, and, by the middle of the century, the sound of *Paradise Lost* was embraced by the elocution movement. Richard Bradford's research has revealed a public fascination with the acoustic power of *Paradise Lost*, evidenced from about 1760 through oral performances and lectures by elocutionists such as John Rice, Thomas Sheridan, and John Walker.

Sheridan, the 'Dublin Orator,' was the leading elocutionist.[5] From 1763 he began to stage his popular 'Attic Entertainments' in Oxford and Cambridge and, for more general audiences, in Dublin, London, Edinburgh, and Bath. Offered in the morning or evening, each entertainment consisted of a public lecture followed by, or interspersed with, Sheridan's performance of poetry, his party pieces being Dryden's *Ode on the Power of Music* and passages from *Paradise Lost*. His 'Attic Evening' at London's Theatre Royal in the Haymarket in 1769 included musical entertainment, and one listener commended Sheridan's careful selection from *Paradise Lost*:

> The first passage he read was to instance the Grand and Magnificent, which he selected from Milton, and was the coming forth of the Messiah to Battle [Book 6]. The second (from the same author) was a Picture of the Sublime and Beautiful, and consisted in the Devil's entering into Paradise [Book 4]. The third Portion, which was to illustrate a mixture

of both the former was that celebrated morning Hymn of Adam to his
Creator [Book 5]. (Benzie 58)

Sheridan's *Art of Reading Verse* (1775), a performance theory of prosody,
went into six editions by 1805 and was a fundamental influence on the study
of poetry in schools and upon the elocution movement, which continued
into the twentieth century (Middleton 281–83).

The nineteenth century saw pronounced admiration for the sound of
Paradise Lost from poets, poet-critics, and academics. A recurring theme is
Milton's acute adapting of sound to sense. Among the Romantics, Coleridge,
Hazlitt, Leigh Hunt, and De Quincey praised Milton's auditory imagination:
'angelic was the ear of Milton,' declared De Quincey, and Hazlitt claimed
that there were more examples in Milton 'of an adaptation of the sound and
movement of the verse to the meaning of the passage, than in all our other
writers, whether of rhyme or blank verse, put together,' with the exception of
Shakespeare (Wittreich 487, 370). In 1838 Edwin Guest, in his monumental
History of English Rhythms, concluded that Milton constantly adapted sound
to sense, and in 1874 David Masson offered the view that, 'in the act of
writing or mentally composing his poetry,' Milton 'obeyed the mood of his
thought, and the instinct of a musical ear as perfect and fastidious as was ever
given to man' (Guest 530; Masson I: cxii–cxiii).

In a study of oral readings of poetry, Peter Middleton found little
information collated from the nineteenth century (273). I have been unable
to find records of public performances, but reading aloud was common in
private groups, as, for example, in the Wordsworth family. In 1802 Dorothy
Wordsworth recorded, 'After tea I read aloud the eleventh book of *Paradise
Lost*. We were much impressed, and also melted into tears' (Wittreich 110).
Her brother William, whose voice was 'deep and pathetic, and thrills with
feeling,' was fond of reading Milton aloud (Wittreich 135, 150 n.13). In
1810, Dorothy wrote:

William read part of the 5th book of *Paradise Lost* to us. He read The
Morning Hymn [5.153–208], while a stream of white vapour, which
coursed the valley of Brathay, ascended slowly and by degrees melted away.

It seemed as if we had never before felt deeply the power of the Poet 'Ye mists and exhalations, etc. etc.!' (Wittreich 123)

The poet Felicia Hemans remembered the older Wordsworth reciting from *Paradise Lost* the passage beginning 'Millions of spiritual Creatures walk the Earth' (4.677): '[h]is tones of solemn earnestness, sinking, almost dying away into a murmur of veneration, as if the passage were breathed forth from the heart, I shall never forget' (Perkins 659). Walter Savage Landor preferred to recite *Paradise Lost* to himself: 'even the great hexameter sounded to me tinkling, when I had recited in my solitary walks on the seashore the haughty appeal of Satan and the deep penitence of Eve' (Nelson 142–43). David Perkins concludes that '[e]verything indicates that the recitation of poetry in the Romantic period was more energetic and impassioned than it usually is now,' and this 'made poetry a more sensuously appealing and a more emotional art than it now is' (664, 666).

Later in the nineteenth century, poets continued to respond to the sound of Milton, and particularly astute appreciation came from the poet-critic, John Addington Symonds, in his study, 'Blank Verse' (1879). Tennyson, whose 'gift of utterance,' according to Gerard Manley Hopkins, was 'truly golden' (95), frequently read *Paradise Lost* aloud, and claimed 'that he knew of no one so well-fitted for reading Milton aloud; as he had a deep chest and long-drawn breath, and could finish the weighty periods of many lines together without a second inhalation' (Nelson 122, 120–21). The responses of Wordsworth and Tennyson to the sound of Milton – respectively, 'a voice whose sound was like the sea' and '*mighty-mouth'd* inventor of harmonies, . . . God-gifted organ-voice of England' – compare with Marvell's experience of *Paradise Lost* and bear out the claim of the poet Francis Berry that poets have 'a peculiarly physical or passional awareness of vocal sound' (5).[6]

In the twentieth century T.S. Eliot, despite his notorious aspersions on Milton, experienced this same physical awareness (Sherry 2008, 139–47; Creaser 2009). In 'Milton II,' he concluded that Milton worked in 'larger musical units' than any other poet, that his verse paragraphs have their own 'wave-length' and communicate a 'peculiar feeling, almost a physical sensation of a breathless leap' (157–58). Poets have been a particularly 'fit audience' of *Paradise Lost*, presumably because they instinctively 'read with [their] ears,' as Hopkins puts it; a great admirer of Milton, Hopkins considered his achievement with rhythm 'beyond any other English poet's' (37–38, 51–52, 79).

From the seventeenth to the twentieth century the numerous accounts of the aural and oral power of *Paradise Lost* highlight three characteristics: the onward pressure of the verse paragraphs, the freedom of Milton's handling of rhythm within the confines of blank verse, and the continual adapting of sound to sense. These views are epitomized in the judgments of three eminent Miltonists: 'What I chiefly want to point out is . . . how [Milton] sweeps us along as though we were attending an actual recitation' (Lewis 41); 'every sound and syllable counted, every pause or silence between sounds. Never has poet known better than [Milton] that sound expresses sense, and that the minutest details of his art must be cared for if he is to render the fullness of his meaning' (Darbishire 1952, I: 5); and 'the best thing [a reader] can do is to read *Paradise Lost* aloud. In no poem in the world is rhythm a more active and essential element of meaning' (Bush 80).

Since the 1970s, Milton scholars have neglected the oral and aural power of *Paradise Lost*.[7] Despite this, the sound of the poem has continued to assert itself outside the bounds of scholarship. Today, performances of *Paradise Lost* are freely audible on the internet, although the standard varies widely.[8] 'Milton marathons,' the practice of reading *Paradise Lost* aloud and entire, has continued for at least forty years.[9] They are usually a one-day event and have tended to remain in the popular culture of academic communities. Less ambitious readings, comprising selected passages, are also performed. Having had experience of both kinds of readings, I now offer some ear-witness accounts from 2000–2008.

In New Zealand, Milton marathons were performed annually from 1992–2004, convened by John Hale of the University of Otago, Dunedin. The 2000 and 2004 marathons, which I co-judged, were organized in teams competitively. In the 2000 event, the dramatic power of *Paradise Lost* was especially well rendered, and the debate in hell in Book 2 was a political spectacular and a high point of the day. Over the course of twelve hours, the range of readers threw into relief the many voices of *Paradise Lost*, and different readers highlighted the development of Milton's characters. There were several Satans, from a desperate fallen angel in Book 1 to a suave, velvet-voiced Satan in Book 9. The melodic rhythm of the hymns and the onward flow of the narrative voice proved more difficult for the readers.[10]

Milton's 400th anniversary in 2008 inspired many public readings, notably a day-long performance of *Paradise Lost* on 23 October at Milton's old college, Christ's, at Cambridge. Fellows of the College featured prominently among the readers, and the convener reported that the performance 'was attended by hundreds and listened to online by nearly 5,000'; through the global reach of the internet, the reading may now be heard by a still wider audience.[11] In Australia, I designed two readings for Milton's quatercentenary, in Brisbane on 17 August and in Sydney on 27 November. Neither was a marathon reading, but both were entitled 'A Life Beyond Life,' inspired by Milton's assertion in *Areopagitica* that 'A good book is the pretious life blood of a master-spirit embalmed and treasured up on purpose to a life beyond life' (*CPW* 2.493).

The Brisbane '*A Life Beyond Life': Celebrating John Milton's 400th Anniversary*, ran from 10 am to 4 pm as a celebratory last day of an international Milton symposium at the University of Queensland and included a festive lunch and a soirée.[12] There was an audience of 140, seventy of them readers, from a wide range of occupations, from a cattleman to a High Court judge. Selected passages were taken from the span of Milton's career, in the morning the shorter poems and prose, in the afternoon *Paradise Lost*. Although the readers had been assigned their lines in advance, they had not rehearsed together, and the standard of reading varied widely. Satan's soliloquy in Book 4 (32–113) was particularly admired, and one listener reported:

> The highlight for me was the long speech of Satan from Book 4, where the reader knew the passage by heart, and captured the muttering/ranting/wheedling/anguish of Satan in an utterly compelling reading. His tone of voice, which was somehow particularly satanic, was one element, but I think what made the difference was the fact that he knew the text so well. Learning it all seemed to enable him to really understand the mind of Satan and project the meaning of that speech with impressive depth

and breadth. He also captured very well the sense that he was talking to himself, not performing for an audience.[13]

Another listener agreed that this was 'the most effective reading,' which 'rendered the inner dialogue alive,' while yet another recalled Plato's account of the rhapsode Ion and considered that this performance 'showed what can be done to bring the English epic into living connection with what we know about ancient Greek epic.'[14]

The Sydney *A Life Beyond Life': Readings from* Paradise Lost *for John Milton's 400th Anniversary*, was of a different order. It was performed in a city church, Christ Church Saint Laurence, for a general audience of more than 240, with the State Premier reading the opening invocation. Given the nature of the audience and the hard church pews, it was designed to last no longer than an hour and a half. It was a rehearsed reading by six experienced readers, and a studio recording was subsequently made at the University of Sydney, now accessible on the internet.[15] Selected passages were chosen, with the principal focus on the temptation of Eve in Book 9. I gave a brief introduction and provided linking commentary, using Milton's text as much as possible. One member of the audience reported: 'the drama of Milton's compelling, persuasive and moving narrative, coupled with the dignity and majesty of the lines, held the listeners rapt. My two seat companions, middle-aged women parishioners, self-confessedly knowing little of Milton, were completely entranced. It was Milton's triumph!' Another reported: 'I found the production lively, engaging and extremely entertaining. The presentations seemed to bring the poetry to life as each character developed and the story unfolded with all its seriousness and gravity. The audience seemed captivated. It was instantly a thrilling, action based piece of drama.' Another listener responded more to the epic narrative and wrote to me that he 'was astounded by Milton's perspective on the cosmos . . . And the subsequent composition and unfolding of the story. I revelled in its telling. You are absolutely right, it needs to be spoken: the ear, to hear its cadence, the body to feel the rhythm.'[16]

Legitimate doubts arise about oral performances. What if the readers mangle Milton's verse? Yvor Winters warns that 'without audible reading, and adequate audible reading, you simply do not have poetry' (83).

Further, do such performances exaggerate the multivocal character of *Paradise Lost*? At the Brisbane event there were contrary responses to a professional actor's performance of Satan in Book 9. For a Shakespeare scholar, it was the outstanding performance of the day, but a Milton scholar offered this judgment:

> It came across more as Shakespearean drama than Miltonic epic. The text is epic, not drama, not a script that is intended to govern performance in theatre, which is how the professional actor treated it. The result was a hyped up, overly dramatic rendering of Satan that violated something essential to the epic genre, and the intentions of the poem's author. I can't imagine Milton applauding such theatrical licence. I think the best readings of the speeches in the poem are sensitive to the characters who deliver them, and the situations in which they are delivered, without obliterating the voice of the epic narrator. That serious, elevated voice must always be there, no matter who is speaking.[17]

This might be balanced against two things, Milton's insistence that an author 'personates' his characters and the fact that *Paradise Lost* is an epic that grew out of plans for a drama (*CPW* 1.880; 8.539–89). Many readers would agree with Edward Weismiller that the narration 'is in a voice so personal and "involved" as to seem, again and again, dramatic' (186).[18] Differing ear-witness responses are valuable because they provoke discussion and test interpretation.

Especially demanding for all readers, and a hallmark of the epic's sublimity, is the onward pressure of Milton's verse paragraphs, with the 'the sense variously drawn out from one Verse into another.' The difficulty is not only to maintain one's breathe but to follow, and to convey the sense of, Milton's syntax. Many readers neglect Milton's light punctuation and insert pauses, thus breaking up the flow of the lines, and few manage to render intelligently the sustained verse paragraphs. There is thus an advantage in listening to expert readers, such as Anton Lesser, in his recording of *Paradise Lost*, and Eric Griffiths, who read Book 4 in the Cambridge marathon. From 4.131 ('So on he fares …'), paradise is described in recurrent waves of verse paragraphs, and this generous amplitude of movement reciprocates the semantic component of the lines, that is, the abundance being described. Thus, partly through 'the sound of sense,' Milton's verse expresses the plenitude of paradise.[19] The effect is highlighted by the periodic separating of the paragraphs by Milton's terse comments—'So little knows / Any, but God alone . . . ' (4.201–04), 'Thus was this place, . . . ' (4.246–47)—and, more spectacularly, by the breaking in of Satan's passionate soliloquies—'O Hell! What do mine eyes with grief behold, . . . ' (4.358 ff.), 'Sight hateful, sight tormenting! . . . ' (4.505 ff.). Both Anton Lesser and Eric Griffiths capture this vocal orchestration of Book 4.

A more intricate challenge for performers is Milton's extraordinary handling of rhythm, which is always for the purpose of embodying meaning. De Quincey rightly asserts that, 'You might as well tax Mozart with harshness in the divinest passages of *Don Giovanni* as Milton with any such offence against metrical science' (Wittreich 486). Milton understood this science intimately, and the audacious licences he takes with the iambic pentameter are always for expressive purpose. John Creaser has made an in-depth study of these deviations and, in what follows, I adopt his method of scansion.[20] The opening line of *Paradise Lost*, for example, is metrically wild, with six instead of five beats, three of which fall on consecutive syllables: 'Of MANS FIRST DIS-o-BED-ience AND the FRUIT.' Yet this weird, arresting rhythm is right, in its sublime weightiness, for the astonishing announcement the bard is making. The alliteration and jolting rhythm of the line, 'And DEV-ils TO a-DORE for DE-i-TIES' – coming at the end of a sustained verse paragraph (1.364-73) – powerfully evoke the narrator's disgust. Yet another metrical deviation combines with pauses to help carry the majestic yet soothing voice of the creator: 'SIL-ence, ye TROUB-l'd WAVES, and THOU DEEP, PEACE' (7.216). These are but three examples, among thousands, of Milton's 'apt numbers.'

The New Zealand marathons enabled me to test a particular interpretation of Milton's rhythms. In a study entitled 'Speech in *Paradise Lost*,' I had argued that before the Fall Adam and Eve speak in the measured rhythms and steady grace of celestial speech, after the Fall in the restless dislocated rhythms of infernal speech. What the marathons demonstrated, however, was a more complex reality within this wider pattern. In the argument about gardening in Book 9, for example, Adam and Eve's speech rhythms are newly assertive. Eve speaks with a kind of mesmerized quietude in Book 4, but in Book 9 she is a mature woman thinking for herself, confidently arguing, and her speech rhythms become emphatic. As for the steady grace of celestial speech, in the course of the all-day marathons, unmistakably strident rhythms were heard in some celestial voices. Readers performing God the Father were unable to hide the sometimes belligerent tone, which often derives from the heavy, draconian rhythm: 'SO will FALL / HEE and his FAITH-less PRO-gen-ie: WHOSE FAULT? / WHOSE but his OWN? IN-GRATE' (3.95–97). And when unfallen angels had to engage with Satan, they got their backs up and so did their speech rhythms; for example, at end of Book 4, the archangel Gabriel spat out these words: 'ARM-ie of FIENDS, *FIT* BOD-y to FIT HEAD' (4.953).

Finally, all performances, including poor ones, can send a reader back to the text to check Milton's finely nuanced auditory effects, for example, the slight rhythmic variation on the word 'infinite' in the line, 'IN-fin-ite WRAUTH, and IN-fin-ITE de-SPAIRE' (4.74). The first 'infinite' has one beat, the second two, which draws out the sense of Satan's despair. Novice readers failed to convey the even iambic pulse of the last line of the poem, which contributes to the chastened effect of the departure from paradise: 'Through ED-en TOOK thir SOL-i-TAR-ie WAY' (12.649). The deep, flatly declarative voice of God the Father in the Sydney *'Life Beyond Life'* sent me back to the dialogue in heaven in Book 3 to hear Milton's nuanced orchestration of the voices of Father and Son. By comparison with the dominating sound and rhythm of the Father's voice, the Son's is a 'still small voice.' Over the course of the dialogue, the two voices gradually move closer together, in sound, thought, and feeling. Mercy tames justice, compassion softens hard self-righteousness, so that, by the end of the dialogue, the two voices are reconciled and at one. Auditory effects thus become part of Milton's justifying 'the wayes of God to men' (1.26).

Today, it is rare to find a scholar who appreciates that *Paradise Lost* is made abundantly of sound. Harold Bloom is one of the few: he closes his eyes and recites the poem aloud and, in this way, comes to share something of his blind students' 'sense of being domesticated in the sublime poem's warmth and light' (206). More pertinently – and typically, I think, from a creative artist – Philip Pullman writes, 'I begin with sound. I read *Paradise Lost* not only with my eyes, but with my mouth. . . . I found that I had to take the lines in my mouth and utter them aloud. . . . Your body has to be involved. . . . The sound is part of the meaning and that part only comes alive when you speak it' (1–3). Orally and aurally, *Paradise Lost* is superlatively 'sensuous,' a word coined by Milton to mean working through the senses (*OED* 1): poetry is 'more simple, sensuous and passionate' than logic or rhetoric (*CPW* 2.403) because more physical, working through the senses. In the past twenty years, much scholarship has been expended on the philosophy of animist materialism that informs *Paradise Lost*, and yet the poem itself, made out of animate sonic matter (sounding words), has only recently been related to this philosophy (Sherry 2010). Milton's animist materialism is best exemplified in the living poem itself, as it flowed out of his body in his voice and continues to live through other human voices, attaining, time and again, 'a life beyond life.'

Works Cited

Barber, Charles. *The English Language: A Historical Introduction*. Cambridge: Cambridge University Press, 1993

Benzie, W. *The Dublin Orator: Thomas Sheridan's Influence on Eighteenth-Century Rhetoric and* Belle Lettres. Menston,Yorkshire: Scolar Press, 1972

Berry, Francis. *Poetry and the Physical Voice*. London: Routledge and Kegan Paul, 1962

Bloom, Harold. *The Best Poems of the English Language*. New York: HarperCollins, 2004

Bradford, Richard. *Augustan Measures: Restoration and Eighteenth-Century Writings on Prosody and Metre*. Aldershot, Hants: Ashgate, 2002

––––––. *Silence and Sound: Theories of Poetics from the Eighteenth Century*. London and Toronto: Associated University Presses, 1992

Bush, Douglas. '*Paradise Lost*.' *A Milton Encyclopedia*. Edited by William B. Hunter Lewisburg: Bucknell UP, 1978–1980. 6.50-80

Creaser, John. '"A Mind of Most Exceptional Energy": Verse rhythm in *Paradise Lost*.' *The Oxford Handbook of Milton*. Edited by Nicholas McDowell and Nigel Smith. Oxford: OUP,   2009. Pp. 462–79

––––––. '"Service is Perfect Freedom": Paradox and Prosodic Style in *Paradise Lost*.' *RES* 58 (2007): 268–315

––––––. 'Verse and rhyme.' *Milton in Context*. Edited by Stephen B. Dobranski. Cambridge: CUP, 2010. Pp. 105–18

Darbishire, Helen (ed.). *The Early Lives of Milton*. London: Constable, 1932

––––––, (ed.). *The Poetical Works of John Milton*. 2 vols. Oxford: Clarendon, 1952–55

Eliot, T.S. *On Poetry and Poets*. London: Faber and Faber, 1957

Fish, Stanley. 'Why Milton Matters: Or, Against Historicism.' *Milton Studies* 44 (2005):

1–12

Goodman, Godfrey. *The Fall of Man*. London, 1616

Guest, Edwin. *A History of English Rhythms*. New ed. London: George Bell and Sons, 1882

Hale, John K. 'Paradise Lost Aloud.' *College Teaching* 42 (1994): 86–89

————. *Milton as Multilingual: Selected Essays, 1982–2004*. Dunedin: University of Otago, 2005

————. *Milton's Languages: The impact of multilingualism on style*. Cambridge: Cambridge UP, 1997

Hopkins, Gerard Manley. *The Letters of Gerard Manley Hopkins to Robert Bridges*. Edited by Claude Colleer Abbott. London: OUP, 1935

Jonson, Ben. *Ben Jonson*. Edited by Ian Donaldson. Oxford: OUP, 1985.

Leighton, Angela. 'Poetry and the Imagining Ear' (F.W.Bateson Memorial Lecture). *Essays in Criticism* 59 (2009): 99–115.

Leonard, John. 'Doing what he Describes: Enactment in Milton's Poetry.' *Cithara* 49 (2009): 7–25.

Lewis, C.S. *A Preface to* Paradise Lost. London: OUP, 1942

Masson, David (ed.). *The Poetical Works of John Milton*. 3 vols. London,1874

McColley, Diane Kelsey. *A Gust for Paradise: Milton's Eden and the Visual Arts*. Urbana: U of Illinois P, 1993

————. *Poetry and Ecology in the Age of Milton and Marvell*. Aldershot (Hants): Ashgate, 2007

————. *Poetry and Music in Seventeenth-Century England*. Cambridge: Cambridge UP. 1997

————. '"The Copious Matter of My Song."' In *Literary Milton: Text, Pretext, Context*. Edited by Diana Trevino Benet and Michael Lieb. Pittsburgh: Duquesne UP, 1994. Pp. 67–90

Middleton, Peter. 'The Contemporary Poetry Reading.' In *Close Listening: Poetry and the Performed Word*. Edited by Charles Bernstein. New York, Oxford: OUP, 1998. Pp. 262–99

Milton, John. *The Poems of John Milton*. Edited by John Carey and Alastair Fowler. London: Longman, 1968

————. *The Complete Prose Works of John Milton*. 8 vols. Gen. ed. Don M. Wolfe et al. New Haven: Yale University Press, 1953–1982

————. *Paradise Lost*. Edited by Barbara K. Lewalski. Oxford: Blackwell, 2007

Nelson, James G. *The Sublime Puritan: Milton and the Victorians*. Madison: U of Wisconsin P, 1963

Perkins, David. 'How the Romantics Recited Poetry.' *Studies in English Literature* 31 (1991): 655–71

Pullman, Philip (ed.). *John Milton: Paradise Lost*. Oxford: OUP, 2005

Shawcross, John T.. 'The Deleterious and the Exalted: Milton's Poetry in the Eighteenth Century.' In *Milton and the Grounds of Contention*. Edited by Mark R. Kelley, Michael Lieb, and John T. Shawcross. Pittsburgh: Duquesne UP, 2003. Pp. 11–36

Sherry, Beverley. 'Milton, Materialism, and the Sound of *Paradise Lost*,' *Essays in Criticism* 60 (2010): 220–41

————. 'Paradise Lost "Made vocal",' *Milton Quarterly* 34 (2000): 128–29

————. 'Speech in *Paradise Lost*,' *Milton Studies* VIII (1975): 247–66

————. 'The Legacy of T.S. Eliot to Milton Studies.' In *The Legacy of T.S. Eliot*. Edited by Barry Spurr. *Literature & Aesthetics* 18.1 (2008): 135–51. Rpt. in *Versification* 5 (2010): 27–38

Steggle, Matthew. 'Paradise Lost and the Acoustics of Hell,' *EMLS* 7.1/Special Issue 8 (May, 2001): 9.1-17. <URL: http://purl.oclc.org/emls/07-1/stegmil2.htm>

Symonds, John Addington. 'Blank Verse.' In *Sketches and Studies in Italy*. London: Smith, Elder, & Co., 1879. Pp. 377–428. Published as *Blank Verse*. London: John C. Nimmo, 1895; rpt. Honolulu: University Press of the Pacific, 2003

Teskey, Gordon. *Delirious Milton: The Fate of the Poet in Modernity*. Cambridge (MA): Harvard UP, 2006

Thorpe, James (ed.). *Milton Criticism: Selections from Four Centuries*. London: Routledge and Kegan Paul, 1951

Walker, William. 'Sounds of Elevation in *Paradise Lost*: God's Commendation of Abdiel.' In *Word and Self Estranged in English Texts, 1550–1660*. Edited by Philippa Kelly and L.E. Semler. Farnham (Surrey): Ashgate, 2010. Pp. 183–94

Weismiller, Edward. 'Blank Verse.' In *A Milton Encyclopedia*. Edited by William B. Hunter. 8 vols. Lewisburg: Bucknell UP, 1978–1980. 1:179–92

Winters, Yvor. *The Function of Criticism: Problems and Exercises*. Denver: Alan   Swallow, 1957

Wittreich, Joseph Anthony, Jr. *The Romantics on Milton: Formal Essays and Critical Asides*. Cleveland and London: Case Western Reserve UP. 1970

Notes

1   Citations from *Paradise Lost* are from Lewalski's edition.

2   *The Complete Prose Works* 1.820–21. Subsequent quotations from Milton's prose are from this edition, abbreviated as *CPW*, followed by volume and page number.

3   Walker takes account of this, and also notes that the rhotic element has survived in North American speech.

4   Darbishire mistakenly attributed the anonymous biography by Skinner to John Phillips.

5   On the elocution movement, see Bradford, *Augustan Measures*, chapters 4 and 5 and *Silence and Sound*, chapter 2; on Sheridan in particular, see Benzie.

6   See Wordsworth's sonnet, 'Milton! Thou shouldst be living at this hour' and Tennyson's experiment with alcaics, 'Milton.' On a change in Milton's voice with age, see the interesting argument by Berry, 'The Voice of Milton' (Berry, chapter VI).

7   The notable exceptions are McColley, Hale, Creaser, and Leonard. See: McColley, *A Gust for Paradise* 109–44, '"The Copious Matter"' 67–90, *Poetry and Music*, chapter 5, and *Poetry and Ecology*, 80–81, 93–94, 118-22; Hale, *Milton's Languages*, chapter 7 and *Milton as Multilingual*, particularly chapter 1. Creaser's expertise is prosody, especially in his award-winning study, '"Service . . ."' My work is also intended to redress the neglect of sound.

8   Some of the best readings are: Anton Lesser's recording of *Paradise Lost* for Naxos (2005) and his readings for Britain's Radio 3 in December 2008; Ian Richardson for the 1984 series, *Six Centuries of Verse* (now accessible on YouTube); and some of the Cambridge readers who performed a day reading of *Paradise Lost* on 23 October 2008. An interesting alternative is proceeding at the University of Texas, where John Rumrich is developing an audio-text of *Paradise Lost*; Books 1, 2, and 9 are now accessible on the internet. <URL: http://www.laits.utexas.edu/miltonpl/> Accessed 3 March 2011.

9   In a letter to me (25 May 2003), Alastair Fowler recalled that Milton marathons began in the early 1970s at the University of Edinburgh.

10   See Sherry 2000, and on earlier Otago marathons, Hale 1994.

11   Personal communication from Gavin Alexander. For the podcast, go to: <URL:http://sms.cam.ac.uk/collection/668015>

12   For details of this event, go to the site for the conference, <URL:http://www.ched. uq.edu.au/index.html?page=70521> and follow links to *'A Life Beyond Life.'*

13   Sarah Holey, company director, also a reader. A young poet, Jaya Savige, recited Satan's soliloquy.

14   Jennifer Arnold, eye surgeon, and John Hale, Milton scholar, both readers on the day.

15   For a transcript of the passages read, and to hear the recording, go to: <URL:http:// www.usyd.edu.au/news/84.html?newscategoryid=6&newsstoryid=2899>

16   Reports from Elaine Moon, academic, Di Robinson, manager, and Kyran David, primary school teacher.

17   The actor Eugene Gilfedder read Satan; the Shakespeare scholar is Peter Holbrook, the Milton scholar William Walker, both readers on the day.

18   Another reader at the Brisbane event wrote: 'I thoroughly enjoyed the day which, on reflection, confirmed my sense that Milton is at his most powerful in his strong, dramatic writing. I am not talking about *Samson,* but about the great speeches, debates and conversations throughout *Paradise Lost* and the creation of those compelling characters and scenes. Somehow I always associate the notion of' "muscular" writing with Milton, and this was reinforced for me in the course of the day.' (Maureen Strugnell, university lecturer in drama)

19   The poet Robert Frost used the phrase, 'the sound of sense,' to emphasize the importance of sound in poetry – see Leighton 104–06.

20   The iambic pentameter is a line of five beats in rising duple movement (x/x/x/x/x/), but in the scansion used in this essay, no feet are marked because Milton did not compose in foot-thinking. Rather, while retaining the pentameter's ten syllables and five beats, he moves the beats around, within patterns shaped by the rhythms of speech, for expressive purpose; 'on average only one line in six scans as a normative iambic pentameter' (Creaser, 2007, 297). Notation is as follows. Capitals indicate beats. Italicised capitals indicate a stressed off-beat, which adds weight to the line. Small capitals are used for a syllable naturally given light emphasis but which, because of its place in the line, is felt as a metrical beat. Underlining is used for two consecutive beats, which are invariably preceded or followed by two unstressed syllables. (See Creaser, 2007, especially 272–76)

Index